THE
OTHER
SIDE OF
THE MIND

THE OTHER SIDE OF THE MIND

W. Clement Stone
AND Norma Lee Browning

A Publication of The Napoleon Hill Foundation

MEDIA

MEDIA

Published 2019 by Gildan Media LLC
aka G&D Media
www.GandDmedia.com

Front Cover design by David Rheinhardt of Pyrographx

Interior design by Meghan Day Healey of Story Horse, LLC

Library of Congress Cataloging-in-Publication Data is available upon request

ISBN: 978-1-7225-0106-8

10   9   8   7   6   5   4   3   2   1

CONTENTS

PART I
The Telepathy Boom
by Norma Lee Browning

PART II
Gullible's Travels
by Norma Lee Browning

PART III
The Crack in the Crystal Ball
by Norma Lee Browning

PART IV
Interlude: Let Your Mind Reach Out
by W. Clement Stone

PART V
From Psi to Science
by Norma Lee Browning

INTRODUCTION

Do Thoughts Make Things Happen?

By Mitch Horowitz

You won't find any direct mention of the work of Napoleon Hill in this book—but its coauthor, insurance magnate and philanthropist W. Clement Stone (1902–2002), not only presided for many years over the Napoleon Hill Foundation but was instrumental in ensuring that Hill's books remained in print and in front of the public eye. Hill called Stone the third most successful person to use the ideas he popularized, following Andrew Carnegie and Thomas Edison.

Yet Stone had another side, reflected in this book: He was a longtime benefactor of psychical research, including the pioneering work of researcher JB Rhine (1895–1980) at Duke University. In his Duke labs, Rhine, with his wife and intellectual collaborator Louisa Rhine (1891–1983), herself a trained scientist and botanist, established in the U.S. the scholarly study of extra-sensory perception, or ESP, a term Rhine popularized.

Hill, too, was a great admirer of Rhine, to whom he refers several times in *Think and Grow Rich*, where he signals his conviction that the mind contains extra-physical properties and potentialities. On this question, Hill had no doubts.

But *The Other Side of the Mind* is not a work of advocacy. Stone's coauthor, journalist Norma Lee Browning (1915–2001), was a pioneering female journalist who capitulated to no one's prejudices or proclivities. Her voice and writing dominate the book, and she expresses earnest agnosticism about the state of ESP research at the time *The Other Side of the Mind* was published in 1964. Browning provides a sort of travelogue of contemporaneous psi research and phenomena, travelling, with Stone's financial aid, to the former Soviet Union, India, Australia, and Fiji. She uncovers dubious accounts, frauds—and some intriguing possibilities.

My only criticism of Browning's approach is that she chooses certain historical targets to rightly demonstrate flimflam, but dedicates comparatively little time surveying the research of key historical figures, including Rhine himself, who was still alive at the time. A profile of Rhine by a skeptical but thoughtful journalist would have benefited the popular literature on ESP.

Clement Stone's sections of the book are concerned, in part, with the application of autosuggestion, which edges us back into the territory that directly concerned Napoleon Hill. Any truly dedicated student of Hill's work ought to have some familiarity with the kinds of psychical study and offshoots that mattered so deeply to him and Stone. And there is a practical dimension to these interests.

You have probably noticed occasions in your personal life where a focused and emotively charged thought—such as a such as a deep conviction or burning question—seemed to bring you in proximity to people and situations that proved directly, even intimately, related to what you were concentrating on. As someone who shares Hill's and Stone's interests, I would theorize that such instances might not simply reflect your heightened awareness of relevant circumstances, or your unconscious willingness to seize upon confirmations of a pre-existing idea (what is sometimes called "confirmation bias"). Rather, at such times it is possible, based on findings in psychical research both before and following this book's publication, that you may be conveying your attitudes in a subtle mind-to-mind fashion, entering a state of rapport with people who can offer assistance, meet you halfway, or provide useful information.

What I am describing, in potential at least, is a form of ESP. It comports with work begun by Rhine in the early 1930s. At Duke, the researcher conducted hundreds of thousands of trials in which subjects attempted to "guess" which card was overturned on a five-suit deck. Certain individuals persistently scored higher-than-average hits in these and other types of trials. These percentage points of deviation, tracked across decades of testing, demonstrated some form of anomalous transfer of information—either that, or the manner in which we compile clinical statistics is flawed in some way that we do not understand.

Rhine labored intensively, and under the scrutiny of critics, to safeguard against every form of corruption in his data—so much so that his experiments far exceeded the controls of most of today's clinical trials. Mathematician Warren Weaver (1894–1978), a former president of the American Association for the Advancement of Science, who directed the allocation of hundreds of millions of dollars in medical research grants, examined Rhine's methodology and concluded: "I cannot reject the evidence and I cannot accept the conclusions." Weaver did not share Rhine's views on ESP; but, as an authentic scientist, he refused to close the door on it. This is the attitude of skeptical engagement we need today.

Clinical researchers including Dean Radin of the Institute of Noetic Sciences (IONS) and Daryl Bem of Cornell University currently continue this line of inquiry, and Rhine's research center remains active as an independent facility.

Again: think back to a time when you experienced a deeply meaningful, emotionally charged concurrence of events, such as urgently needing to see someone who showed up at an uncannily propitious moment. Statistical tools can measure the odds of such an event, but they cannot fully capture the emotional import to one or more of the individuals involved, and hence the occurrence's truly anomalous nature. Clinical ESP research, of the kind considered in *The Other Side of the Mind*, suggest that such events may be far more than happy accidents. They may be the ESP of daily life.

Hill took such prospects seriously, as his careful readers know. Reviewing this aspect of Hill's broad catalogue of interests, as the authors do in this book, will deepen your appreciation for, and ability to benefit from, the master teacher's ideas.

Mitch Horowitz is a lecturer-in-residence at the University of Philosophical Research in Los Angeles, a writer-in-residence at the New York Public Library, and the PEN Award-winning author of books including *Occult America* and *The Miracle Club: How Thoughts Become Reality*. Visit him @MitchHorowitz.

I Dare You!

by W. Clement Stone

I dare you to accept the challenge!" said Myron Boardman, an executive of Prentice-Hall, Inc. He had come to Chicago to discuss an exciting book idea with Norma Lee Browning and me.

"A hard-headed businessman and a woman newspaper reporter investigate mind phenomena . . . that's the working title. But I'll make the assignment only if you two co-author the work. I dare you to accept!" he repeated.

What a challenge! It involved an exploration of all phases of mind phenomena, and a linking of them to the practical art of motivation, in one book. It meant research into psychic phenomena as well as the physical sciences and psychology—in fact everything pertaining to the functioning of the human mind. Our field would include all that was known or even conjectured about the mind's mysterious forces. From this we were to attempt to evaluate present knowledge about the powers of the human mind and to speculate about what these powers might accomplish in the future. And we were to try to motivate you, the reader, to relate, assimilate, and apply certain principles for developing and maintaining physical, mental and moral well-being.

The scope of the suggestion was unexpected and amazing. But it intrigued me.

There was a long silence. Norma Lee and I were thinking. Here are some of the thoughts that ran through my mind:

The key words in the whole project, for me at least, were *mind phenomena*. I knew, for instance, that over a million copies of the famous book, *The Law of Psychic Phenomena*, by Thomas Jay Hudson, had been sold since its first publication in 1893, and that it still affects the thinking of men and women in all walks of life. It seemed to me that it was time to update the material in this great work.

Hypnosis, for example, no longer belongs strictly in the realm of psychic phenomena, as it did in the early part of the century. And perhaps we could do what Hudson failed to do: help certain readers protect themselves from the real danger of harming their minds when they explore ESP (extrasensory perception) and other forms of psychic phenomena. For these are *mental dynamite*.

In such a project, I would be helping myself as a person. I would be forced to learn. It would be necessary to engage in research into many sciences bearing on brain-mind function—many of which I had not studied in depth.

The knowledge gained from research on mind phenomena would help me in my role as a director of certain other projects that were very important to me: The American Foundation of Religion and Psychiatry, The Foundation for the Study of Cycles, and Foundation for Research on the Nature of Man.

If I went into the project, I knew that Norma Lee would do most of the writing. She had a reputation for getting the facts, and she enjoyed a deserved popularity among readers of *The Chicago Tribune* and various magazines, including the *Saturday Evening Post* and *The Reader's Digest*.

Her daring exposés of phony spiritualists, mediums, healers, con men, and gyp artists who prey on the public had earned her recognition as one of the country's top reporters. She was the first woman to win the *Tribune's* coveted Edward S. Beck Award for her series exposing the operations of quack doctors, and she is one of the few woman to be included on the invitational list for the nation's top medical science writers at the National Congress on Medical Quackery, sponsored jointly by the American Medical Association and the Food and Drug Administration. I felt it would be a privilege to work on a book with such an author.

Way back in the depths of my mind, however, there were even more personal reasons for the strong attraction I felt toward Myron Boardman's idea.

When I was a boy, my mother had a dressmaking establishment in our apartment. One of her best clients was the wife of a well-known professional magician, who taught me card tricks and magic. Every time his wife came to our apartment for a fitting, he accompanied her. To pass the time, he would perform for me. I was enthralled! He enjoyed my interest and enthusiasm too.

One day we were talking about magic and he stimulated my interest with: "I have a bird cage and I put a live bird in it. When I do a certain trick the bird disappears and I can never find him or make him re-appear." He never did demonstrate this trick to me, but I believed he had the ability to do it. In fact, I bragged to the kids in my neighborhood about this great mystery. For I had full confidence in what he said.

Later I realized that in the entertainment field, *anything* a magician says is just part of his act. He is under no moral obligation to adhere to the truth. But deception by authority or experts, upon whose integrity we rely to make important decisions, is despicable. Yet many people on whom the public relies have made deception an art, and some are as skillful as Houdini in their machinations. Perhaps, I thought, I could render a real service by winnowing out the false from the true in mind phenomena, by separating the worthless from the valuable.

Also as a boy, I had time to daydream—many wonderful dreams. Perhaps it was because I was an only child and my mother was busy during the day making our livelihood. Daydreaming stimulated my *imagination*, and when I read stories, such as those written by Horatio Alger, I could imagine myself the hero. In my early years at school, I reenacted in my dreams the achievements of warriors and heroes who had changed the course of world events.

But a history teacher in the sixth grade awakened me to some concepts that have played an important part in my life ever since. In searching for truth, she said, search for *primary* authority and evidence; try to determine the *motives* of the authors. Don't believe it *just* because it's in print.

Be an individual, this well-remembered teacher would insist. *Think!* Think for yourself, regardless of authority. But when you think, be *logical* and practical; and always be at least respectful of authority.

It was a long time ago that I first heard those thoughts expressed. Through the years I had seen the value of them in operation time and again . . . and it now occurred to me that this was exactly the approach that was most needed today in the field of mind phenomena. Too often, what is written about mind phenomena is a mere parroting of prejudiced, uninformed opinion. And many of the "investigations" have been nothing more than searches for "evidence" to support preconceived notions. Perhaps it was time to take a shovel to the foundations and dig for the facts, I thought.

In my later school years, my imagination was stimulated by the study of ancient and medieval history. To me, these were thrilling, exciting stories through which I could associate myself in more adult manner with other heroes, particularly the patrons—noblemen, kings, emperors, and popes—whose financial support and protection were so important in the development of philosophy, the arts, and the sciences.

Today, as always, a wealthy man can love art; and when he buys paintings and donates them to a museum, he is called "a patron of the arts." But a patron of old, unlike the patron of today, gave his encouragement, understanding, support, and protection to deserving persons of talent in the fields of literature, the arts, the sciences, and the professions. And he would often participate personally in these fields to some extent.

In my reading, I was inspired by the story of Maecenas, the patron of Virgil and Horace, whose very name has become synonymous with the idea of patron, notably in literature and the arts. I knew that Dante had had his Cangrande della Scala of Verona, and Shakespeare his Earl of Southampton.

It's great to beat a drum for the Salvation Army on South State Street in Chicago . . . to try to change the lives of human derelicts as a worker in a city mission . . . to help boys and girls become decent citizens by doing social work in the Boys Clubs of America, Boy Scouts, Girl Scouts, the YMCA or YWCA . . . to dedicate your life to the ministry or become a missionary in far-off lands . . . to become an outstanding inventor, scientist, teacher, author, musician, sculptor, or artist. But what one person, by himself and in a short single lifetime, can do *all* of these wonderful things?

A patron!

When, eventually, I acquired wealth, I determined to use part of it as had the patrons of old—in sponsoring talents and projects that stood chances of adding to the happiness and betterment of the world. The idea that Myron Boardman had now suggested would take a large sum of money and much time and effort—probably more time and money than any one magazine or newspaper or foundation could afford to put into such an endeavor. I realized that here, in a subject of great importance to mankind, was a new and fine opportunity for me to act on the inspirations I had received years before.

The long period of silence was broken when I said: "I certainly had no intention of getting involved in professional writing now. But here's an opportunity of a lifetime. I'll accept the challenge if it's OK with Norma Lee . . ."

That decision has already proved to be a good one. For if this book were never published, I would still be amply repaid for the time, money, and energy expended. I have already been recompensed through the persons I met, the knowledge I gained, and the inspiration I experienced—most of all because of my trip to the shrine of Lourdes, which you will read about in Chapter Fifteen.

Myron Boardman had hardly left my studio when Norma Lee and I began to work out our plans. Here's what we decided:

Norma Lee was to ask for a leave of absence from her employer, *The Chicago Tribune*, for one full year, so she could devote her efforts to the project exclusively. She and her husband, Russell Ogg (a professional photographer), were to make a trip around the world to investigate, witness, and record information and activities pertaining to the subject of brain-mind phenomena.

They were to interview government officials, scientists, university professors, inventors, authors, psychic sensitives, and newspaper editors . . . to check particularly on what was really going on behind the Iron Curtain in Russia and Czechoslovakia . . . to obtain first-hand information on the yogi and mystics of India, the fire-walkers of Fiji, the aborigines in Australia . . . to run down the authority of psychic experiences and experiments reported in the world's press . . . to collect helpful books and scientific papers that were not available here in the United States.

I was to: finance the project . . . employ experts in specialized fields where necessary . . . interview scientists and university professors in this country . . . obtain information from Taegu, Formosa, and about the Maori in New Zealand, where I had contacts . . . visit Haiti and check on voodoo . . . read and study what turned out to be a sizable library of books and scientific papers . . . check on faith-healing among the several religious denominations . . . and visit Lourdes to study the subject of miracles.

Together, Norma Lee and I would interview sensitives who were reputed to have special psychic powers, and psychologists, psychiatrists, and parapsychologists.

We agreed that each author was to have complete freedom in the style and content of his portion of the book, and that we would employ a format where the work of each could be identified.

And now we dare *you!*

We dare you to keep an open mind as you read this book from beginning to end . . . then to reread it and question any statements or theories before you come to definite conclusions.

You will be exposed to the thinking, experiences, and customs of peoples different from yourself: Russians, Indians, Japanese, Chinese, Africans, Australian aborigines, and others.

You will explore with us many sciences relating to the functioning of your body and mind, among which are physiology, biology, psychology, physics, chemistry, electronics, mathematics, and engineering. You will take a look at concepts you may have feared to be informed about because of self-imposed taboos—knowledge of such subjects as hypnosis, telepathy, levitation, yoga, voodoo, and the like.

We dare you to relate the facts in this book to your own life, to assimilate whatever is true in them, and—*when you are ready*—to use those down-to-earth principles that you can apply to achieve your specific worthwhile objectives.

We dare you to have the courage to realize that even the most intelligent persons can be tricked and deceived by what they see, hear, and read—especially when their confidence and faith are wrongly placed in honest-appearing cheats, frauds, phonies, and charlatans who prey upon the gullibility of good people.

We dare you to accept the premise: *truth will be truth regardless of any person's belief, ignorance, negligence, or misunderstanding, or the failure of scientific proof.*

If you accept these challenges, you will have nothing to fear, but much to gain. For, *if you are ready*, you will expand your horizons, develop and use your latent abilities, and tap unseen external forces that may now be unknown to you.

You may, like many before you, become more mature, logical, and tolerant. And you will be motivated to use these powers more successfully to achieve your worthwhile aims.

PART I

The Telepathy Boom

by Norma Lee Browning

CHAPTER 1

Will the Russians Harness Telepathy?

Early in 1960 an eminent Russian physiologist, Professor Leonid L. Vasiliev, read some amazing articles in a French journal of popular science. They described a sensational experiment in telepathy that had taken place aboard the American atomic submarine *Nautilus*. The news jolted him. His country had been first in space; it also had to be first to harness the hidden powers of the mind.

It wasn't necessary to *believe* the claims coming from capitalist countries, said the professor, but it wasn't reasonable to ignore them, either. Russia must find out what was being done about the "phenomenon of mental suggestion" and give the problem the correct materialistic explanation so necessary to Soviet science.

Professor Vasiliev, head of the physiology department at Leningrad University, lost no time in conveying his sentiments to the Kremlinites who pull the strings in such matters. Before the year was ended he had established within his department a special laboratory for the study of "telepathic phenomena." It was the first laboratory of its kind in the Soviet Union—probably the first of its kind anywhere.

By 1963 the whole world knew about Russia's claims of success with long-distance telepathic experiments. What the whole world did not know was that the Russians had fallen—hook, line and sinker—for a hoax. There was not an iota of truth in the *Nautilus* story. It has been repudiated by government sources, and *This Week* magazine, in September 1963, published denials by all the people supposedly involved. Captain William Anderson, first skipper of the *Nautilus*, pointed out that the sub was laid up in dry-dock during the very days in which the French story had her far at sea in the great experiment. But the fable went over big behind the Iron Curtain, and, ironically, launched a whole new era in the tumultuous history of psychic studies. Now the entire world is wondering just how far the Russians have really gone in their efforts to crack the secret of human telepathy.

If the Russian reports are even partly true, if telepathy—or mind-to-mind "thought transference"—can be used for such things as interplanetary communications or the guiding of intercontinental space ships, the reports will obviously have overwhelming significance.

A first-hand look behind the Iron Curtain confirms certain facts. The Russians are indeed pouring unbelievable amounts of money and manpower into the race to harness something more awesome than the atom—the human mind. They are giving research in telepathy a top-priority rating in their space program, under the heading of biological sciences. If the harnessing of telepathy turns out to be nothing more than a pipe dream, it will not be because the Russians didn't try. They spare nothing in their efforts toward the goal of world mastery by whatever means possible—from nuclear power to mind power.

For many years, any attempt to study telepathic phenomena was denounced in Russia as mysticism and idealism. But today, under the impetus of a Communist decree to push ahead with the biological sciences in conjunction with space research, telepathy is getting the full-scale treatment as a form of "biological radio communication." In fact, the Russians' telepathy research program is highly endorsed by top Soviet space-flight scientists. Rocket flight pioneer K. A. Ciolkovski has stated publicly:

"The phenomena of telepathy can no longer be called into question. We must highly esteem the attempt at elucidating them in the light of science. Especially in the coming era of space flights, telepathic abilities are necessary, and they will aid the whole development of mankind."

Early in 1963, I went to Russia to investigate reports of the telepathy experiments. Besides my passport and introductions from American and British scientists, I went armed with a crate full of books—the most useful entrée to scientific communities behind the Iron Curtain. The Russian people are hungry for books. An Agatha Christie whodunit or a Tennessee Williams play will mellow a cab driver or an Intourist guide almost as much as a pack of American cigarettes, and Soviet scientists are cautiously eager for books in all fields of science and technology.

The Russians spend millions of rubles on scientific translations and they seem to know more about what is going on in American science laboratories than the average American does.

In exchange for books I was granted interviews with some of the leading Soviet scientists, doctors, and researchers in telepathy, among them scientists from Professor Vasiliev's "mental radio" laboratory.

It is Professor Vasiliev more than anyone else who is responsible for snatching telepathy from the realm of occultism and bringing it to the forefront as at least a fit subject of inspection by orthodox scientists. Before we examine Vasiliev's work in detail, it should be emphasized that possibly no one outside Russia knows with certainty the precise nature of his experiments or just how much he has accomplished to date. What the Russians *claim* to be doing is one thing; what they actually are doing may be something else.

Doctors and scientists from other countries are generally not welcome as observers in Soviet laboratories; science writers and news correspondents stationed in Russia must depend largely on handouts from the Communist press corps. The Russians are cagey about answering specific questions. Some of my information concerning Russian experiments was obtained from non-Soviet scientific sources in Russia, and from other investigators whose impressions and findings largely confirmed mine.

The best evidence of what the Russians are doing or planning is to be found in their own scientific papers, journals, and books—a collection of which I acquired in exchange for the books I took with me. Translations are expensive but well worth it, for only a careful analysis of the Russians' own scientific claims can give anything like an accurate indication of the facts. From these translations, as well as dozens of interviews with scientists, one important fact stands out: There is no doubt about the *scope* of the Russians' *research* in telepathy. There is still room for doubt, however, about how much they have actually accomplished.

As this is written, telepathy in Russia, according to the information available, is still in the exploratory stage. But to the extent that anything the Russians are doing can be confirmed, it is safe to say that already they have:

1. Established at least eight known research centers specializing in telepathic experiments, and all on an academic—scientific level. The best known is the one at Leningrad University.
2. Established an exchange program with India to study the physiological and mental disciplines of the yogis and their alleged capacities to transmit ideas at will.
3. Organized teams of scientists—physiologists, physicists, psychologists, zoologists, biologists, neurologists, mathematicians, cyberneticians, and electronics engineers—to investigate telepathy, find out how it works, and devise means of practical application.
4. Conducted experiments that, if the results are half as good as the Russians claim, indicate that they may be the first to put a human thought in orbit, or achieve mind-to-mind communication with men on the moon.

There is one major and significant point of difference between the Soviet approach to telepathy and that of most western scientists. The Russians do not accept telepathy as psychic in character. They do not regard it as a "sixth sense." They want nothing to do with ESP (extrasensory perception) or, as Professor Vasiliev has said, any other "superstitious concepts about the soul" such as are "exploited in capitalist countries by ardent idealists." The Soviet people, he says, have "freed themselves of superstitious religious notions," and telepathy must be studied in light of its "ideological, antireligious significance," on a sound physiological basis.

Although telepathy research has been going on in earnest since 1960, when Professor Vasiliev established his "mental radio" laboratory, it was given an even bigger boost in early

1963 by a Kremlin edict that placed the biological sciences on an equal footing with aerodynamics.

An official "decision" adopted by the Central Committee of the CPSU and USSR Council of Ministers—"On Measures to Further Develop Biology and Strengthen Its Links with Practical Work"—specified increased allocations for biological research, improved training of new scientists, and opening of new scientific centers equipped with first-class apparatus.

Biological research, of course, takes in a vast territory.

Its scope, so far as the Russians' experiments in telepathy are concerned, is perhaps best expressed in the words of Academician N. Sisakian, head of the biological department of the Soviet Academy of Sciences: "The main tasks of biology are to find out the essence of the phenomena of life, to comprehend and control the vital processes . . . Once scientists have discovered the biological laws of governing the development of organic life, they will be in a position to control that development, to modify it in the interests of man."

The reason for including telepathy as a subject of investigation in the biological sciences was based on the work of two eminent Russian scientists, B. Kazhinsky, an electrical engineer whose book entitled *Biological Radio Communication* was published by the Ukrainian Academy of Sciences, and the even more eminent physiologist Vasiliev, whose recently published works, *Long Distance Suggestion*, and *Experiments in Mental Suggestion* set the stage for the revival of a metaphysical concept in a modern science laboratory.

An indication of Russian interest in the subject is shown by the fact that Vasiliev's first book, *Long Distance Suggestion*, had an initial printing of 120,000 copies—probably because it contains information about western research as well as a summary of Russia's. The book is now being translated into

English, French, and German, so the rest of the world can learn what the Russians are doing.

Since the establishment of the Leningrad laboratory in 1960, at least eight other research centers—probably more, but this is all I could confirm, have been opened for specialization in telepathic experiments. They are located in Kiev, Tbliski, Omsk (Siberia), Saratov, Tarty, Odessa, and of course, Moscow.

The Pavlovian Institute of Higher Nervous Activity in Moscow has incorporated telepathic research into its program under the heading, "The Problem of Transmission of Information." The Durov Institute, named for the Russian scientist famous for his telepathic experiments with animals, now has a group of 50 scientists studying the "transmission of biological information" through telepathy.

In Moscow there is also an "Institute of the Problem of Transmission of Information" conducting research on telepathy from the point of view of "subliminal perception," and another scientific group studying the "transmission of biological information" with the following objectives: to find the medium of telepathic transmission, to discuss theoretical aspects of telepathic research, to analyze works being carried on outside the USSR, and to educate public opinion. The Russians leave no doubt that their prime interest in telepathy is not as a "spiritualistic hypothesis" but as a specialized method of transmitting information.

Although they claim "peaceful intentions," they do not overlook the opportunity to remind themselves in their scientific publications that "aggressive intentions are ripening in the capitalist world"—this is based on the false *Nautilus* reports—and the rumors are that the Russians plan to use telepathy (after they learn how) for the guiding of space ships and for interplanetary communications with their own spacemen and with whatever species of life they find on other planets.

One report is that the Russians intend to place a pigeon inside the control pit of a rocket, and the pigeon will direct the movement of the rocket via telepathic instructions from an agent at a distance. The pigeons are supposed to be in training now at the Durov Institute in Moscow, although so far no one on this side of the Iron Curtain has figured out how to send thought waves to pigeons.

It is very probable, in view of the Russians' intense interest in any kind of scientific research going on abroad, that they have heard of Harvard's famous psychologist, Burrhus Frederic Skinner, the world's leading exponent of Pavlovian behaviorism, and are trying to copy his pigeon experiments. Skinner, who is the principal inventor of the teaching machine, is also an ardent disciple of Pavlov, the great Russian physiologist whose experiments with conditioned reflexes in dogs set the course of modern psychology. Pavlov received the 1904 Nobel Prize in physiology and medicine for his work on the digestive glands. It was while he was experimenting with the glands of digestive secretion that he discovered accidentally that a dog could learn to salivate at the ringing of a bell which had been rung repeatedly while the dog was being fed.

Skinner, one of America's best known experimental psychologists, has advocated that human behavior can be shaped and controlled, and Utopian communities engineered, by Pavlovian principles of conditioning. Skinner uses rats and pigeons for his studies on animal behavior. He and his associates have trained pigeons to play table tennis, dance together, and to peck out tunes on a piano.

Shortly after the outbreak of World War II, it occurred to Skinner that pigeons might even be trained as navigator—

bombardiers. He obtained financial help from the government and then rigged up a simulated missile with a translucent screen in its nose. The steering mechanism was arranged so that a pigeon placed in the nose of the missile could guide it toward a specified target by pecking on the image of the target when it appeared on the screen. In 1944, Skinner and his collaborators put on a demonstration for a group of the government's chief scientific advisors. Although it went off without a hitch, the scientists decided the project should be dropped—possibly, Skinner speculated in *Harper's* of April 1963, because "the spectacle of a living pigeon carrying out its assignment, no matter how beautifully, simply reminded the committee of how utterly fantastic our proposal was."

There is an extraordinary similarity between this report of the 1944 Skinner pigeon demonstration and reports of the current Soviet pigeon-research program. The major difference is that the Russians apparently are trying to add telepathy to the pigeons' repertoire. Neither Skinner's nor Pavlov's experiments, of course, had anything to do with telepathy. It is difficult in fact to see how the conditioned salivation of Pavlov's dogs could be applicable to psychic phenomena like telepathy, but the Russians seem to be relying heavily on Pavlovian principles in their telepathic research program.

There are indications also of intense research into "telecommunications in the animal world" in newly established telepathy research centers in both Leningrad and Moscow. And there is no doubt about the extensive animal research going on behind the Iron Curtain in areas other than telepathy. Most of the world has already heard of the fantastic organ transplants, for example, that Soviet doctors have performed in dogs.

In one experiment involving 67 dogs, each with two hearts, one lived as long as five days. More spectacular have been the experiments with animal head grafts. In one case the head and forequarters of a smaller dog were grafted onto the neck of a large German shepherd. It survived 29 days, the grafted head barking, eating, biting, and to all appearances normally healthy.

One of the most important animal experimental stations is the Sukumi Ape Colony, an hour's drive from Khrushchev's villa, where scientists are studying the action of radiation on the brain and testing the preventive actions of various drugs. At Sukumi also has been established a nuclear station of the future, where technicians are trying to perfect a type of controlled fission that will relegate atomic energy, as it is conceived today, to the junk pile. This, of course, has no direct bearing on Russian research in telepathy, but it is all part of the same picture—the drive to control nuclear energy, brain energy, and any other kind of energy in the Soviet's race for complete mastery of both mind and space.

It is evident that the problems involved in many of the Russians' fields of research, as for example in their organ-transplant experiments, touch on physical problems. A dog with two hearts or a new head, gruesome as it may seem to some, arms the scientist with another line of attack on the mysteries of brain and mind functioning and learning and behavior processes, as well as the mystery of the compatibilities and incompatibilities of different tissues and organisms. Soviet scientists are bent on solving all these mysteries.

Most of Vasiliev's experiments in telepathy have been conducted jointly with scientists from the Bechterev Brain Institute in Leningrad. This is affiliated with the Institute for Experimental Medicine, where Pavlov conducted his famous dog experiments, and where the granddaughter of the great Soviet scientist Bechterev now has her own neurophysiology laboratory.

Ironically, in spite of Vasiliev's long and close identification with this same Bechterev, he has failed to convince Bechterev's granddaughter of the genuineness of telepathy. Apparently her grandfather didn't convince her either.

I was granted an interview with Dr. Bechterev in Leningrad. When I asked her about Professor Vasiliev's work, she gave a little smile of tolerance and said: "We do not believe in telepathic communication. We have had no proof of it yet."

Moreover, she seemed about as little concerned with the human psyche as the great Pavlov before her had been, and certainly far less concerned than her grandfather had been—although as a modern neurophysiologist she deals in problems of brain research that were undreamed of in Pavlov's time. "Neurophysiology," she said, "should be more concerned with the diagnosis and treatment of brain diseases than with the psychological aspects of mental activity."

"There is no doubt," she added, "that the riddles of the brain are going to be solved by physics, mathematics, engineering, and cybernetics, all working together. But the approach has to be physiological, not psychological."

This might indicate that in spite of all the furor over Russian telepathy, there are still some Russian scientists who are no more sold on it than scientists anywhere else. In fact, a careful analysis of Professor Vasiliev's own works reveals that the wild claims of the Communist propaganda machine are not made by Vasiliev. He *tentatively* commits himself to a belief in the existence of mental suggestion—nothing more.

CHAPTER 2

Russian Telepathy—or Is It Hysteria?

In an age popping with scientific miracles too awesome and incredible for the human mind to grasp, a cocksure attitude is considered neither popular nor proper. It is safer to steer the middle course and say that nothing, but absolutely nothing, is impossible. For all I know we *may* be riding some space ships manned by telepathic pigeons even before this chapter is finished. On the other hand, it may be a long wait before such miracles come to pass.

There is nothing unique about good minds going astray; it has happened often in the past, but usually only one at a time. Only a country like Communist Russia, with its goal of conquering the world, could afford to throw so much money and manpower down the drain, chasing what may be nothing but a will-o'-the-wisp. The nature and contents of the human psyche, it seems, are as puzzling to the Russians as to anyone else.

The whole telltale drama of Russian telepathy unfolds meticulously and with painful scientific solemnity in Professor Vasiliev's *Long Distance Suggestion*, published in Moscow in 1962. On the second page of his book, Vasiliev tells in his own words the reason the Russians decided to do something about telepathy:

> In foreign countries, particularly in the USA, Great Britain, France, Holland, India, Argentina, and also in some social-ist countries, the research in this phenomena is being given great attention. In capitalist countries there are institutions, specialized laboratories, even university departments (e.g. in Utrecht), which explore mental suggestion and other "para-psychological phenomena" cognate to it. [*Note that Vasiliev puts "parapsychological phenomena in quotes.*]
>
> As time passes, reports about sensational experiments and discoveries in the field of research of the brain and psy-che have reached us from abroad. Thus, for instance, in De-cember 1959, and February 1960, articles appeared in the French popular-scientific journals giving the description of a sensational experiment, which was said to have been con-ducted on board the American submarine "Nautilus" . . .

Once started, Russian research in telepathy went full steam ahead. Vasiliev admits in his book that he was unable to verify the *Nautilus* experiment, but he repeatedly makes it clear that the Russians should take no chances. During my own stay in Russia I was quizzed persistently about the *Nau-tilus* experiments.

What happened immediately after Vasiliev read the *Nautilus* fairy tale is obvious to anyone who reads his reports and compares them with those put out by the Kremlin press corps. In the first place Vasiliev got busy doing some research and writing his own book. Apparently, he somehow managed to assemble enough lit-erature on the subject to get himself fairly well informed about parapsychology, extrasensory perception, and the "paranormal" claims regarding "psi phenomena" made my Dr. J. B. Rhine in the United States and Dr. S. G. Soal in England.

He was alternately awed, puzzled, and filled with apprehensions. He repeatedly expressed his presentiments in comments such as, "Soviet scientists are now faced with the not easy task of critically evaluating all present day statements of foreign 'parapsychologists.'" And—"It is hard to decide what is truth in [these] reports, and what is fiction. Only one thing is clear: It is not possible to neglect similar research work."

One can understand the consternation of Professor Vasiliev—he was 70 when hit by the *Nautilus* news—as he conscientiously weighs and ponders all the parapsychological "marvels" that are going on in capitalist countries.

Vasiliev's book is crammed with case histories of "spontaneous" telepathic phenomena—all culled from reports of American, British, Dutch, and French parapsychologists. And just to show the world that Russia is no laggard in these things, Vasiliev has included a number of "sensational" experiences and experiments involving his own countrymen.

"Very few people know," he wrote, "that in the very early thirties, when Dr. Rhine started his research in the USA, similar experiments to the same end, i.e., to prove the very existence of mental suggestion, were conducted at Leningrad . . ." Instead of card-guessing, the Russians used a roulette wheel.

The experimenter would spin the wheel, which would stop at either a black or white disc. The experimenter would then try to communicate "black" or "white" to a blindfolded subject to test the effect of "mental suggestion." Vasiliev studiously avoids using the term ESP in connection with any of the Russian experiments, and only cautiously uses the word telepathy, preferring the more scientifically acceptable term "mental suggestion," or sometimes, "nonverbal" suggestion.

Vasiliev's book apparently hasn't been read much outside the USSR. If it had been, there would not be such an uproar over Russian telepathy. For the clamor revolves around Vasiliev's purported success with "long-distance mental suggestion," and is based mainly on one experiment between Leningrad and Sevastopol, a distance of about 1200 miles.

In typical glowing terms, the Soviet press issued a news release on the Vasiliev book.

"Imagine yourself in a quiet park with an attractive young woman," it began . . . "And then the lady, who had just been talking with such animation, lapses into a silence, seems to forget your very existence and stares vacantly into space. 'I'm falling asleep,' she declares. Ten minutes pass, twenty, half an hour. In forty minutes the woman opens her eyes.

"'I'm sorry,' she says. 'I don't know what happened to me. I could swear that I was hypnotized . . .'" And indeed she was, the report stated. She had been put to sleep and awakened by "sheer willpower" in an experiment in "long-distance hypnotism" between Leningrad and Sevastopol.

"If you want to learn more about telepathy," the release continued, "read Professor Vasiliev's book. You will find out many amazing things. It seems that observant people in many countries have recorded many cases of so-called spontaneous telepathy, when sensations and vivid optical images were instantaneously transmitted from one person to another over tremendous distances . . .

"Page after page there passes before the reader an engrossing story about the most mysterious properties of living matter . . . Once you begin reading you will hardly lay the book aside until you get to the last word . . . More, you will surely wish to learn more about attempts to provide a scientific explanation of telepathic phenomena . . ."

There is no doubt that Vasiliev's book is an engrossing story up to the very last word, and the reader who takes the trouble to read the book instead of the Soviet reviews will indeed find out many amazing things—the most amazing of which is the fact that Vasiliev's highly touted, world-shaking "telepathy" experiments that have people quaking in their boots actually took place 30 years ago—between 1932 and 1937—while Vasiliev was working with V. M. Bechterev. And they boil down to something started by a Frenchman named Franz Anton Mesmer long before that.

At the age of eleven, Vasiliev saw someone hypnotized, and he apparently has never recovered. Hypnosis is his principal tool of research for investigating telepathy, and his experiments in "mental suggestion" fall a little short of what is commonly known as telepathy—a fact that Vasiliev himself admits. In fact, the most he claims to have achieved is "nonverbal hypnotizing" of a few subjects, and he admits that good subjects are "very hard to find."

Anyone conversant with this subject must feel a twinge of compassion for Vasiliev as he walks the scientific tightrope of contradiction and indecision—and all because he isn't sure what the capitalist countries are going to come up with next. But the ultimate irony, for those who are counting on Vasiliev to provide the gospel for modern, advanced, space-age telepathy, is that after all his troubles, he has concluded that the telepathic faculty, if it exists at all, can be of "biological significance" only for some animals, especially those living in muddy water. For these animals, he says, the telepathic faculty "may have some significance for the preservation of the race."

"But it does not play any significant biological part for people at the present time," he concludes, . . . because . . . "man possesses devices much more reliable for the long-distance transference of information."

Vasiliev has found that most of his successful subjects are hysterics and has concluded that telepathy is a symptom of hysteria. In fact, the much publicized long-distance experiment between Sevastopol and Leningrad did not take place with a young woman in a quiet park, as the Soviet news release indicated, but with a patient at the psychotherapeutic hospital connected with the Bechterev Brain Institute, where Vasiliev has found most of his best subjects.

Vasiliev claims to have long ago mastered the techniques of verbal suggestion in hypnosis. It is no longer necessary for him to say aloud to the subject, "Go to sleep. Go to sleep. You are falling, falling, falling. Now you are asleep." He merely *thinks* or wills the subject into a hypnotic trance without saying a word. This is what he calls "nonverbal" suggestion. When the subject is in another room or in a distant city, as in the Leningrad-Sevastopol experiments, the term "long-distance suggestion" is used.

In one series of experiments conducted jointly with scientists from the Bechterev Brain Institute and using as subjects patients suffering predominantly from hysteria, Vasiliev demonstrated, at least to his own satisfaction, that it is possible to hypnotize a subject in another room by mere mental suggestion. A rubber balloon filled with air was fastened to the subject's right hand and connected by a rubber hose and metal pipe to a registering device called a kymograph, which was in another room with the hypnologist. The subject, unaware of the nature of the experiment, was instructed only to press the balloon rhythmically. At a certain moment unknown to the subject, Vasiliev would transmit the mental order, "Go to sleep." Later he would transmit the order, "Wake up."

The electromagnetic registering apparatus showed that the balloon rhythms were interrupted during the subject's state of hypnotic sleep, and resumed upon waking. Vasiliev said that out of 260 such experiments, only 10 percent failed to respond to the mental hypnotizing or awakening. But Vasiliev does not claim that mental suggestion or mental influence on another person is the same thing as telepathy. Of far more importance in his opinion is whether specific *information* can be transmitted from mind to mind. In one experiment he mentally projected the picture of a bird to the subject, who was enclosed in a screening chamber in another room. The subject's telepathic antenna picked up the word "crow."

Similar experiments have led him to believe that subjects under hypnosis are able to perceive persons, movements, and objects in another room, and to pick up visual images projected by the hypnologist through nonverbal suggestion. It is not usually a word-for-word "thought transference," Vasiliev explains, but simply a two-way biological rapport that indicates the *possibility* of communicating information, in the form of images and ideas, from one human mind to another. Vasiliev's apparent honesty and sincerity are impressive, and his own personal conclusions regarding the possibility of developing or training a telepathic faculty for practical use are extremely conservative.

The exaggerated claims for telepathy experiments come from other Soviet sources, not from Vasiliev. He commits himself only to such cautious observations as, "Suggestibility is exceedingly increased during hypnosis"—a fact commonly known and accepted by scientists everywhere—and "The most conclusive method of investigation to date is nonverbal hypnotizing of subjects, but they are very hard to find."

A logical question might be whether hysterics or psychopaths—who seem to make the best subjects for experimentation—are the best suited for practical application of telepathy, and this is possibly one reason for Vasiliev's restraint in his conclusions.

How can telepathy be explained physiologically if ever its existence should be scientifically confirmed? This, of course, is the question that has stumped everyone concerned.

Neurologists say the electrical charges generated by brain cells are too minute for use as telepathic carriers.

Vasiliev emphasizes that the electromagnetic hypothesis, with which some have tried to explain telepathy, remains experimentally unproved. In fact, he specifically confirms the present-day stand of all serious scientists everywhere in these words: "A matter of 85 years of experimental research work has proved to be insufficiently long for long-distance suggestion to be generally recognized as a scientifically established fact."

However, he adds that it took a whole century to satisfy the scientific world of the existence of *mental suggestion* and of hypnotic trance—"which are the most common phenomena and more easily to be produced than long-distance suggestion." By mental suggestion, he clearly means just that—mere mental suggestion or mental influence on another person, which is not the same as telepathy.

For his own part he seems convinced of the *existence* of long-distance suggestion, though at present, he says, it is still difficult to guess what importance for science and life the practical mastering of the phenomena would have—since it would be "incomparably less exact and suitable for the realization of communication than a telegram or a telephone call."

Vasiliev feels that any rational, scientific, and materialistic explanation of telepathy must come either from cybernetics— the new science of control systems—or from the discovery of some yet unknown form of brain energy.

He and most Soviet scientists are working on the theory that there is still a new form of brain energy to be discovered. Discussing this theory, he says:

"Long-distance suggestion could be of gigantic significance for science and life in case the hypothesis based on our experiments should prove correct, namely, that telepathic transmission is accomplished by some kind of energy, or factor so far unknown to us, yet belonging to the highest stage of development of matter, i.e. to the substance and structure of the brain. To discover such energy or factor would be tantamount to the discovery of nuclear energy."

This is the direction in which scientists should concentrate their endeavors, he says; but he adds, "The solution of this question is still far ahead." In fact, on a final note of irony and honesty, he admits there is nothing whatever to indicate that the results achieved in his long-distance suggestion experiments were in any way connected with the activity of the brain. But, he concludes, "This means that something else, something new must be looked for. It has not happened only once in the history of science that the discovery of new facts which were inexplicable by the experience known until then entailed further discoveries of new, unknown aspects of being."

In Vasiliev's second book, *Experiments in Mental Suggestion*, published in 1963, he carries on the same fearful theme he expressed earlier: "We in the Soviet Union must not only keep abreast of that which already has been, and is being, done in the field abroad, but also gain our own experience."

In January 1963, British newspapers carried an announcement that plans were being made for a long-distance telepathy experiment between Cambridge and Leningrad. In August 1963, the *New York Times* carried a story headlined RUSSIANS REJECT TELEPATHY TESTS, and quoting Professor Vasiliev as saying that plans for the experiment were "a bit premature."

In January 1963, I spent several hours with three members of Vasiliev's staff—a physicist, a physiologist, and a psychologist. They told me, "We have not established whether telepathy exists. We want to find out. Then we can say yes or no."

CHAPTER 3

Can Hypnosis Explain Telepathy?

Psychologists and physiologists generally agree that in the twilight zone of hypnosis are locked many of the brain's unfathomable mysteries; but nowhere are scientists concentrating so much attention on hypnosis as in the USSR. Russian psychologists and physiologists have traditionally shown a great deal of interest in hypnotic phenomena, probably because of Pavlov's interest in it and the continuing predominance of the Pavlovian school in the USSR.

Scientific interest in hypnotism has had its ups and downs, possibly because of its long association with magical powers, particularly in primitive societies, and its use by stage entertainers. Hypnotic suggestion had been around a long time before Mesmer began his wild claims with "animal magnetism," thus bringing the whole subject of hypnotism into disrepute. Serious investigation into hypnotism was revived in the latter half of the nineteenth century under the leadership of two French psychopathologists, Hippolyte Bernheim at Nancy, and Jean Charcot at the Salpetriere Hospital. The Nancy school explained hypnotism in terms of suggestion; the Salpetriere school considered hypnosis to be a pathological state analogous to hysteria. Though "war" was declared between the two schools, both turned out to be right, according to most modern investigators.

For the whole problem of hypnotism is inextricably bound up with the problem of suggestion. Hypnotism is, in fact, merely a particular method of inducing an increased state of suggestibility in an individual. And hysteria can be regarded, for purposes of comparison, as a state of high suggestibility accompanied by a tendency towards mental dissociation.

The main difference between hysteria and hypnosis in this respect is that the effects or symptoms of *genuine* hysteria are due to a pathological state of mind, while in hypnosis the effects are produced artificially.

Psychic phenomena such as telepathy or general ESP have sometimes been identified with hysteria, mental dissociation, or other psychopathic characteristics that can be induced through hypnosis.

When scientists can explain hypnosis, they will have unlocked the door to the mind. When they can explain the phenomenon of *suggestion*, they will have solved the riddle of *mind power*.

In a deep hypnotic trance—or a heightened state of suggestibility—the hypnotized subject can be made to experience all kinds of delusions, to carry out the most absurd and unreasonable actions, to assume a totally different personality, to remember events that he has long ago consciously forgotten, to fall into a rigid cataleptic trance, to become insensible to pain, or to impersonate, dramatically, the multiple personalities that inhabit his subconscious being.

The hypnotic nature of "possession," as it is usually called in reference to primitive cultures, or personality dissociation, as it is known in modern psychology, is unquestioned.

Nearly everyone has seen this phenomenon demonstrated by stage hypnotists, who can produce multiple personalities on demand in a hypnotized subject merely through the simple and incredible technique of suggestion. Most of us have seen samples of what is generally known as age-regression under hypnosis.

Age-regression, in which a subject recalls or relives events from his past that he has consciously forgotten, has been the subject of constant controversy ever since this strange hypnotic phenomena was discovered in 1887 by Krafft-Ebing. The controversy has centered around how much of the phenomena is valid and how much is role playing.

The debate is irrelevant in the overall picture, for it has been firmly established that age-regression is a genuine mental phenomenon that can be produced by hypnosis—or, perhaps more important, by chemicals or by electrical stimulation of certain areas of the brain. In fact, modern research into the effects of drugs and electrical stimuli on the brain has reinforced the science of hypnology with new evidence that the normal, nonhysterical human brain can be made to produce on demand—by stimulation—many of the same mental aberrations associated with genuine hysterics or produced artificially by hypnosis.

In this respect, the observations of Wilder Penfield, of Montreal, one of the world's leading neurologists, are intriguing. Penfield found during operations on epileptics that when certain small regions of the temporal lobe were stimulated, some of his patients could remember in vivid detail scenes, dreams, and tunes from their distant pasts, and even acquaintances' voices from childhood.

Psychologists have used hypnotic age-regression in psychotherapeutic treatment. Perhaps one of the best known of recent cases was that of Eve White, recorded in *The Three Faces of Eve*, the fantastic true story of a housewife who was "three women in one body." Eve found her real self only after she was led back through age-regression psychotherapy to remember and relive a terrifying event from early childhood—her grandmother's funeral. There are well-authenticated cases of subjects being carried back to the age of one month in hypnotic age regression—but there are no authenticated cases of a subject being regressed to a foetal existence or to some previous life, as the sensational Bridey Murphy story claimed.

Despite the popular and sensational aspects of hypnotism, serious researchers no longer question the genuine effects produced under the strange power of hypnotic suggestion. Major surgical operations have been performed on patients in deep hypnotic sleep, without the patients feeling the least pain. Analgesia, or the inability to feel pain, can also be induced locally—in an arm or a leg, for example—through hypnotic suggestion. Similarly, hypnotic suggestion can induce localized physiological inflammations, blisters, and nose-bleeding.

In fact, so enormous is the force of suggestion and so highly suggestible are some people that among primitive tribes *death by suggestion* is an established fact. The "curse" of the witch-doctor is no myth. "Thanatomania," the anthropological name for death by suggestion, is still prevalent in the Stone Age culture of the Australian aborigines. The witch doctor's "curse" can get such a hold on the suggestible mind of primitive man that it can result in death within a few days. He believes he will die, and die he does—unless his friends manage to persuade the witch doctor to "lift" the curse.

The overwhelming implications of the power of hypnotic suggestion are obvious, and apparently more so to Soviet scientists *en masse* than to scientists elsewhere. There are thought-provoking reports of Russian research in hypnosis in many directions—particularly in medicine, space research, the training of astronauts, and telepathy.

One Russian astronaut, when asked by an American interviewer whether he had been hypnotized for his space trip, replied, "I did not have to be put to sleep. I was thoroughly conditioned." It is believed that the Russians subject their astronauts to long periods of conditioning through hypnosis before their space flights, and appeals have been made to the U.S. Defense Department to do the same. During the first Invitational Congress of Hypnosis in November 1962, in Las Vegas, a telegram was sent to Defense Secretary Robert A. McNamara urging the use of hypnosis on astronauts.

The appeal asserted that hypnosis would enable American astronauts to match Russia's efforts in space by helping them to achieve concentration and peace of mind, to use less oxygen, and to require less rest.

Some experts also believe that hypnosis could be valuable in offsetting the possibility of a psychotic condition developing during a space flight. Actual experiments have shown the effects of "stimulus deprivation" similar to that endured by space pilots. For example, in some experiments a subject is immersed in a tub of water at body temperature, to remove all extraneous skin stimulation, he is blind-folded, and he has his ears blocked. The experience is wonderful—for the first hour. After that the subject develops hallucinations and seems headed for a psychotic crisis.

The astronaut's space suit, his relative lack of mobility, the use of his eyes only to look at his instruments and of his ears only to listen to radio communications—all these deprive him of the normal stimuli of everyday life. He may tolerate such deprivation for a while—as Gordon Cooper did for 34 hours, and apparently quite well—but in trying for more orbits or a shot to the moon, posthypnotic suggestion might well provide a built-in escape valve of artificial stimuli that could be turned on and off on demand.

Although the Russians are very hush-hush on points dealing with specific technical information, it is known that a great deal of their research in hypnosis is based on Pavlov's conditioned-reflex principles and findings of EEG studies. Those who are at all familiar with the Russian research say that in the past ten years, much work of value has been accomplished, almost all of which is unknown in the U.S.

You are probably wondering how hypnosis can explain telepathy. From all indications, the Russians are still wondering, too.

The theory is that if the phenomenon of telepathy exists, as some believe, it is activated through the unconscious, or subconscious mind, and thus hypnosis would be the device with which to tap it and bring it under control of the conscious mind—at least for repeatable experiments. But can it produce telepathy? Can it *cause telepathy to occur?* This is the crux of the problem. It is also the gossamer thread of hope that spans everything from mesmerism to cybernetics in the Soviet drive toward conquering mind power.

To date there is no evidence that either hypnosis, vision-producing drugs, ESB (electrical stimulation of the brain), or cybernetical machines have been able to produce, imitate, recreate, or cause to occur the mental activity known as telepathy—the direct transference of thoughts from one mind to another.

Professor Vasiliev's experiments in nonverbal suggestion have sometimes been compared to those of Dr. James Esdaile, a well-known medical hypnologist of more than a century ago.

It is believed by some that both Vasiliev's and Esdaile's work in hypnotizing subjects without verbal commands offers proof that hypnosis can be induced by telepathy. However, a careful study of Esdaile's work with mesmerism in India would indicate that his successful results in nonverbal hypnotizing of patients were based on conditioning, expectation, and autosuggestion—not on telepathy. In fact, nowhere does Esdaile indicate any relationship between his method and telepathy.

Approximately the same can be said of Vasiliev's experiments in long-distance mental suggestion; his results may be due to hypnotic conditioning, expectation, and autosuggestion. Nowhere does he claim they are due to telepathy.

The term "mental suggestion" was first used in France in 1884 by Charles Richet, the 1913 Nobel Prize winner in physiology and medicine, who was also interested in psychical research and whose brilliant scientific mind also gullibly accepted the brazen trickeries of many famous spiritualist mediums.

From the standpoint of modern telepathy research, so far as concrete results are concerned, mental (or nonverbal) suggestion amounts to the same thing as mesmerism, or animal magnetism, in pretty much its original form. That is, a subject can be mesmerized, or hypnotized, or induced into a state of trance—in varying degrees—merely by *suggestion*. The hypnotist does not need to wave a wand or wear a lilac-colored cloak or speak a word or even be in the same room with his subject. The suggestible subject is hypnotized just the same, through conditioning, expectation, and/or autosuggestion. But again it must be emphasized that this is not the same as telepathy, nor is it evidence that hypnosis can be induced by telepathy.

One of the popular misconceptions concerning hypnotism is that a subject's senses are sharpened under hypnosis. For example, it has been claimed that hypnosis can improve the memory. But modern investigation has shown that despite extraordinary results of hypnosis in recalling past events (more effective in hysterical subjects), hypnosis has, *if anything, a slightly deleterious effect* on the memories of normal persons.

Some also believe that under hypnotic suggestion a subject's senses are so sharpened as to become extrasensory. One of the most talked-about experimenters in telepathy in countries behind the Iron Curtain is Milan Ryzl, a young Czechoslovakian chemist whose card-guessing experiments with hypnotically trained subjects have attracted wide attention. Ryzl is a graduate of the University of Prague, where he majored in chemistry and natural sciences. As a sideline he became interested in hypnosis and discovered in working with the blind that a blind person could apparently tell time rather accurately under hypnosis simply by touching a watch and, presumably by some means other than normal sensory perception, ascertaining the positions of the hands on the watch.

For the past few years, Ryzl and Dr. J. G. Pratt, who for many years was J. B. Rhine's assistant at Duke University, have been engaged in a series of experiments to test the hypothesis that telepathic powers, as well as other extrasensory faculties, can be developed or improved under hypnotic conditioning.

Meantime, however, there is little foundation in claims that hypnosis can "sharpen" the senses to the point of telepathy. Most alleged cases of "hyperacuity" or "hyperaesthesia" (an unusual degree of sensitivity of sense organs) can be traced to minimal cues or involuntary articulations by the hypnotist.

Apparently, hypnotized subjects have not yet passed the real test of telepathy. In 1962, *Hypnosis Quarterly* magazine (Vol. 7, No. 4) offered $1000 to anyone who could call out three words the editor would write on a piece of paper.

Although the offer was published and remained open for several months, no one accepted the challenge.

It is perhaps also significant that in the literature on hypnosis the word telepathy is rarely mentioned by any recognized authorities on hypnosis. In a random selection of ten books, only one mentioned telepathy, and it stated: "Telepathic tests under hypnosis have been conducted by nearly every dabbler in hypnotism, mostly with no controls and unscientifically. Results reported are often astounding—and completely worthless as proof that hypnosis increases a telepathic faculty." (*Hypnotism Today*, L. M. LeCron and J. Bordeaux)

There still remains the fact that Russian scientists, who obviously are more than mere dabblers in hypnotism, are seriously exploring all avenues to the brain's mysteries. If some of their theories seem to be ridiculous and preposterous—well, so did some of those of Galileo.

CHAPTER 4

Whither Parapsychology?

In the tumultuous race to conquer space and the mind, it would be foolish to discount, dogmatically and categorically, *anything* as impossible. It once seemed impossible to fly in the air. Nevertheless, people do now fly in the air. It is very possible that all the researchers in telepathy are dead wrong and are being mislead by a will-o-the-wisp, as were those who believed in alchemy and phrenology in another day. It is also possible that the worldwide telepathy boom may result in the discovery of a new form of energy, a discovery that, as Professor Vasiliev speculated, would be equal in importance to the splitting of the atom.

One fact in this maze of unknowns stands out as certain: at no time in history have men of science and world governments taken such a penetrating look at the mental phenomena known collectively as telepathy. As Professor Vasiliev has pointed out in his second book, *Experiments in Mental Suggestion:* "Nowadays, mental suggestion . . . also finds support in the most recent branch of scientific thought—information theory and cybernetics."

It is significant that in September 1963, scientists at the Massachusetts Institute of Technology set a precedent by holding a two-day symposium with six of America's leading parapsychologists in attendance. Also, researchers at the Newark College of Engineering, alerted by the Russian experiments in telepathy, have scientifically explored several intriguing and promising avenues of "nonconventional communication"—or telepathy.

In New Delhi, the Indian government has launched a major research program within one of its leading universities to study the riddles of the mind in terms of practical application. Its approach is similar to that of the Russians—through the physical sciences. There are even rumors of secret National Aeronautics and Space Administration projects in levitation, or table-tipping. But so far there have been very few authenticated cases of U.S. government projects in this area.

At Bedford, Massachusetts, the Cambridge Research Laboratories of the U.S. Air Force conducted a series of ESP experiments with the aid of an electronic device called the *Veritac*. The results proved nothing, and the equipment, reports said, turned out to be useful for experiments other than ESP.

A U.S. space official, Dr. Eugene B. Konecci, reviewed the Russian experiments in "information transfer" by telepathy at the International Astronautics Federation in Paris and noted the widespread interest in the subject. Dr. Konecci, who is director of biotechnology and human research for NASA and also chairman of the IAF's bioastronautics committee, told me in an interview that the U.S. government had no projects afoot to test scientifically the validity of nonphysical information transfer, but indicated that he did not consider telepathy or mind-to-mind communication between people on earth and astronauts on the moon an impossibility. The worth of such studies, he said, should not be discounted, adding that nonphysical information transfer is a "highly interesting problem in modern science."

The reaction I have encountered throughout Europe and America to the Russian experiments in telepathy ranges all the way from "Hogwash!" to an honest avowal that the Russians just might have something.

Dr. W. Grey Walter, director of the Burden Neurological Institute in Bristol, England, and one of the world's leading brain physiologists, told me: "We must confess at this stage that no study of brain activity has thrown any light on the peculiar forms of behavior known variously as second-sight, clairvoyance, telepathy, extrasensory perception and psychokinesis (mind over matter). It has often been suggested by those seeking a material basis for otherwise unaccountable behavior that the electrical activity of the brain might be the mechanism whereby information could be transmitted from brain to brain . . . The actual scale and properties of the brain's electrical mechanisms offer no support for this theory."

In Vienna, I talked to Dr. Arthur Kline, former Boston neurologist and now dean of the Postgraduate Medical School, University of Vienna. He said, "We know there are electronic impulses in the brain cells which can be conveyed. We know the power of mind over matter. This is the basis of psychosomatic medicine. When we discover how brain cells generate energy to control the entire body we will have discovered the secret of existence."

Medical scientists, he added, are interested in the physiological mechanics of the brain—not metaphysics. As for telepathy: "You can *train* the mind to do anything." But he doubted that it could be trained for long-distance telepathy.

In Paris, leading French cybernetician Louis Couffignal, inspector general for the Ministry of Education and president of the Association for Cybernetical Pedagogy, said: "Telepathy is not at all impossible. But the difficulty is how to transmit a telepathic language or sign signals recognizable in a normal sensory way. I wouldn't want to be on a space ship manned by telepathy."

In Breda, Holland, Dr. J. M. Kooey, a Dutch physicist and specialist in rocketry, astrodynamics, and orbit calculations at the Royal Netherlands Military Academy, told me: "Beyond any doubt telepathy could be used for military purposes. But it would be unreliable and dangerous."

At the University of Freiburg in Germany, Professor Hans Bender, head of the psychology department, commented, "We have made scientific investigations of sleep, dreams, and memory functions. Why not telepathy? I think the experiments in telepathy behind the Iron Curtain may be more significant than we realize."

In London I talked to Gordon Pask, one of the world's top experts in cybernetics, who is working on brain-simulating machines for the U.S. Army and Air Force. In his opinion there is nothing absurd or far-fetched in including telepathy as a field of solid scientific research. "Either the whole concept is nonsense," he said, "or if not, the consequences can be enormous. If telepathy can be demonstrated scientifically, it can also be used to control space ships."

This divergence of opinion expressed by scientists with whom I have talked is representative of the varying opinions held by laymen. The number of individuals interested in ESP must be astronomical, for who among us has not talked at some time with someone who either believes he has experienced extrasensory perception or knows someone else who thinks he has? The opinions of these individuals, it seems, range all the way from utter scorn to complete belief, with the vast majority lying somewhere in between and characterized by a questioning "there-may-be-something-to-it-but-prove-it" attitude.

As this is written, there can be no doubt that scientific opinion is still preponderantly against the belief in these psychic phenomena—but science-fiction these days is hard put to keep up with reality, and there are many serious-minded individuals who are convinced that a breakthrough is imminent in the field of human telepathy.

The word telepathy, defined as thought transference or apparent communication from one mind to another otherwise than through the channels of sense, was invented in 1882 by F.W.H. Myers, one of the founders of the Society for Psychical Research in London. Myers was also author of the book, *Human Personality and Its Survival of Bodily Death*, one of the classics in psychic literature. Thus, as Professor Vasiliev and many others have pointed out, telepathy has had an intimate association with spiritualism, which could not be accommodated in the modern sciences.

Thus, too, parapsychology was born as a specialized branch of study and research dealing with beyond-the-grave questions. Parapsychology, in brief, is the study of such purported phenomena as telepathy, precognition (foretelling the future), clairvoyance, psycho kinesis (mind over matter), and the occult powers of mediums. Most of these are lumped together under two popular alphabetical categories, ESP (for extrasensory perception) and PK (for psychokinesis); and together they are included in the broad overall catch-phrase "psi," meaning psychic abilities. The term extrasensory perception originated with Dr. J. B. Rhine, director of Duke Uni-

versity's Parapsychology Laboratory and a central figure in the
continuing debate over ESP.

While parapsychology—the modern term now given to
psychical research—has attracted many reputable and well-
informed scholars and scientifically trained minds, it also has
been subjected over the years to a great deal of criticism. Psychologist C.E.M. Hansel of the University of Manchester in
England, for example, has charged that "no experiment yet
reported satisfies the basic requirements of science."

In the spotlight of publicity identifying ESP with Dr. Rhine
and Duke University, few among the general public have realized the true scope of parapsychological research now going on.

One of the most active research centers, for example, is
connected with the famed Menninger Foundation in Topeka,
Kansas, and is headed by Dr. Gardner Murphy, who is recognized as one of the nation's leading psychologists. One of
its projects is a study of the relation between creativity and
extrasensory perception. Another, being conducted jointly
by Dr. Murphy and Dr. Karlos Osis, director of the American Society for Psychical Research in New York, is called the
"ESP and Creativity" and involves the interviewing of New
York artists to determine what goes on psychologically during
their peak periods of creativity.

Two little-publicized groups that have over the years
attracted the interest of men of integrity in virtually every
profession are the American Society for Psychical Research
and the Parapsychology Foundation, both in New York. The
A.S.P.R. is the American counterpart of the Society for Psychical Research in London, the oldest and perhaps most highly
esteemed of any of the psychical-research societies.

Dr. Karlos Osis, director of the A.S.P.R. in New York, is
recognized as one of the outstanding men in the field. He has

recently been engaged in conducting surveys on "deathbed observations," and these investigations have turned up some thought provoking information on the most common emotions, visions, hallucinations, and personality changes in the dying.

The surveys are aimed at learning more about the psychology and behavior of a dying person in his last hours before death, and although this is perhaps not the most enchanting area in the world to research, the surveys shed light on a hitherto unexplored area of the mind. The surveys indicate, for example, that not fear, but pain and discomfort followed by elation is the common pattern at the hour of death.

In one case reported, a patient suffering from severe schizophrenia and out of touch with reality for two years regained normal mentality shortly before death. If the observation was accurate, this would indicate an extremely important area for psychiatrists to explore.

It is not entirely inconceivable that these deathbed studies might illuminate certain areas of psychical research that to date have not been explained by ESP of PK experiments.

Dr. Ian Stevenson, head of the department of psychiatry at the University of Virginia, is also engaged in a long-term project on a subject that even some parapsychologists consider taboo—reincarnation. He has personally and with collaborators investigated cases of alleged reincarnation in many countries, and has accumulated a massive amount of unusual case histories and carefully sifted facts. Dr. Stevenson is cautious in his approach and has reached no conclusions. His project is still in its infancy, but it is possible that it may one day provide some of the answers to the mystery of death, which has been one of the greatest challenges to man's intellect through the ages.

The work of Dr. J. G. Pratt also may one day shed new light on the mental processes lumped together as ESP or psi.

Dr. Pratt's experiments in collaboration with Milan Ryzl of Prague have caught the attention of scientists who heretofore have been dubious about ESP. He is the only parapsychologist in America to receive an official invitation from Professor Vasiliev to visit his laboratory in Leningrad, late in 1963.

There are many other highly respected researchers studying various aspects of ESP problems from diverse angles.

In most cases parapsychologists must carry on their research independently, supported by private grants, and with little if any academic recognition or encouragement from the institutions with which they are associated.

A notable exception to this is Professor Hans Bender, of the University of Freiburg, one of Germany's leading psychologists. He has won academic recognition, respect, and support for his careful, scientific approach to a subject whose scientific status is still being debated.

The University of Freiburg is one of the few places—perhaps the only one with the possible exception of Rhodes University in South Africa—where parapsychology has achieved a genuine academic status as an integral part of a university teaching curriculum. Professor Bender is permitted to schedule classes and lectures in parapsychology, in addition to his regular courses in psychology. He is also director of the University's Institute for Border Areas of Psychology and Mental Hygiene. At Freiburg, parapsychology is classified under the "border areas of psychology," and the research emphasis has been on dream analysis as a tool in psychotherapy. Both Professor Bender and his assistant, Dr. Inge Strauch, are well known in America as well as in Europe for their depth research in dreams.

Curiously enough, some of the most important contributions in the entire field of psychical research have been made possible by a woman who was once a well-known medium, Mrs. Eileen J. Garrett, head of the Parapsychology Foundation in New York. Mrs. Garrett was one of the first mediums tested by Dr. Rhine at Duke in the early years when his main interest was focused by the question of survival after death. In fact, it was the result of his tests with Mrs. Garrett that led him to develop his famous ESP card-guessing tests.

Up to that time it was often asserted that mediums obtained their supernormal knowledge from the spirits of the dead. Many, of course, still believe this. But Dr. Rhine theorized that Mrs. Garrett could have obtained her information not by spirit communication, but by clairvoyance or by telepathy from living persons. However, as Dr. Rhine later explained, evidence for telepathy and clairvoyance at that time, "though suggestive, was not conclusive." The obvious need, he decided, was to develop tests to show whether or not they were alternatives to the survival hypothesis. He then developed the ESP cards and the experiments to establish whether telepathy and clairvoyance existed.

Meantime, Mrs. Garrett turned her talents and her wealth into other parapsychological channels—which at times, ironically, have proved a major source of embarrassment to psi researchers. One of her principal projects has been the sponsoring of investigations of phony mediums. It was Mrs. Garrett who sponsored and financed the calamitous exposure of the Sir William Crookes-Katie King affair, the details of which are given in Chapter Eleven. Mrs. Garrett's Parapsychology Foundation also sponsors and finances a wide range of projects in serious psychical research, from psi-hunting among the Australian aborigines to psi-development under hypnosis.

From all of this it can be clearly seen that the modern field of parapsychology embraces some areas that would have little appeal for Soviet space scientists with their materialistic attitudes. Therefore, it is not surprising that they disclaim western concepts of ESP in their telepathy-research program. They have admitted that their interest in telepathic communication was based on a fear of what the capitalist countries are doing; and now, ironically, the capitalist countries, apprehensive of what the Russians may be doing, are trying to catch up with them.

Experiments at the Newark College of Engineering, for example, have stressed the significance of the Vasiliev experiments in Leningrad, in applying for grants to further their own telepathic research. The Newark experiments, conducted by Douglas Dean and Robert Taetzsch, involve the use of the plethysmograph, an electronic research instrument first used about 100 years ago and now a psychiatrist's tool for testing emotional responses.

Dean and Taetzsch claim that tests with the plethysmograph show a connection between the thought of one person and the unconscious physiological reaction of another. Their ultimate goal is to perfect a "psi communication system" that will permit the sending of telepathic messages through the use of coded signals and electronic computers. No actual telepathic message has yet been communicated, but the Dean-Taetzsch plethysmography research is regarded as one of the brightest new leads on the horizon of parapsychology—and of telepathy as a means of nonconventional communication.

Perhaps the most sensible summary of the problem is expressed in Professor Vasiliev's words:

"Every year more and more researchers are becoming convinced of the real existence of mental suggestion and study the various aspects of these complex phenomena. This does not, however, mean that mental suggestion has yet found general recognition by scientists—not in the least. Arguments for and against are still going on. The question of the energetic nature of mental suggestion is not a futile problem: it is beginning to exercise the minds of outstanding representatives of the most advanced branch of modern science—physics. And this provides a guarantee that, in one way or another, sooner or later, the problem will be solved."

Meditative Yogis in the public square of Jaipur, India, surrounded by smoldering firepits which have a spiritual significance in the development of their ascetic philosophy. Modern science has established the genuine and astounding nature of many of the Yogi's physiological and mental feats.

India, cradle of mysticism, abounds in esoteric beliefs and practices, turbaned Swamis, "rope tricks," and fortune tellers. Here a man famous as the King of the Astrologers gives Norma Lee Browning a reading at the Rambagh Palace in Jaipur. He scored well on fortune telling, but failed the ESP card test Miss Browning gave him.

Yoga training is a long and difficult process, involving several stages, including semi-acrobatic postures, complicated breathing exercised, and specialized mental exercises. In this sequence, a Yogi demonstrates various phases of his physical training. Scientific studies being made of Yogis at the All India Institute of Medical Sciences have shown that they can voluntarily slow their heart-beat, reduce their oxygen requirements by 45 to 50 percent in air-tight box experiments, and voluntarily control certain automatic functions of the nervous system.

H. N. Banerjee (*left*), research director in Parapsychology in the State of Rajasthan, India; Dr. K. Sampurnanda, Governor of Rajasthan; and Norma Lee Browning. Dr. Sampurnanda, a scholar of both Sanskrit and Yoga, maintains that Yogis do not have extrasensory perception, but rather a highly refined extension and development of the normal sensory organs and powers that are latent in everyone.

PART II

Gullible's Travels

by Norma Lee Browning

CHAPTER 5

The Psychic Life of the Aborigines

In the desolate, forbidden, outback bush country of northern Australia lives the most archaic human race in existence, the Australian aborigines. They are a Stone Age people believed to have evolved from a Neanderthaloid people who lived in Java 150,000 years ago.

They eat pythons by the yard, trade wives for tins of tobacco, practice the most pagan forms of tribal black magic and witchcraft, and are superabundantly endowed with mysterious mental powers that are widely accepted as genuine and have defied scientific explanation. Missionaries, government workers, skeptical newspaper men, cattle ranchers, geologists, and even staid anthropologists who have worked or lived among the aborigines all will testify unequivocally that these incredibly primitive people really do communicate over long distances by some form of mental telepathy.

All can verify cases of death by "pointing the bone." All know of natives who have been "sung" to death by a malevolent Doctor Blackfellow. All are familiar with the terrible curse of the Wilgin Woman and the evil powers of the Mulunguwa executioner and the sorcerer's menacing threat: *I'll have your kidney fat.*" (And he does!) All have experienced the strange and unfathomable silent-communications system of the aborigines—their ability to send and receive messages through finger talk, muscle-twitching, smoke signals, footprints, message sticks, and their Dream-Time totems.

In man's race to unlock the secrets of the human mind, biologists have been mobilized for an accelerated research program with special emphasis on the study of primitive societies. It is doubtful whether they could find a society more primitive than the aborigines or any better subject for studies in such genuine mental phenomena as hypnosis, autosuggestion, the posthypnotic trance, mind-over-matter and extrasensory perception. The aborigines are undoubtedly the most hypersensitive race of people in the world, and the most highly suggestible, the most nontalkative, and the most psychic in the truest literal sense of the word. The word psychic is derived from the Greek word *psychikos*, meaning *of the soul or life, spiritual.* It also means: sensitive to nonphysical forces. Nothing could fit the aborigines more perfectly.

Most of us will admit that it is possible to be cured and live by faith, but the aborigines do it in reverse and go on dying by faith—only because they have been "sung" or cursed by "bone pointing." Incredible as it may seem, it nevertheless is a fact that in the year 1963 aborigines were still "willing" themselves to die after the curse of the Medicine Man; and the Mulunguwa, or tribal executioner, was still carrying out tribal murders with the aid of posthypnotic suggestion. And they were still communicating silently in ways that white man will probably never fathom.

At 2:30 one morning, Tommy Two Fingers awakened his boss, a mining prospector, and said, "Got 'em go now. My uncle bin got 'em bad trouble. Bin kill'm properly-dead-finish."

Later, it was verified that his uncle had been killed in an accident at 2:30 that morning, 75 miles away.

Queenie, an aborigine dog woman (one who takes care of her clan's dogs), wandered into the superintendent's office of the Maningrida government settlement early one morning and said, "My brother bin properly-dead-finish." The superintendent knew that Queenie's brother was in Cape York, over 200 miles away. "You've been dreaming again, Queenie," the superintendent said. Just then a wireless message came through: "If Queenie's still around, tell her that her brother died at 5 o'clock this morning." The superintendent turned to Queenie and asked, "How did you know that, Queenie?" "I just knew," said Queenie.

Fully verified reports of this kind are so common in the aborigines' strange never-never land that it is difficult to discount them. In nearly a month of living among the aborigines, I asked hundreds of them how they did it—how they could know what was happening sometimes hundreds of miles away. Long Billy and his wife Peggy said, "We know. We just know." Donkey, a tribal executioner with seven wives, said, "It's the Dreamin'." Michael, a Kunapipi headman, said "The Dreamin'."

The answers were always the same: "We just know." or: "Dreamin'."

The word *dreaming*, however, does not mean the same to aborigines as to most people. The secret life of the aborigines is intricately interwoven with their pagan mythology, the core of which is their sacred Dream-Time, or creative past. It was the Dream-Time that gave them the great Earth Mother Goddess and the Rainbow Serpent, which they worship in the most sacred of all their religious corroborees, the Kunapipi.

The Earth Mother was the source of life in man and nature, both in the Dream-Time and now; it was she who brought the totems into being, who breathed life into animals, birds, reptiles, spirits, and inanimate objects; it was she who created all the totemic heroes and sky gods and spirit children after the Rainbow Serpent "made the road." Animistic, totemistic, and spirit beliefs are part of the Dream-Time way of the aborigines. They believe in a spirit-double in the animal world and a spirit preexistence before birth. They do not know or believe that conception occurs through sexual intercourse; for them it is achieved by spirits.

The aborigines have sometimes been called "the lowest race of mankind" because their brain cavity is smaller and their quantity of brain matter 20 percent less than in Europeans; because they practice wife-lending, blood-sucking, scalp-biting, and sorcery; because their circumcision or initiation rites and corroborees (ceremonials) are the most pagan of any primitive peoples; and because their Dream-Time way of life is incomprehensible to white men. Nevertheless, Kunapipi, the Earth Mother, and the Rainbow Serpent are a reality and a living faith for the aborigines, and quite inseparable from the pattern of everyday life and thought. The Kunapipi religious ceremony, for example, goes on for six months—compared with the one-hour-a-week religious services in many modern civilized societies.

Anthropologists have written voluminously on the aborigines' complex customs and beliefs—much more than can be condensed in a chapter. But it is important to know a little of their culture and mythology before even trying to understand their strange mental magic.

Many aborigines have never seen white men. In fact, except by special government permit usually granted only to missionaries and anthropologists, white people are not allowed to enter Arnhem Land, the home of the few aborigine tribes least touched by civilization. It took two weeks of negotiations with government and church officials in Sydney, Canberra, and Darwin for my husband and me to obtain the required written permits to enter Arnhem Land. And these were granted only after a guarantee that we would provide our own transportation—a chartered bush plane—as well as camping equipment and guides.

During "the wet," as the rainy season is known, there are no roads into Arnhem Land, and we were there during the wet. It is a land of brimming billabongs (land-locked lakes), weird rock escarpments, and mangrove swamps infested with snakes and crocodiles. We had to wear high-topped shoes to avoid snakebite, and we never went out at night without flashlights.

The plane we chartered was a double-winged model of Wright Brothers vintage that was ordinarily used for transporting buffalo meat out of the bush. In spots it was held together with bailing wire, safety pins, and adhesive tape. The door dropped off once, but Ding Dong Bell, who was our pilot—and the best bush pilot in the Northern Territory—kept reassuring us that the plane would hold up until we got back to Darwin.

We had three guides with us—René Henri, a Frenchman famed in Australia as a big-game and crocodile shooter; Allan Stewart, who operates a buffalo camp at Nourlangie in western Arnhem Land and who acted as our interpreter; and Young Nim, a full-blooded aborigine from the Mailli tribe who apparently was accustomed to communicating by telepathy or sign language. During our entire trip with him, we rarely heard him utter a sound.

We spent a week at the Nourlangie campsite on the Alligator River, where we lived mostly on wild-buffalo meat and barramundi, a kind of fish the natives catch in the billabongs. We then flew on to Maningrida, a government settlement in the heart of one of the largest aboriginal reserves in Australia. Maningrida is in the primeval bushland at the mouth of the Liverpool River in north-central Arnhem Land on the Arafura coast, and as remote from "The Whitefeller Way" as Lambarene was for Dr. Albert Schweitzer when he first sailed up the Agowe River in the Belgian Congo. This is the tribal territory of the Berara and the Gunavidji tribesmen, the most warlike of the aborigines.

We were permitted to pitch camp with our swag and tucker (camp-cots and food) in an abandoned schoolroom. The pickaninnies had "gone bush" or on "walkabouts" with their families, leaving the schoolroom vacant. They might return in a few months, a few years, or—more probably—never. The government's new policy of "assimilation" for aborigines has been frustrating. Not only is the aborigine not literate but his capacity for learning is limited by his smaller quantity of brain matter, as well as by his ancestral customs and beliefs. The aborigines are biologically nomadic; they walk as much as 35 miles a day and do not live in permanent settlements or villages. They are divided into tribal groups and spend most of their time on "walkabouts," wandering over their tribal lands to attend intertribal functions, fights, and corroborees.

The aborigines' means of livelihood is hunting, fishing, and food-gathering. They do not plant crops or gardens, nor do they engage in any form of agriculture or stock-raising, preferring to find their food where nature gives it, with no assistance from them except through their religious and ritualistic magic and corroborees. Because of their prehistoric background and primitive features, anthropologists have eliminated the aborigines from the three main divisions of mankind—Negroid, Mongoloid, and European—and have put them in a special racial category of their own—the Austroloid.

Their empire once numbered 250,000 but has dwindled to 50,000, of which 19,000 are scattered throughout the Northern Territory, an area covering one-sixth of the Australian continent. Others are called "fringe dwellers," living on the outskirts of country towns and working spasmodically in mining camps or on cattle stations, but it is Arnhem Land that holds the last remnants of the most primitive and archaic of the aborigine tribes, those who are still comparatively untouched by "civilizing" influences.

No one knows for certain how many Aborigines still roam the 31,200-square-mile area of Arnhem Land. The Australian government's estimate of 4000 is a stab in the dark, literally, for Arnhem Land, besides being one of the most remote and isolated spots in the world, is itself an impenetrable heart of darkness, with rugged escarpments, towering ranges, and terrain so inhospitable that much of it has never been seen by white men.

It would obviously require remarkable mental and sensory powers merely to survive in this primeval bushland. The aborigines have developed these powers from sheer necessity. They cannot read or write, nor can they count above ten. But they can live for long periods in parts of the bush where white men would die of thirst and hunger. They can put up a paperbark shelter in minutes or fashion a boomerang as accurate as any modern missile.

They can spot a wallaby or a kangaroo or a mopoke bird quicker than any white man. The bush has sharpened their senses. Sights, sounds, smells, and touch sensations have special meanings for them. They have hypersensitive eyesight and acute hearing, they can easily distinguish between natural background sounds and those made by moving animals, and they can read footprints or tracks on the ground as other people read newspapers and books. As one told me, "My wife's footprint was the first thing I remembered about her."

They have never heard of January or June or March or December. Their seasons are simply *Wet Weather, Cold Weather,* and *Hot Weather,* with variations: *The Green Grass Time, The Long Grass Time, The Burnt Grass Time, The Turtle Egg Time,* to indicate precise periods. They know instinctively when it's time for the flowering of the nutwoods, the coolibahs, and the mountain ash, and they know when their favorite delicacy, sugarbag (wild bees' honey), will be plentiful in the trees. They can pick up spears with their toes. They can ask for food by touching the mouth, for water by bulging one cheek, and they can describe most animals and birds with movements of their hands and arms.

Their finger talk, by which they can communicate with people miles away, is too subtle and too quick for white men's eyes. They have at least eight different methods of finger talk, and can ask, "Who is it?" "What is it?" "Where is it?" "What is going on?" by merely raising a thumb and index finger and revolving the wrist in a semicircle. A hospitable man may tell a visitor from another tribe to borrow one of his wives without opening his mouth, simply by clenching his fist at the breast and tapping his belly and thigh. The finger talk goes on constantly. It not only saves unnecessary speech but has the added advantage that evil spirits cannot hear it.

The much talked about smoke signals for which the aborigines are famous are not actually a refined method of communication messages over long distance. They are simply an announcement of a man's whereabouts. The aborigines are not fond of unauthorized strangers crossing their boundaries; and any native walking through the land of another tribe sends messages ahead to let them know of his approach. Every tribe has special messengers—or diplomats—who are accredited to neighboring tribes. They are often sent into another tribal territory carrying a message stick—a sort of presidential note—containing an invitation to a corroboree or a request for permission to cross the neighboring tribe's country.

Such an emissary always lights a fire every hour to inform the neighboring tribe of his approach. The fires can be seen up to 100 miles away on clear days, and the neighboring tribe can identify the approaching guest—or at least his tribe—by the direction of the smoke. If the smoke is from the direction of the Roper River, for example, they will know that it is someone from the Alawa tribe—and so on.

There is no mystery or magic in the smoke signals. They are simply a means of announcing a man's approach and of keeping track of kinsmen. The aborigines are limited in numbers; most of them are interrelated, and their nomadic life has taught them to identify approaching visitors by smoke signals and by logical deduction.

While we were at Nourlangie, for example, we were told that old Gudjiwa from the Wulaki tribe would be arriving in a few days. How did the natives know? By the smoke fires coming from Jim-Jim Creek, about 75 miles away. Besides, old Gudjiwa had been gone on "walkabout" since *The Turtle Egg Time*—about four months—and it was now time for Kunapipi to begin.

I also had a chance to be an emissary with a message stick. The message sticks, which the aborigines send to their kinsmen by anyone who happens to be going in the right direction, mystify white men—because white men read printed words rather than sticks and notches on pieces of tree bark. At Nourlangie, the Kunapipi headman, Michael, of the Wulaki tribe, gave me a message stick to deliver to his brother-in-law Johnny at Maningrida. I watched him carve the thin lines and notches on a piece of tree bark about two inches long and half an inch wide; and I made notes as he explained, one by one, what each line and notch meant.

"This bin for Number Two Missus Nellie, and Number Three Missus Peggy," he said. "Peggy got 'em two pickaninny, Nellie two—Toby, Judy, little Nellie and Kathleen . . . Got 'em four brothers, Jackie, Charlie Number One, Billy, Toby . . ."

Each tiny notch or line indicated a different kinsmen or wife. Michael had three wives. One, Margaret, was the dog woman at the Nourlangie camp, caretaker of the 55 dogs that belonged to a clan of only about two dozen aborigines. Two other wives, Nellie and Peggy, were at Maningrida.

"Tell 'em Michael and Margaret bin stay camp till Cold Weather Time," he continued. "Then go walkabout to Maningrida. Tell Johnny and Charlie and Jack go get 'em white missus properly-big crocodile."

He explained to me, since one of our guides was René Henri, the crocodile shooter, that, "White man he don't know what billabong for crocodile. Only blackfellow know. Blackfellow know Rainbow Dream Time big water hole. If Dreamin' place, don't go in. Might be Somethin'. ("Somethin'" is the aborigines' expression for fear of evil spirits.) "Allis Dreamin' we don't go in. If swim we bin properly finish. But all-a-right here no Dreamin' and blackfellow know water hole for properly-cheeky-feller big mob crocodile. Good tucker."

The aborigines call any place they believe to be inhabited by evil spirits a "Dreamin'" place, and they won't go near it.

Michael was trying to explain that the aborigines know better than white men where to hunt for crocodiles, and that he would have his brothers in Maningrida get one for me. He made one final little knick in the message stick and said, "Tell 'em be careful of black-fellow doctor." He asked me to give the message stick to Nellie's brother, Johnny, in Maningrida.

How do you go about finding a man named Johnny among 700 aborigines encamped in paperback shanties around a government reserve? It was easy. I merely put in my request for Johnny through Allan Stewart, our interpreter, who told the bland-faced tonguetied Young Nim that I wanted to find a man named Johnny who was the brother of Nellie who was the number-two wife of Michael in Nourlangie. This was the only information I gave. Young Nim had never been to Maningrida before. His face was blank, but we could sense rather than see the finger-talk radar go into action.

He did not move. He did not speak. He did not go looking for Johnny. But we were aware that somehow Young Nim must have passed a message along to a native a few yards away, who in turn apparently passed it on to another, and so on down the line among the natives roaming the settlement. In such a manner, which completely escapes the untrained eye, they can ticktack messages with finger talk for miles. We stood in the same spot and waited. It was only a few minutes until the news was flashed back by sign signals that Johnny had been located. We knew it only because another native suddenly appeared beside Young Nim, and then the two of them motioned silently for us to follow them. We found Johnny playing blackfellow poker in the shade of a stringy bark tree a mile away.

We told Johnny about the message stick and asked that he collect the whole family before I gave it to him. Silently the sign-signal wireless went into operation again, and Johnny nonchalantly went back to his poker game while we waited. In a short time various men, women, and children were straggling in from all directions and collecting in a group of their own, all eyeing us curiously and silently.

When the family group was complete, Johnny left the poker game and went over to them, with me, and identified all the relatives to match the notches carved on Michael's message stick. There were both Michael's wives, Nellie and Peggy (who didn't seem to be too happy about posing side-by-side in the family picture), their four children, an uncle, brothers, and assorted kinsmen. Only after making sure of their identifications did I give Johnny the message stick from Michael.

He read it all accurately enough to be quite impressive, but there are things other than telepathy that can explain his accuracy. Naturally, Michael would have sent regards to both his wives, his children, and his other relatives. They could have assumed, perhaps, if they knew Michael well, that he and Margaret would have stayed at Nourlangie until Cold Weather Time. They probably knew when Michael started his walkabouts, and that he was leery of certain blackfellow doctors, and that he was familiar with the water holes and places where one could or could not hunt crocodiles. The message stick, of course, is not telepathy. Like the smoke signals, the reading of footprints, and the finger-talk, it is simply another means of communication among primitive tribes who have no telephones, telegraph, radio, post office—or even a written language.

It was from Waipuldanya, or Wadjiri-Wadpiri, whose whitefeller name is Phillip Roberts, that I learned the aborigines' secret of telepathy.

Waipuldanya is a full-blooded aborigine of the Alawa tribe at Roper River in the Northern Territory. His body has been through the fires of tribal initiation. He has been subjected to many taboos. As a child he was "sung" to death by a Doctor Blackfellow, a medicine man who wished to destroy him in order to punish his clan. He was saved by another blackfellow medicine man.

He still worships Kunapipi, the Earth Mother, in the tribal pagan ceremonies, and he believes in the Rainbow Serpent. In his youth he was taught to track and to hunt wild animals, to be self-reliant in living off the land, and to provide for his family with the aid of his spears and woomeras only. He is now known as the most literate and knowledgeable of all aborigines, because in 1953 he was chosen by a white doctor as his driver and orderly. Waipuldanya speaks English fluently from his association with whitefellow doctors in Darwin and he understands, at least vaguely, the meanings of such words as hypnosis and telepathy. Mention these words to other aborigines and they completely fail to comprehend.

Roberts explained to us how the Mulunguwa, or tribal executioner, kills through a third person with the use of hypnotism. The Mulunguwa entices his victim into the bush, renders him unconscious with a blow on the back of the neck, hypnotizes him as he recovers, and removes his kidney fat with a knife. The wound is stitched with string and wiped over with a wax that makes it invisible. While the doomed man is under hypnosis the Mulunguwa implants a message in his subconscious mind: "*Your enemy is Budjirindja. Even his dogs are against you. Next time one barks at you, kill it at once. Otherwise you will not know peace.*"

Back at camp a few days later one of Budjirindja's dogs barks loudly.

"Why don't you stop your dogs from barking?" the hypnotic demands angrily.

"Because they like to bark."

"Well, stop them!"

"I won't."

"Then I will." He throws a spear. It is an unpardonable offense to deliberately kill another man's dog. Budjirindja's white-hot rage is unquenchable. He spears the Mulunguwa's victim at point-blank range while the Mulunguwa, sitting in his camp, placidly observes a killing he has arranged but not executed. With his kidney fat already removed, the doomed man would have died anyway, but with the aid of posthypnotic suggestion the Mulunguwa cleverly achieves his mission with an innocent intermediary—while he sits back mournfully bewailing the victim's demise in a death corroboree, thus detracting suspicion from himself.

Douglas Lockwood, one of Australia's top award-winning newspapermen, has described all this in detail in his book, *I, the Aboriginal*, which is based on the life of Phillip Roberts, or Waipuldanya. As Lockwood points out, it is well known that in aboriginal murders, especially those involving Mulunguwas and Kadaitja Men (even worse tribal killers), the wrong man invariably goes to jail under the white man's law—because of the deceit and cunning of the tribal executioners and the extreme suggestibility of the aborigines.

This suggestibility perhaps has its most extreme manifestation in muscle-twitching, the method by which the aborigines use their so-called powers of telepathy. As Waipuldanya explained it: "When I get a twitch in my left shoulder, I know it's my uncle. (Relatives are symbolized in various parts of the body.) If it twitches for several hours I know something is wrong. Then I begin to worry. I tune in. When I go to sleep maybe I see my uncle or his Dreaming (totem), the *dugong* (sea cow). (The word Dreaming is used for animal totems as well as for places inhabited by evil spirits.) If the *dugong* is being speared or bitten by a shark, I know that my uncle is seriously ill and is going to die. That's how we talk to each other—through Dreamings."

Crazy? Well, apparently it works. At least no one else has come up with a better system of communicating through Dream Time totems or through muscle-twitching.

As Roberts said, "If my right shoulder twitches I know that my father has thought of me. If it persists, I know that he may be ill. My left shoulder represents my Uncle Stanley Marbunggu, my mother is in my right breast, my thighs belong to my wife, my calves to my brothers and sisters, my right eyelid to brothers-in-law, and the left to my cousins. When a muscle twitches I throw out my flexed arm violently to straighten it. If the elbow cracks I know that I will soon see or receive news of the person represented by the muscle which has twitched . . . This is the Dream Time way."

Implausible as it may seem, there are some reasons for the aborigines' art of silent communication that make sense. First, of course, the aborigines' nomadic life requires some elementary forms of communication. But back of it all is the aborigines' well-programmed lessons in self-control and self-denial when they are youths and as they mature. An aborigine, for instance, is never permitted to look at or speak to his mother-in-law. This law is scrupulously observed and saves endless speech. Moreover, immediately after the tribal initiation rites, the newly circumcised boy is forbidden to eat certain foods and talk to certain relatives (especially female)—not only for a month, two months, six months, but two years! The tribal speech taboo explains much of the reticence of the aborigines. A man who is half-dumb for two years is seldom garrulous thereafter.

It also explains something of what most people take for granted about the aborigines—their system of so-called telepathy. The aborigines have developed the art of contemplation to a much greater degree than most people. They seem to understand instinctively the power of faith and the influence that can be exercised by mind over body. As Phillip Roberts told us, "We have no radios or motor cars or telephones to pass on messages. So we do it with our finger-talk and our muscle-twitching. When we are lonely we just sit by ourselves and contact our people, whatever their Dreaming is. Maybe it's a tree, or the lily root, or the dingo. It's all in the Dream Time. We just know."

Who can say that Phillip Roberts of the Kangaroo Dreaming, whose father was Barnabas Gabarla of the Frilled Neck Lizard totem of the Alawa tribe, has not mastered the mind's mysterious secrets that puzzle scientists? The aborigine's philosophical powers span space and time. As Roberts, who does not know his own age, says, "Age does not worry us. Everybody has a start and a finish. That is why we don't worry about anything. We always know when it's time for corroborees. We just *know*."

Primitive peoples have more time for contemplating than those in modern civilized societies. Could it be that the aborigines' Dream Time way of life has developed in them mental and sensory powers lost to non-Stone Age people from disuse? Certainly it seems that these people have, at least to some degree, found an answer to the question of the power of the mind.

CHAPTER 6

Firewalking on Fiji

The reports of Soviet experiments in long-distance telepathy have led some skeptics—including me—to take another look at alleged "supernormal" phenomena—when these unique occurrences can be pinned down long enough to look at, which is not often. In several months of diligent sleuthing around the world I was unable to locate a ghost, a poltergeist, or a glimmer of real telepathic communication. But I did see the firewalkers of Fiji, and they are for real.

The firewalkers do not claim telepathic powers, but like the yogis of India they can demonstrate at will the power of mind over matter. So far chances seem very slim of ever getting the primitive Fijians into a scientific laboratory—or of Soviet scientists getting close enough to their firepit for an on-the-spot investigation.

Many people have observed the strange rites from an uncomfortably close distance and have come away completely mystified as well as scorched. "I have brought many doctors and scientists over to this island to see the firewalkers," Captain Stanley Brown told us. "On the trip over they have all kinds of explanations—hypnosis, tough feet, special fire-resistant ointments, stones that cool off fast . . . On the trip back they're usually very quiet. They don't try to explain it."

Captain Brown is an Englishman who came to Fiji with the Navy during World War II and stayed because he liked it. He operates charter cruises to the outer islands of Fiji on his 89-foot ketch, the *Maroro*. He has brought many scientific expeditions to Beqa (pronounced Mbengga) to investigate the firewalkers.

There are no interisland tourist cruise boats stopping at Beqa, so we chartered the *Maroro* for a visit with these barefoot believers in their own magic. We could see the smoke rising from the firepit as we sailed through a cobalt sea and anchored in a small inlet inside the coral reef on the south coast of Beqa. Fijians rowed us part way to shore in a dinghy. We took off our shoes and walked the rest of the way in low tide to the village of Ndakuimbengga.

The village chief, Ratu Timoci Cola, met us and took us to the *vakatunaloa* (a palm shelter or pavilion) lavishly decorated with tropical greenery and flowers for our ceremonial welcome. The chief wore a freshly pressed white linen sulu (sarong), a tan tropical-print shirt, and a salu-salu (garland of hibiscus blossoms). The other men of the village wore skirts of dyed grass and hibiscus fiber, sashes of black and white bark cloth, and chaplets of shredded pandanus leaves in their hair. Their bodies glistened with coconut oil.

Immediately following the kava drinking ceremony—the traditional welcome to all visitors—we were led through the village (population 80) to the *lovo* (earth oven) or firepit.

"Are you walking today?" we asked a young boy beside us.

"No," he replied sheepishly.

"Why not?"

"Because today is Tuesday," he said.

"What difference does that make?"

With downcast eyes he confessed, "I ate coconut on Saturday."

Four is a magic number with the Fijians and for four days before firewalking they must give up coconuts and women. They must live lives of chastity, secluded in huts apart from their wives, and anyone who has domestic problems or whose wife is pregnant may not walk on the firepit. Anyone who breaks a taboo will get his feet burned. In 1950 one of the firewalkers blistered his feet; it was later discovered that his wife was pregnant.

Chief Timoci escorted us to the cool, green, earthen-terraced steps reserved for distinguished guests, about 20 feet away from the blazing *lovo*. The fire had been started at 3:30 A.M. The walkers would go on at 11:30. The fire must be lit exactly eight hours before the ceremony.

The circular pit, fifteen feet across and five feet deep, was filled with huge blazing logs from the native *Dawa* tree and stones as big as a Fijian's fuzzy-mopped head. The air simmered with heat. The closest we could approach without being singed was about five feet from the firepit's edge. Yet Fijians in grass skirts were leaping around the rim, fishing out smouldering timbers with nooses made of vines tied on the end of long poles, and leveling the jumble of red-hot boulders to provide a roughly even surface on which to walk.

The walkers, six of them, were secluded in a nearby *bure*, (house) awaiting their signal to come out. At exactly 11:30 they emerged, and in a hushed silence complete except for the swishing of pandanus kilts, we watched them walk straight to the firepit and onto the searing hot stones.

They did not hop, skip, or jump. They did not flinch or tread lightly. They walked strong-footed with their full weight in every step across boulders that no one would dare touch. They walked for 20 seconds.

Quickly the other men of the village flung freshly gathered green leaves and masawa vines into the pit, and then leaped in on top of them, shouting and chanting, sitting and standing in a great outpouring of steam, while others shoveled fresh black earth over the smouldering pit. The ceremony would not be finished until four days later, when the villagers would open the pit and feast on masawa pudding from the leaves and vines cooked in the *lovo*.

Many have witnessed the firewalking with critical eyes. No one has found evidence of trickery. Doctors have examined the firewalkers' feet and found that although toughened from walking barefoot, they were not abnormally thickened and responded normally to pain when pricked with pins or touched with lighted cigarettes. Nor were they smeared with any unguents or protective coatings. The stones used have been inspected and found to be perfectly normal andesite rock, capable of retaining heat for a long time.

Most scientists who have witnessed the Fijian firewalking attribute it to a kind of self-hypnosis induced by great faith, which seals them off from any feeling of pain. The firewalkers themselves would not understand the meaning of the words *hypnosis* or *autosuggestion*. Their explanation is more simple: *faith*.

The Fiji firewalk has its roots in an ancient Fijian legend in which a little "spirit god" promised the people of Beqa Island the gift of firewalking. The islanders still have a simple child-like belief that no man is truly a Beqa man until he becomes a firewalker—and they all do. In all the Fiji islands—more than 300—only the Beqa islanders are firewalkers. Other Fijians regard them as possessed by "little devils."

We examined their feet. None bore the slightest sign of being even slightly burned. All of them said that their feet felt cold on the oven-hot stones.

"The body is warm but the feet are cold. The little god is only in the feet," they explained.

Could anyone else walk the firepit?

"Yes, if you believe," they said. "Plenty of belief and you can walk. No belief, your feet burn." No one but a Beqa man has believed it enough to try the Fiji stone walk, but the ember-walk of Indian firewalkers has been duplicated with some success in England.

Some of the mysteries of firewalking were cleared up by experiments conducted in England by Harry Price in 1935 and 1937. (See "How I Brought the Firewalk to England" and "Science Solves the Firewalk Mystery" in Harry Price's *Confessions of a Ghost Hunter*.) First of all it was proved that the firewalk was not a deception. An Indian, Kuda Bux, walked quickly along a 20-foot trench of glowing embers, several inches deep, four times. His feet were medically examined before and after the walks, and there was no sign of blistering. More significant were tests made in 1937 in which three Englishmen followed an Indian firewalker across the burning coals. All showed traces of slight burns, but one British volunteer, Reginald Adcock, showed only slight signs of burning on a fire that was supposed to be *nearly twice as hot* as that used for the Indian firewalkers, thus disposing of the idea that there were mysterious agencies involved.

Among the conclusions reached in the report on the 1937 tests were:

1. The firewalk is in no sense a trick; the walk is performed in a normal manner with bare and chemically unprepared feet.

2. Because the surface of the fire is very unstable and the feet can sink in several inches, it is impossible to walk so that a constantly changing portion of the foot is in contact with the hot embers (this would be possible on a firm plane surface), and skill of this kind is not a factor necessary for success. Nevertheless, steadiness in walking is an advantage in that the steady walker avoids remaining with his weight on one foot for too long an interval.

3. Moisture on the feet is a disadvantage, since it can cause hot particles to adhere to the skin and thus produce blisters.

4. The "spheroidal state"—that is, the sudden formation of an insulating cushion of vapor between the foot and the hot embers—does not occur.

5. No abnormal degree of callosity (callouses) of the feet is required.

6. Fasting or other initial preparation is not necessary.

7. No evidence was shown that immunity from burning can be conveyed to other persons.

8. The fall in the temperature of the surface of the soles of the feet during the experiment was possibly the result of a number of steps being taken on the grass after leaving the fire, before the place of examination was reached.

9. Immunity is not due to contact with layers of relatively cold ash in which combustion has ceased, since in experiments with Kuda Bux, the ash was removed; in any case, the feet sink in sufficiently far to be in contact with the burning embers and small flames below the surface.

An important significance of all these findings is that they are the results of research with the Indian ember-walk, *not* the Fijian stone-walk. The practice of firewalking—walking over glowing embers—has been a custom of many countries, including China, Japan, many parts of India and Malaya, and even Bulgaria. But only in Fiji does the stone-walk occur.

Even so thorough a skeptic as D. H. Rawcliffe, Britain's conscientious and classic debunker of anything that science cannot explain, has been constrained to admit:

"Stone-walking is indeed a feat to be wondered at, and it is doubtful whether any European has succeeded in actually walking the stones. The intense heat given out by the stones puts it on a level altogether different from the ember-walk." In reaching for a rational explanation, Rawcliffe advances the theory that if Europeans, accustomed to wearing shoes, can do the ember-walk as experiments have proved, then it would be far easier for the habitually barefoot Fijians, with their toughened feet, to walk the stones.

However, in 1935, two members of the British Medical Association visited Beqa to investigate the stone-walkers and found that although the soles of the Fijians' feet were toughened from walking barefoot all their lives, they were not abnormally thickened. Yet they walked unharmed on stones hot enough to ignite paper and sticks instantly.

One of the doctors thought that by repeated practice the men had become inured to the heat and could therefore endure temperatures that would be intolerable to untrained persons. The other was of the opinion that the men could perform the strange rite by means of autosuggestion or by means of suggestion by their chief or leader.

I questioned Chief Timoci and the village priest, as well as the stone-walkers themselves, on these points. It would appear that repeated practice is not the explanation, as there is no practice or training period for the stone-walking—except, of course, the short period of mental conditioning based on taboos. But there is no practice before the actual walking on the stones. In fact, a Beqa man is not required to walk the stones more than once in his life, and Chief Timoci himself has declined to walk more than once. He admitted that he was frightened before he stepped on the stones, but then the priest told him, "Go ahead, you can do it. It won't hurt you." And it didn't.

Of the six firewalkers who performed for us, only two could be called veterans. One was 30 years old and he had walked the stones seven times. The other was 27 and had done the stonewalk six times. The youngest was Tiaki Vakrarawa, 18 who walked the stones for the first time on the day of our visit. How did he feel? "Okay," he said, proud of his English. Was he scared? "No. The priest says go ahead, it won't hurt. But you have to *want* to go. If you believe it, you can go. If not, you can't." These were the answers we heard over and over again from the firewalkers.

Among the most surprising aspects of the Fijian firewalk is that it is not, as many people commonly assume, a part of any Fijian initiation rite or religious ceremony. Nor is it performed with any regularity or with any higher purpose in mind than to carry on tradition, and to prove that every Beqa man can walk the stones. This is *Kavakavanua,* the Fijian way, the custom of the land.

The Sawau tribe, which founded the firewalk, is one of the oldest tribes of Beqa, and any Beqa man would be banished in disgrace if he did not walk the stones. Thus, every Beqa man does it. It is as simple as that. Beqa women are not obligated to carry on the tradition, but there are two women of the village, Liliviwa Kasa and Salaniyata Davutu, so old they cannot remember their ages, who in their youth also walked the stones—one of them three times, the other only once—just to prove they could.

In the Harry Price experiments in England, a great deal was made of the theory that weight is a decided disadvantage in the firewalk. Those who weighed most were burned most in the British ember-walk. The Indian Kuda Bux weighed only 120 pounds, and Reginald Adcock, the most successful of the European volunteer ember-walkers, weighed only 40 pounds more. The Fijians disprove this theory; Fijian men are famous for their handsome, strong physiques, and their average weight is undoubtedly far more than that of European men, and certainly more than the Indians. This obviously has made no difference in their ability to walk the stones.

The Fijians were once ferocious cannibals, but they are now among the most gentle people in the world, and they are possibly the most honest. In trying to find the words to explain to us the real reason for walking the stones, since the performance has no connection with initiation or religious rites, Chief Timoci said simply: "We do it because we *believe* in it. And we're proud of it. And because Beqa is the only place in the world and my people are the only ones in the world who can walk the stones. And we do it because we can collect money and we need money."

Before you jump to conclusions, let me say that this in no sense implies tourist commercialism. Beqa is so far off the beaten track that tourists rarely get there. The tiny island, with a population of less than 100 in its main village, has no tourist facilities, hotel, snack bar, modern plumbing, or motor car. The only way to get there is by chartered boat from Suva, the capital of Fiji.

Preparations for the firewalk are elaborate, lengthy, and expensive. The *dawa* tree logs must be cut and brought down from the mountains, the *masawa* vines gathered, the river stones collected, and the pit dug. Sawau tribesmen living in other villages around the island must be notified and firewalkers recruited.

The Beqa islanders require two weeks' notice from anyone wishing to see the stone-walk, and during this time all adult men and women of the village are busy preparing for the ceremony. At the time we were on Beqa, there were only 38 adult men in the village. The visitor must pay the Fijians for their two weeks of time and labor (the fee of approximately $300 per visitor is set by the Fijian government and is not paid directly to the Fijians but is paid through the Fiji Visitors Bureau), and the visitor must also pay for the boat charter. The money the Fijians make from their firewalks all goes into village improvement, principally for their school and church and for the rethatching of their reed and pandanus houses.

The Beqa men, quite reasonably, see no point in performing the firewalk for their own amusement. This would not buy them the things they need for their school and church, nor would it get their *bures* rethatched. It would only cost them the loss of two weeks' time when they could be doing something else more to their liking—such as fishing, drinking kava, and eating coconuts. Even a Beqa man doesn't walk on the stones just for fun.

Because of the remoteness of the firewalking island and the time and expense involved for both visitors and islanders, the Beqa firewalkers probably average no more than ten or twelve performances a year. These necessarily would involve different walkers, to give each one his turn to prove his skill as a Beqa man. And because of the island's small population, there would be no problem of a Beqa man not getting his chance to prove it, even with such a limited number of visitors. There are usually six to ten men who walk the stones at one ceremony.

From all of this it would seem obvious that repeated practice is not the reason for the Fijian's immunity to burns when he walks over the fiery furnace of red-hot stones. As for autosuggestion or hypnosis, there was nothing even remotely resembling a trancelike state or any of the other familiar effects of hypnotic suggestion in the stone-walking performance I saw—either before, during, or after the event. In fact, one of the disconcerting elements was the casual, almost comical air of light-heartedness at the ceremony. No South Sea islander, of course, can be expected to take life too seriously. They are the clowns of the Pacific, bubbling with dark-eyed laughter and immersed in an enchanting folklore of their own that should never be subjected to psychological probing.

They can call up turtles and sharks from the depths of the sea merely by singing to them. They can call up red prawns and eels, and they can predict infallibly the annual two-day rising of the balolo worm. Only certain Fijians possess this mysterious rapport with sea creatures. Their secret is their own. White men cannot fathom it, nor can they fathom the Beqa man's power to walk over the fiery stones.

It is perhaps significant that two leading investigators and skeptics, D. H. Rawcliffe and Harry Price, both of whose reputations have been built on exposing the frauds and fallacies of mental phenomena, have reluctantly concluded that not only is the firewalk performance genuine, but even more important, that it is probably based on one word that is rapidly vanishing from the sophisticated space-age scene.

The word is *faith*.

Rawcliffe himself does not go so far as to use the word. Instead, he says, "Absence of fear is a vital point in all types of firewalk." And he emphasizes that the Fijian stone-walking is far more impressive and inexplicable than the ember-walks.

Price is so frightened of the word "faith" that he puts it in quotes followed by a parenthetical synonym: . . . "After all, 'faith' (or confidence) plays some part in the performance. I think that may be the secret of the firewalk . . . I think there is some obscure relationship between physical and mental forces."

Certainly the Beqa man's faith in his ability to walk the stones when his time comes, or when he is ready, is not the same as the yogi's prolonged physical and mental conditioning for *samadhi*. The Beqa boy knows almost from infancy that someday he is going to have to walk the stones to prove he is a Beqa man—and that's about all. Perhaps the knowing that he has to do it helps give him faith. Perhaps the knowing and the faith are a form of prolonged mental conditioning. Perhaps Beqa men are more highly suggestible than other Fijians. And perhaps their fathers have taught them a special heel-and-toe technique so that the soles of their feet will not be burned.

Like all the others who have witnessed this strange ceremony, I can offer no rational explanation for the stone-walk. I can only report what I saw on the island of Beqa.

Science, which does not claim to be either infallible or omnipotent, has yet to explain many strange nuances of mental energy, or mind power. And modern space-age scientists are probing these brain mysteries from every direction. Could it be that what they hope to achieve has already been mastered in the faraway islands of Fiji, or in the yogi retreats of India, or in the Australian outback country of the Stone Age aborigines?

CHAPTER 7

What Can We Learn from the Yogis?

If I were placing bets on where the missing links in mind power will be found, if ever, I would bet that they will be found in India—a strange, exotic land of ancient and esoteric beliefs, the land of the mongoose and cobra and the "ropetricks," a land whose culture is inexorably interwoven with the theme of reincarnation, and the land where even Prime Minister Nehru still stands on his head every morning in the ancient custom of yoga.

No country conjures in Western minds more mystical associations than does India. No country gives such an impression of a no-man's land of science. There is some basis of truth in these popular conceptions. But there is also a sound basis for believing that the Indian yogi may hold the key that scientists everywhere are looking for—the key that can unlock the hidden reservoirs of human efficiency and energy.

There is widespread belief in the occult powers of the yogi. This belief is unfounded. The true yogi is not at all interested in occultism, magic, supernaturalism, or any aspects of psychic phenomena; in fact, he would merely laugh them out of court if given the chance. But modern science has definitely established the fact that many of the yogi's physiological and mental feats are indeed genuine—and astounding. This scientific truth may one day shed new light on the nature of the mind, its motivation, its alleys and labyrinths. It brings into sharper focus, and with the transfusion of new hope, the significance of the age-old questions: Are we fully aware of the limits of our powers? Are there deeper reservoirs of mental energy in all of us that we can tap and channel and master as some religious ascetics have apparently done?

Many of the alleged miracles of the yogis can still be chalked up to fiction or fakirs, but this does not deny the fact that modern medical science has finally recruited the yogi into the laboratory—a feat almost as miraculous as those claimed by some yogis—for an experimental look at what makes him tick. The verdict: the yogi somehow seems to be able to develop, probably through prolonged conditioning and practice, unusual voluntary control of certain physiological functions.

The true yogi is as indifferent to the curiosity of scientists as he is to everything else in the world outside his own *dhyana,* or meditation. But doctors at the All India Institute of Medical Sciences in New Delhi have finally succeeded in persuading a few yogis to be guinea pigs in their newly established yogic section of neurophysiologic research. The institute is supported largely by Rockefeller and Ford Foundation grants for studying reproductive physiology in relation to India's overpopulation problem. Most of its work is being done with monkeys, and in this respect the All India Institute is unique because of the availability of large quantities of monkeys and the advantages of using monkeys—rather than rats, for example—in physiological research.

The monkey's biological makeup is more like that of humans than is the makeup of other lower primates, and monkeys are therefore of great usefulness to scientists—especially in the study of biological drives, hypersexuality, and reproductive cycles.

Again through chemical and electrical stimulation of the brain—the monkey's brain—scientists have found that there are various centers of the brain that control hormone release and sexual behavior, and much of the work currently going on at the All India Institute of Medical Sciences is concentrated on trying to map out these specific control centers to determine how they are susceptible to the influence of various stimuli and whether they can be affected by prolonged conditioning.

How does the yogi fit into the research picture of India's overpopulation problem? By the study of biological opposites.

For the yogi's chaste physical and mental self-discipline, his withdrawal from all external sense impressions, and his consequently truly *supernormal*—not *supernatural*—feats of bodily control and endurance are all the result of intense and prolonged conditioning. And they are all *physical*—not *metaphysical*—proof of the indomitable power of the human mind.

At the All India Institute, yogis have been tested for respiratory and vascular muscle control, basal metabolic rate, lung efficiency, heart action (by electrocardiographs), and brain waves (with electroencephalographs). Here are some of the medical findings.

+ The yogi subjects were able voluntarily to influence their heartbeat. They were able to stop the heart sounds, if not the heart itself.
+ A few of those tested have shown "some signs" of actual heart-stopping for a few seconds, although doctors are cautious about confirming this.

+ More significant from the standpoint of repeated experiments and definite medical confirmation is that many yogi subjects have been able to *slow* their heart rate voluntarily, which is much more difficult to achieve than voluntary acceleration or quickening of the heart.

+ The brain-wave patterns of meditative yogis were distinctly different from those of normal persons in repose. Moreover, the brain rhythms were not disturbed by various stimuli such as flashing lights and clicking sounds, as would be the case with normal subjects.

+ Tests of activity of sweat glands showed that some yogis can produce perspiration at will on underarms and forearms.

+ In airtight-box tests in the laboratory, conducted with yogis who claimed the ability to remain buried alive underground for long periods of time, it was found that yogi subjects could reduce their oxygen requirements by 45 to 50 percent of normal requirements; under similar conditions a normal person's oxygen needs would increase rather than decrease.

+ In the airtight-box tests comparing yogis with normal subjects, the sealed cage was equipped with a buzzer system to signify discomfort. Maximum endurance time for normal subjects was seven hours. The yogis pushed no buzzers, were still apparently perfectly comfortable and ready for more than ten and a half hours, at which time the experiment was terminated.

"We were not interested in endurance tests, nor proving how long a yogi could remain in the box," one of the institute doctors told me. "We were interested only in trying to find the physiological mechanism by which the yogi can exercise such control over the autonomic nervous system." (The term autonomic applies to those sections of the nervous system that are generally a law unto themselves and cannot be controlled by voluntary effort. The function that is most apparently in this class is the heart rate.)

There is a great deal of medical-scientific speculation about the exact nature of the psychological and physiological factors which account for the yogi's phenomenal powers of body control and endurance, but there is no longer any question that they are genuine and that they are the result of prolonged conditioning through rigid and austere physical and mental self-disciplines. Some European and American psychiatrists, in fact, have advanced the theory that anyone can achieve similar powers through practice.

There is an excerpt from Sir William Brown's *Mind, Medicine and Metaphysics* that bears an astonishing resemblance to the tenets of yoga: "You can gain power over involuntary muscles, stomach, heart, or whatever it may be. I believe that we can get more and more power, through our sympathetic nervous system, over the different parts of our body, if in earnest about it, and if we carry out a certain amount of self-training. You can only convince yourself of this by doing it for yourself.

"This is not hypnotism, but a genuine development and increase of the power of the will over the body. One can influence one's own digestion, heart-beat, the processes of elimination, and general functions of almost every part of the body by resolution and calm determination. The important thing is to avoid spasmodic effort, to get muscular and mental relaxation; to imagine success with calm certainty, and then to affirm it with conviction."

It is well known that the yogis can do all these things at will, and more. Although "burial alive" and lying on a "bed of nails" are not part of genuine yoga practice, and are in fact frowned on by the true yogi philosophers, it nevertheless is true that some yogis who have deviated from the ascetic path for the sake of showmanship have been able, through autosuggestion, to induce states of extreme catalepsy for the purpose of burying themselves underground in coffins. Apparently a similar state of self-induced catalepsy or extreme autohypnotism is used for lying on a bed of nails, a feat that I personally saw demonstrated in Benares by a 27-year old yogi named Shambhu Nath Yadava, a champion wrestler of the province of Uttar Pradesh.

Yadava has studied yogi for nine years, concentrating on a yogic exercise called *Kumbhak*, through which—he told me—he has learned to "stiffen" the body as well as the nerves for lying on the bed of nails. There was no doubt about the authenticity of his demonstration, nor the sharpness of the long spikes that were driven into the long board—sharp end up—on which he reclined. His bare back was splotched afterwards with imprints from the spikes, but the skin was not punctured, he denied feeling any pain, and he said the spike marks would disappear in two or three hours. Yadava does not give demonstrations for entertainment. He started the *Kumbhak* stiffening exercises to keep physically fit, practices 15 or 20 minutes a day, and performs the bed-of-nails feat just as a hobby!

Some yogis have also apparently learned the art of psychosomatic control of body temperature. For example, by a certain technique of breathing and by fixing their thoughts on cool scenes, such as mountain streams or snow-capped peaks, they are able to keep cool in even the hottest weather. The lamas of Tibet do the same thing in reverse, concentrating their thoughts on the hot sun or on fires, which helps them withstand frigid winters living in caves among snow-covered mountains and clad only in cotton garments—or completely naked.

It is clear that intense autosuggestion or self-hypnosis plays a leading role in the physical and mental disciplines of the oriental religious ascetics, although many yogi adepts are perhaps not aware of this.

The word yoga means, literally, "to yoke," and in ancient Hindu philosophy, yoga can be described as a system of ascetic practice, abstract meditation, and mental concentration all aimed at spiritual purity and union with the supreme spirit. One of the best known modern authorities on yoga is K. T. Behanan, an American who is originally from eastern India and who was granted a fellowship from Yale University for two years of first-hand study of the yoga discipline in India, and whose thesis on the subject gained him his doctor's degree.

Behanan describes the yogis as sound, sensible men with poise and insight, radiating quiet power, and with capacities for enjoyment and humor in spite of their self-imposed austerities.

Yoga is one of the six classical systems of philosophy stemming from the Upanishadic teachings of ancient India. It is, in fact, a psychological, moral, and physical system of training designed to emancipate the individual from the needs, wants, and desires that are the lot of the average man, and to develop certain unusual states of consciousness.

The yogi neophyte goes through a long series of graduated mental, physical, and respiratory exercises in the belief that by such means the mind can be made to function at far higher than the normal levels. The ultimate aim is supreme mystical experience.

There are many types of yoga practices and beliefs, but perhaps the best known is *Rajah Yoga*, which also is the most universally respected because of its depth of philosophy and the obvious soundness of many of its practices. Its philosophy stems from the oldest of all Indian philosophical systems—Samkhya—and it has evolved into a brand of religious metaphysics that even a great many Western people regard as greatly superior in some ways to the metaphysics of any of the other of the world's great religions.

Yoga training is a long and difficult process, and it involves several stages, including difficult and sometimes semiacrobatic meditative postures (*asanas*), complicated breathing exercises, and specialized mental exercises. These comprise:

(a) *Pratyahara* or sense-withdrawal. The yogi learns to restrain the flow of external sense impressions to his mind.

(b) *Dharana* or concentration. This does not have the same connotation as concentration in the Western sense. Its final phase is characterized by the highest state of complete *thoughtlessness*, or a totally blank mind.

(c) *Dhyana* or contemplation. In Dhyana, the yogi begins to perceive new and subtle aspects of the objects of his contemplation.

(d) *Samadhi* or trance. The desire of all yogis is to reach this stage. Many fail. There are five stages of this trance, according to the manuals, and the final stage is that of *Kaivalya*, or total liberation. In the final stages of *Samadhi*, the yogi is supposed to achieve an ecstasy of the highest form attainable, sometimes characterized by "superconscious" or "supernormal" perception, transcending space and time. It is this more than anything else that has given rise to the widespread but mistaken belief in the yogi's powers of extrasensory perception.

Behanan, who himself undertook a part of the yogic training in India, and who is sympathetic to the practice of yoga, emphatically disclaims and disparages the association of "psychic phenomena" (the quotes are his) with yoga. He points out that most experiences of illusions, hallucinations, visions, levitations, and other mystic "miracles" of the yogis are essentially no different from those of their "spiritual comrades" in the West, who, in states of complete relaxation, may experience feelings of "floating" or levitation. Most of these "supernatural" experiences, he adds, can be traced to physical causes.

Physiologists believe that some of the same strange forms of mental activity, such as illusions, hallucinations, and "visions," which can be produced artificially by chemical and electrical stimulation of the brain, can also be produced naturally at will, as the yogis apparently do, through prolonged conditioning and with a great deal of help from autosuggestion or self-hypnosis.

This brings up again the important role of hypnosis in brain and mind research, or more precisely the role of mental suggestion. For the yogis have demonstrated time and again what they can do with their highly developed powers of mental suggestion.

In what way, and by what brain-nerve mechanism can simple *thinking* (or concentration, contemplation, meditation, or even pure thoughtlessness) charge the electrochemical substance of the brain to produce the same kind of mental illusions that can be turned on by artificially stimulating certain areas of the brain with electronics and drugs? There is ample evidence that intoxicating drinks and drugs have been used by many mystics of ancient civilizations to create "visions" and other mystical experiences. But the yogis are strictly forbidden to use intoxicating drinks and drugs for the very reason that they may cause supernormal experiences.

Although in the process of attaining *Samadhi* the yogi may in fact also develop genuinely supernormal physical powers, or even experience some of the so-called psychic phenomena, these are, as Behanan has stated, "merely distractions to be overcome. They are not gifts but obstacles." The yoga trance, although undoubtedly a source of great happiness and inspiration to those who achieve it, has the modern psychiatric interpretation of autohypnosis.

"Hypnosis," writes Behanan, "comprises various stages ranging from mild drowsiness to deep trance. Yoga, likewise, has its gradations of experience."

Although there are some differences between hypnosis and the yoga trance, he points out one striking similarity:

"It is well known that hypnosis can be induced by staring steadily at an object or by thinking exclusively of one idea. This monoideism has its parallel in yoga during the meditative period when the yogi aims to eliminate from the mind everything but the thought of the minute object of concentration."

If the phenomenon of telepathy is genuine it might be reasonably expected that the yogi would make admirable subjects. This obviously is one of the reasons for the present interest of Russian scientists in the mystical Indian yogi—plus, of course, the yogi's other more demonstrable powers of physical and mental control.

Nowhere in Russia did I find that the Russians are going in for the practice of yoga as a fad, such as has happened in America in recent years. But there were indications that Soviet scientists engaged in research in telepathy have become interested in studying the yogis, and this was confirmed in India by Dr. H. N. Banerjee, research director in parapsychology in the state of Rajasthan.

Dr. Banerjee was invited to Moscow in 1962 as a "nonofficial" guest of a group of Soviet scientists interested in yoga, and subsequently he assumed charge of coordinating a yogic-research exchange program with the Russians. He told me when I was in India early in 1963 that some yogis already had been sent to Moscow for laboratory observation, and that arrangements were being made for a team of Soviet scientists to visit India to study yogic practices.

Banerjee was a former professor of philosophy of Rajasthan State College and is one of India's leading researchers in the field of parapsychology. He is now director of the Department of Parapsychology at the University of Rajasthan in Jaipur. He has collaborated with Dr. Ian Stevenson, chairman of the Department of Psychiatry and Neurology at the University of Virginia, in studies of reported cases of reincarnation, and with Dr. Hiroshi Motoyama, director of the Institute of Religious Psychology in Tokyo, in depth psychology studies of yoga in relation to its mental and autonomic nervous functions.

Partly because of the growing interest in brain-mind phenomena, India is setting up the first nationally instituted and supported research center in the world for the scientific study of mental activity. Two branches of the Indian government, the University Grants Commission and the Ministry of Education, have instituted the program.

In New Delhi, Dr. D. S. Kothari, chairman of the physics departments at the University of New Delhi and head of the University Grants Commission, told me that the new Indian center—which was then still in the planning stages—was to be a fully equipped research center for "studies of the mind," and that the research would be conducted by teams of physiologists, biologists, engineers, and statisticians.

One of the first goals, he said, would be to devise better experimental methods for studying the mind. "We can't depend on metaphysics. It's experimental answers we want," he said. "We know there is a relationship between the human mind, the nervous system, and the logic of mathematics. But we seem to have an outer logic and an inner logic. The computer machine works on the outer logic of the human mind, which is communicable, and it took us thousands of years to discover this. It now seems that there is an inner logic ingrained in the evolutionary process. It may take us a few thousand more years to find the link between the computer-machine outer logic of the human mind and the inner logic ingrained in the evolutionary process. It may be on some other planet that we'll unravel this mystery, but it must be done according to physical, not metaphysical, laws."

On the question of whether the yogis possess the faculty of telepathy or other forms of ESP, he gave the same answer that is usually given by scientists, "ESP, if it exists, is still to be discovered."

In the beautiful Pink City of Jaipur I was a guest for a while in the governor's palace. Dr. K. Sampurnanda, governor of the State of Rajasthan, has for 30 years been a scholar of both Sanskrit and yoga. It was Dr. Sampurnanda who gave me one of the most meaningful interpretations of yoga and its relationship to extrasensory perception.

"The yogi does not develop extrasensory perception," he said. "What is sometimes mistaken for *extra*sensory is purely sensory, a highly refined extension and development of the normal sensory organs and powers that are latent in everyone, if we wish to develop them. As for perception, the physiology of the yogi is no different from others. There is no new set of nerves involved. The yogi's perception is not different from ordinary perception except that some become hypersensitive.

"This can only be explained in the background of yoga. According to the yogic way of thinking, the senses are much more powerful than we normally find them to be. Man has developed and evolved as he is today because he is subject to certain desires. His psychological and physiological apparatus is conditioned for the satisfaction of his desires; thus he makes a very limited and selected use of the power of his senses. There are things he does not wish to hear, things he does not wish to see. He uses his sensory organs only to the extent that they satisfy his desires.

"Nature is a great economist. She does not give what does not have to be used. In the practice of yoga there are many restraints put upon man. He has to practice a strict self-discipline and subdue his desires as much as possible. Therefore, through great practice, and sometimes painfully, he may, little by little, gain use of these sensory powers that have lain dormant from disuse. Some of his sensory organs become hypersensitive. The powers of sight and sound come back automatically in greater force. Not that they were dead; they were there all along. But they are normally not used to their fullest capacity.

"The person who really comes to grips with these powers is the yogi. But the powers that come to him are not any added or *extra*sensory powers of perception, no sixth or seventh sense. They are his own normal sensory powers developed by self-discipline to higher stages of sensitivity than in most people."

Could the yogi's highly developed sensory powers be harnessed for practical use, such as for "biological long-distance communication" or telepathy, as the Russians hope?

Dr. Sampurnanda's handsome face seemed to mirror all the austerities and the inscrutable wisdom of the ages as he gently replied: "The approach of the yogi is, to a large extent, completely different from the approach of a research student. The practice of yoga is not maintained for the development of psychic powers, physical powers, or any other kind of powers. These powers are only obstacles to spiritual progress and could be put to bad purposes. The yogi disciple is never told what powers he will develop, nor is he interested in helping anyone else develop similar powers. It can be definitely stated that the one and only aim of the true yogi is spiritual progress toward self-realization.

It might be assumed that such a philosophy could definitely be a stumbling block in the Russians' research into yoga.

PART III

The Crack in the Crystal Ball

By Norma Lee Browning

CHAPTER 8

Sensitives I Have Known

Little has been scientifically established in the area of psychic phenomena. With the upsurge of scientific interest in telepathy it is more important than ever to know how to separate the wheat from the chaff, the real from the ethereal, the physical from the metaphysical, the natural from the supernatural, and the sense from the nonsense. The challenge of the unknown sometimes obscures these borderlines.

At Oxford, seat of learning and lost causes, students in a "psychophysical research unit," for example, are being subsidized to "research" astral projection, or "out-of-the body experiences." For many years I had naively assumed that astral projection went out with Madame Blavatsky, whose spiritual double frequently floated around one country while she, in the flesh, was in another. Such phenomena have been identified in the past with a few famous mediums and inmates of mental institutions.

Even ghosts, once thought to roam only in graveyards and deathbed visions, have invaded seats of learning and culture for investigation by dedicated disciples of psi. And poltergeists, those noisy, mischievous little spirits that go around knocking down chandeliers and crockery, are enjoying a new boom of popularity.

Some of my best friends are "sensitives." One is a psychiatrist in New York who regularly attends Ouija board séances to communicate with the departed spirit of a former Harvard professor of psychology. Another said to me recently, "If we could just call a meeting of about 50 of the world's best sensitives in a kind of summit conference and have them all concentrate for a week on reading Khrushchev's mind, we could halt the march of Communism." I politely agreed that it was certainly an idea worth exploring. I know many sensitives who have assured me that all it takes to write a book is to go into a trance and let the "higher intelligences" take over in a phenomenon known as "automatic writing." I am told that quite a few truly marvelous manuscripts are written this way, and I am green with envy.

My only problem with all these sensitives, "psychics," and mediums is that either they have just lost their "gifts" or simply are not in the proper cosmic frames of mind to demonstrate them when I arrive on the scene.

Perhaps the most highly publicized psychics of modern times are: the late Edgar Cayce of Virginia Beach, Virginia, who in a state of hypnotic trance could purportedly predict the future or diagnose and treat human ailments at a distance; Arthur Ford, a trance medium who won overnight fame for supposedly "breaking" the Houdini code in 1929; and two famous Dutch clairvoyants, Peter Hurkos and Gerard Croiset.

Edgar Cayce, posthumously, is going stronger than ever, with Cayce cults springing up in many cities across the country and reportedly doing a booming business in the sale of Cayce "life readings," as well as mail-order psychic diagnoses and cures. Cayce's life readings touch on everything from drugless therapy to the lost Atlantis. In the growing Cayce legend there seems to be no doubt about Cayce's sincerity, and he has spun an indestructible web of enchantment even among skeptics. He died before my own cosmic sojourns began. I can only report what one of the leading sensitives, who knew him well, told me: "Cayce damned near killed me. He misdiagnosed my ulcers." But it is folly indeed to try to shake the faith of a Cayce believer.

Many consider Arthur Ford the greatest living trance medium and many have also been persuaded that Ford broke the famous Houdini code. I might have accepted this, too, if I had not been one of the last reporters to interview Mrs. Houdini before she died in 1943.

Harry Houdini, the master magician, was one of the most passionate exposers of mediums in his day. He declared that all mediums were fakes and he had turned his fabulous tenacity and his physical-mental powers toward exposing the whole spiritualist movement. Before his death in 1926, he left a widely publicized message that if there were anything to spiritualism, he would get through to his wife with a code message that only she would be able to decipher. Houdini's last request was that his wife attempt to reach him at a séance. If a medium could supply the words of the code, he said, then spiritualism would be proved.

On January 9, 1929, newspapers across the country carried a story that the spiritualist medium, Arthur Ford, had received the code message from Houdini's spirit. There were subsequent charges that in addition to the prearranged code between the Houdinis, there were other prearrangements between Mrs. Houdini, Arthur Ford, and the press. It was no secret that Mrs. Houdini and Arthur Ford were well acquainted. The whole matter was aired publicly in the nation's press, and on her deathbed years later, Beatrice Houdini then admitted that she had *never* made contact with her dead husband. This, too, was widely publicized at the time. But years dim the memory of yesterday's headlines.

What about those two famous Dutch clairvoyants? Well, I have had illuminating sessions with both Peter Hurkos and Gerard Croiset, but to interpret them properly it is important first to understand the climate for psi in Holland.

The Dutch people evince great interest in psychic phenomena and the supernatural. Early in 1919, a young German named Rubini gave some "telepathic" performances in many Dutch cities and evoked an enormous amount of interest from the public. A young undergraduate student at the University of Groningen was present at one of these performances, and afterwards claimed to his costudents that he could do the telepathic trick just as well as the German telepathist. And he did.

The student was subsequently "discovered" as Holland's best ESP subject. In fact it was the public interest in telepathy in general and in that student in particular that led to the founding of the Dutch Society for Psychical Research; the society was founded for the express purpose of conducting experiments with the student. Professors from the leading Dutch universities were invited to be on the SPR council; so were psychiatrists and prominent Dutch spiritualists. The organization followed the pattern of the English SPR pioneers in 1882—and led to the same psychic pitfalls.

There were constant bickering between the spiritualists and nonspiritualists (a common ailment of many psychical research groups), and personal squabbles within the council. The late H.J.F.W. Brugmans, one of the pioneers in the

Dutch group and secretary of the SPR council, got so fed up with squabbles that he resigned from the council in 1935. He also became curiously quiet about his earlier experiments (the reports of which now form part of the classic literature in psychical research) after it was pointed out to him that the student's success in the ESP experiments could have been due to "motor automatism" or involuntary movements.

The public ardor for psi in Holland, which could hardly be dampened by any academic dousing, continued to be oiled by stage telepathists and clairvoyants, some of whom pulled stunts so remarkable that they made news headlines throughout most of Europe. In the early 1940's, a mysterious event involving telepathy in Holland was widely publicized.

The story appeared the day following a symphony concert during which two soloists suffered "pitiful" breakdowns in the middle of their performances, and the orchestra fumbled its notes in a fashion that brought highly critical reviews from music editors. The guest artist seemed to be in good form, until suddenly she got up, flung her arms and cried to the audience in substance. "I can't remember anything. What's wrong with me?"

One of the other soloists also, who usually had flawless technique, lost his memory in the middle of a part; and another member of the orchestra became rattled and misplayed his part because, as he reported later, he "felt something strange in the air."

Somehow word got out that the musical debacle was caused by a telepathist who won a bet from three cronies that he could disrupt the concert with his powers of telepathic concentration. He reportedly went to the concert, sat in the audience, and just concentrated—successfully. There were reports in Rotterdam that he also had stopped a train with telepathy, merely by putting his psychic powers of concentration to work on the man who pulled the stop cord.

Authorities instituted a search for the phantom telepathist who had ruined their symphony concert, and who was mystifying all of Holland. The Dutch and British press carried a colorful running account of the search. There was a parenthetical mention that one of the soloists had suffered tortures in a German concentration camp and as a result was sometimes subject to mental lapses, and that the guest artist also periodically suffered from loss of memory and had been treated for ill health. The great Dutch telepathy mystery that held the public entranced for weeks was probably the brain child of a clairvoyant press agent, and in the manner of most psychic whodunits, it was never "solved."

Comes now the new twist—mysteries solved by clairvoyance.

The stage was set, the audience palpitating, when Peter Hurkos and Gerard Croiset made their full-blown debut as clairvoyant crime-solvers.

Croiset has fared well with the psychic intelligentsia because of his collaboration with Professor W. H. C. Tenhaeff, who is highly esteemed in serious psi circles as director of the Parapsychology Laboratory at the University of Utrecht.

Hurkos, on the other hand, has been severely criticized by parapsychologists for his "deviation from the scientifically straight and narrow paths of modern psychical research." He has never submitted his psyche to the ESP card and dice tests at Duke University. He has been criticized for his "multifarious American contacts."

Despite this handicap, however, Hurkos catapulted to popularity as the matinee idol of the psychic clan in America. His life story has been well publicized. He claims to have been a Dutch house painter who fell on his head in his native Holland and became psychic.

Thus, he can gaze intently into a person's eyes and warn, "Be careful of your car. You may have some bad trouble with your differential." It's the sort of thing that gives a man pause.

Even reputable parapsychologists were impressed with the prediction he made in April 1959 that the Los Angeles Dodgers would beat the Milwaukee Braves for the National League pennant. The anti-chance odds on the prediction coming true were 1440:1. When it did come true, parapsychologists pointed to it as one of the "best bits of psi evidence anyone could hope for." The prediction has helped to secure Hurkos some notice by intellectuals in the field.

As one of these intellectuals said, "Hurkos probably has some degree of spontaneous extrasensory ability, and he makes a little bit go a long way."

I had read a great deal about Peter Hurkos and General Croiset before I met either of them. My first meeting with Hurkos might have made a psi convert out of me if I had not once had a similar baffling experience with that amazing master mentalist, The Great Dunninger. It takes a Dunninger or a Hurkos to convert long confirmed skeptics—at least those who haven't yet read the classics on the tricks of the magicians' trade.

There is a difference, of course, between Dunninger and Hurkos. Though Dunninger calls himself a mind-reader, he doesn't claim any supernatural powers, and he had no association with the metaphysical group, either on the academic or spiritualist level. In fact, he used to be ejected regularly from spiritualistic meetings for giving away trade secrets from ringside seats, and like Houdini, he has boasted that there are no spiritualistic phenomena produced by mediums that he cannot duplicate by trickery. He once announced a standing offer of $10,000 to anyone who wanted to take him up on it. No one did.

At his peak, Peter Hurkos seemed to demonstrate cerebral convolutions that were practically on a par with Dunninger's in their mystifying impact on an audience, and many were convinced—some still are—that he is endowed with at least some small measure of genuine extrasensory perception. I can only report that from my own experiences he seemed as adept as Dunninger in the magic art of picking people's craniums, and whether what he got was the result of magicianship or psychic powers still remains a puzzle to many who have watched him perform.

Personally, I belong to an old-fashioned school that is still reluctant to attribute a psychic explanation to things that might seem otherwise unexplainable only because of lack of an expert's knowledge.

Hurkos has claimed 85-percent accuracy in his psychic powers. On close inspection this could be chalked up to an 85-percent combination of simple guesswork, good psychology, and generalities—such as, in examining your wristwatch, "It's a good watch, but I see a repair in the spring."

In my first meeting with Peter Hurkos I had brought with me from Chicago, a city of unsolved crimes, an envelope containing photographs of victims in some of Chicago's well-known murder cases. Hurkos lightly rubbed his fingertips across each picture, one by one, and as he did so, beads of perspiration broke out on his face, his look of horror increased, and he came up with some astonishing clairvoyant surmises, most of which had been reported in gory detail in the daily press.

One psychiatrist told me, "There is absolutely no question about Peter Hurkos' unusual powers. I think in time he will be recognized as one of the greatest and most gifted men of modern times." There are many who feel, however, that some psychiatrists need their own heads examined.

I also talked to the chief of the homicide squad in a city where Hurkos once worked on crime cases.

"I don't believe in this stuff," he told me, "but this guy's got *something*. I can't say he's really helped solve a crime, but he comes up with things that give you the shivers. And please don't use my name. They'll think I'm nuts."

Whoever heard of a cop that doesn't want his name mentioned in a story?

It has always puzzled me why, if all clairvoyants are as good as they claim to be—and as many believe them to be—they aren't cleaning up in the stock market.

I have also wondered sometimes why it is that Dutchmen seem to be more psychic than others—and, more important, why it is that so many psychics are not psychic enough to predict, or at least anticipate, their own personal problems and exert a better control over their own mixed-up lives.

With high hopes I rang the doorbell at No. 21 Willem de Zwygerlaan Street in Utrecht. The name on the shiny brass nameplate to the left of the door was GERARD CROISET, who for a long time, confidentially, had been my ESP idol. If anyone had the "gift," it must be Gerard Croiset, I thought, inspired in moments of irrationality by all I had heard and read about him.

Although a skeptic by nature and training, I am no exception to the rule of wish over wisdom. A basic urge of mankind (and womankind, too, of course) is to believe in the mystical, and some people search for realities to support their beliefs. For several years I had harbored a secret ambition to meet Gerard Croiset. The time was here.

The light was on in the Croiset manse, but no one answered the doorbell, so I walked in. From a nondescript hallway, I took a left turn through a door that opened into an empty room. At one end of the room was another door beyond which I could see lights and hear voices. I knocked on the door, at first quietly, then loudly. The door opened abruptly, and standing there, with one hand on the knob and his eyes on his wristwatch, was a harried, impatient man obviously in the throes of important business that my arrival had clearly interrupted. He was lean and muscular, with reddish brown hair and flinty blue eyes under bushy, overhanging brows. Somehow, although he didn't fit the preconceived picture I had of him, I knew instinctively that this was Gerard Croiset.

He hurriedly ushered me into a large room, the walls of which were lined with 50 straight-backed wooden chairs, most of them occupied by women. He pointed to an empty one for me and spoke quickly in his native tongue to the audience.

A woman crossed the room and sat down beside me. "You speak English?" she asked. "The doctor asked me to sit next to you. He said to tell you this is ladies' hour. After dinner it will be for both men and women."

In the center of the room stood a large, dark green leather chair and foot rest that appeared to be medical equipment for examining patients.

Croiset did a toe-whirl and snapped his fingers at the women in a gesture that apparently meant "Who's next?" A plumpish, pale-faced woman came forward and squeezed into the chair. With his eyes closed and his head tilted upward, as though in prayer, Croiset began massaging the woman's temples, then her neck and shoulders, then her hips and thighs, and on down to her ankles.

My lady interpreter leaned over and whispered, "Polio. Very bad. She's much better now."

"What's the doctor's name again?" I asked, just to make sure.

"Dr. Croiset," she whispered. "He's wonderful."

By this time Croiset had the lady out of the chair and on her feet. He did a quick crescendo up her spine as though it were a piano keyboard, fingered a grand finale on her neck, gave her a little pat on the posterior, then waved his arms in an arc and snapped his fingers again. Next! He spent two minutes per patient.

Once, squatting low (he was at the lady's knee), he looked up at me with a broad grin and gave me a big wink. He then directed a question to the sitter next to me, who interpreted, "He wants to know what you are thinking." This seemed a little peculiar, coming from one of the world's greatest clairvoyants, but I murmured as politely and enthusiastically as possible, "Amazing!"

Croiset treats many patients in his "spiritual healing" séances and apparently earns many thousands of guilders a year. His schedule includes a children's hour, ladies' hour, and men's night, and special sessions for mixed groups, business groups, and other assorted categories.

The woman next to me said that she had been taking Dr. Croiset's treatments for a year and felt a thousand percent better already. I asked what her trouble was.

"Nerves," she said. "I was a nervous wreck and I had pains in my face. Now I feel fine."

"Then why are you still coming for treatments?"

"I know I'd get worse if I didn't," she said. "He's such a wonderful doctor. It's all in his hands. He has electromagnetic waves in them . . ."

Croiset had only a few moments to spare before his next group came in for spiritual healing. But he was willing to answer a few questions. When I asked about his work on solving crime cases, he pointed to his telephone and tape recorder and said, "That's for police work. But I don't do much of it anymore. There's no pay for police work." He gave me another big wink and added, "It's mostly all healing now."

Meantime I had deliberately and casually dropped on his desk my large brown envelope containing pictures of some of Chicago's best-known murder victims—and some not so well known. I also saw him accidently-on-purpose reach over and feel the envelope; then, as I was about to leave, he said, "You have pictures of three little boys, haven't you?"

"*How* did you know?" I asked in wide-eyed wonder.

"The envelope. You saw me touch it? I can tell. It's the psychic power. You have a girl's picture, too."

He then proceeded to give me a few psychic details of the Schuessler-Peterson case in Chicago, in which three little boys were brutally murdered, and of the well-publicized Judith Anderson murder case, which has never been solved. Nor could Croiset solve them. My envelope did indeed contain pictures of the Schuessler and Peterson boys, Judith Anderson, the Grimes sisters, and other principles in Chicago's better-known crime cases.

Of course, anyone in Holland could keep abreast of America's most famous murder and missing-persons cases, particularly with Americans calling on them for help and supplying details. The envelope also contained pictures of principles in some less well-known crime cases, but Croiset said nothing about these. I asked one of the crime-solving clairvoyants if he belonged to the Dutch Psychical Research Society. He replied, "Oh, no. Only the Gerard Croiset Society." He explained that this was the society that "worked with" Professor Tenhaeff. He volunteered, however, that he himself did "police work" only—no healing.

Croiset's healing work can perhaps best be described in his own words. He has written voluminously on the subject of himself, most of it published in pamphlet form and in a Dutch journal called *The Paranormal Healer*, copies of which I obtained and had translated.

"A Spiritual, or Paranormal, Healer," he says, "is endowed with a special extrasensory perception which gives him a paranormal means of communicating with others . . . My personality is closely related to my powers of extrasensory perception . . . Persons who can perceive motivating causes without first having studied their past history and interworkings formally, and who can differentiate among these causes through their extrasensory perception, we call Psychoscopic Diagnosticians. If such persons have, as well, the gift of being able to bring back together the dislocated interworkings of these principles, we then call them Paranormal, or Spiritual, Healers, or, as we still sometimes say today, Mesmerizers.

"A Spiritual Healer is somehow not fettered by his human form. He stretches himself up, and can sometimes experience something of God-like Love when his perceptive power is active in him. The more the Healer can turn unawareness to awareness, the more he can help his fellow men . . ."

There are subjects other than himself discussed in Croiset's writings. They include everything from nuclear fallout and manmade smog to the "Herb of the Month," the importance of Vitamin-D in daily diet, and "visionary dream experiences"—all wrapped up in the timeless beauty of the kind of obscure verbiage that has always deluded credulous minds.

After leaving Croiset, I went to the University of Utrecht to find Professor W. H. C. Tenhaeff. There was no office or laboratory listed for him. I finally located his quarters in an office building several blocks from the campus. After I pounded on the door for some time, a secretary came to the door and told me to come back in an hour.

The professor, rotund and dapper, with goatee and monocle, greeted me with the warning that he did not like journalists and would give me only 15 minutes of his time. It was long enough. He gave me the answers I needed. What did he think of Croiset's work? "Remarkable." He added that he had "discovered" Croiset, developed his ESP abilities, and that they had continued to collaborate closely on laboratory experiments.

He would not be pinned down on the precise nature of his laboratory experiments, except to say that the ESP card tests were out of date and that he was concentrating more now on "healing." In the registrar's office at the University of Utrecht, I learned that Professor Tenhaeff teaches no classes at the university in parapsychology (or anything else), and that his salary is paid neither by the university nor by the Netherlands government, but by a "sponsor." The "sponsor," I learned, was the Dutch Society of Spiritual Healers.

Croiset and Tenhaeff have not fared well in the official investigative reports of commissions who have checked into their activities.

One of these is the distinguished Belgian Committee for the Scientific Investigation of Phenomena Reputed to be Paranormal. This committee is in fact a well-knit organization of 40 active and about 100 associate members, including scientists, lawyers, criminologists, scholars, medical doctors, mathematicians, and others—including a chief of police.

The Belgian Committee approaches the paranormal from the standpoint of science rather than as a study of the supernatural. It has performed a remarkable service, largely ignored by psychical researchers, in investigating objectively and scientifically the phenomena that emerge from occultism, and in trying to bring the results of these investigations to the public's attention.

In Brussels, I talked with some of the committee's members, including S. Moulinasse, a retired army colonel; and Dr. M. J. Bessemans, a doctor of medicine and surgery, professor (and former rector) at the University of Ghent, and professor at the Brussels School of Criminology and Scientific Detection. The committee, whose work is supported by grants from scientific foundations, has investigated everything from table-tipping to clairvoyance in more than 1500 experiments, the designs of the experiments depending on the types of cases under investigation. The total results?

"The results are always negative," they told me.

The formal statement in their official report is: "Up to the present time, none of the completed experiments under the control of the committee have shown clear evidence of paranormal phenomena. To the contrary, all the attempts have failed . . . The only concern of the committee is the recognition of the truth."

Such conclusions, unfortunately, rarely make any impression on psi believers. And the paranormal impact of Tenhaeff and Croiset goes on with undiminished zeal. Their influence, in fact, now extends all the way to South Africa, where parapsychologists at Rhodes University are going in for the study of telepathy, psychometry, and something they call "psychoscopy"—a word they admittedly picked up from Croiset.

It seems that while a couple of South African psychical researchers were guest-researching with Tenhaeff and Croiset at Utrecht, Croiset demonstrated still another of his many remarkable talents by dramatically analyzing the contents of a sixteenth century manuscript—without even opening the book. He only touched the sides. In this experiment he referred to himself as a "psychoscopist," which impressed the South Africans—if one is to believe everything one reads in the psychical-research journals.

Should there remain any question about these noted clair-voyant crime-solvers, I can only add this written confirmation from *De Hoofcommissaris Van Politie Te Amsterdam,* which roughly translated, means the chief of police of Amsterdam:

> In reply to your letter, I inform you that the Amsterdam po-lice have never cooperated with clairvoyants. In general there is not any tendency by the Dutch police to become connected with clairvoyants. There are no Dutch crime cases known here which were solved by clairvoyants.

CHAPTER 9

A-Ghosting We Did Go

My deepest regret about my associations in the world of psi is that I've never met a real ghost. I feel on cozy terms with hundreds of fascinating apparitions described to me by psychical researchers as paranormal phenomena. And I have listened, full of envy, to the wondrous accounts of those who are lucky enough to know at least one, and sometimes a whole collection, of ghosts.

Why am I so unlucky?

Ghosts are comparatively harmless. There is nothing wrong in believing in them. In fact, anyone who has never seen a ghost is generally regarded as a dud in tall-tales-by-the-fireside circles.

The eminent psychiatrist Carl Gustaf Jung considered ghosts a vital part of mortal man's existence. In his memoirs he wrote, "Why should not there be ghosts? How did we know that something was 'impossible'? Myself, I found such possibilities extremely interesting and attractive. They added another dimension to my life; the world gained depth and background."

The ghosts I have met in séances have been interesting enough. Possibly they would have added another dimension to my life if I had not seen how they were manufactured in a magic-spook shop.

I have gone sleuthing for ghosts—the real thing—all the way from the Tower of London to the Taj Mahal, always in the hope that I would at least see *something*. I've slept in haunted houses, perched on tombstones in long-forsaken graveyards, and scanned lonely, moonlit battlefields for some sign of a phantom. No luck.

But I have met some fabulous phantoms by proxy, through friends who are personally acquainted with them.

Not long ago I was invited to lunch at the Fine Arts Club in London with a pretty little white-haired woman whose large blue eyes gazed trancelike into space as she talked about her favorite ghosts. I was enchanted, but at an opportune moment I could not refrain from asking, "You mean you have *really seen* all these ghosts?"

"My dear," she replied, "I've seen them by moonlight, daylight, gaslight, and lamplight. I'm psychic, you know. My people are Highlanders from the Isle of Skye and I'm the seventh child of a seventh child and was given the gift of seeing. My granny used to dream dreams and tell fortunes in egg whites." In spite of her long association with ghosts, she appeared to be perfectly normal. It was impossible not to believe her.

The Tower of London, where heads once rolled willy-nilly, is said to be infested with some spectacular ghosts. Only a few years ago, a sentry at the number-four post had just heard the clock chime a quarter to midnight when he saw a puff of white smoke emanating from the mouth of an old cannon a few yards from him. The puff of smoke hovered for a moment and made the shape of a square. Then, as if noticing the sentry, it made a beeline for him. The frightened guard left his sentry box and called the guard from the number-three post. They both saw it then, a strange vaporous shape dangling on the side of the steps leading to the top of the wall. It was quivering and moving, but was nothing human. The frightened guards-men returned to the number-three box and rang the alarm bell, calling out the entire guard. By the time the guard turned out, the apparition had vanished.

I haunted the tower for a while, waiting for something dramatic to happen. I was accompanied by London's well-known ghost expert, Guy Lambert, and his ghost-detecting machine.

Lambert is a member of the London Society for Psychi-cal Research and has spent many years tracking down all the famous phantoms that roam through England's musty castles and ancient houses knocking over tables, blowing out candles, and producing sudden moans, groans, wails, and rappings. His ghost-detecting machine is a small, caged instrument, similar to a seismograph; it registers the eerie movements— the shakes, quakes, and shocks—usually attributed to ghosts and poltergeists.

After all his years of personally haunting haunted houses in search of ghosts, Guy Lambert admitted to me rather sadly, "No, I have never seen a ghost. I guess I'm not the sort." Not only that, but he has stripped ghosts of their aura of mystery and deglamorized them with a mundane and earthy hypoth-esis. Their *raison d'etre*, he says, is strictly geological—the result of underground rivers, streams, and brooks—clogged drainage pipes.

There are forces—not psychic—beneath the ground, he explains, that cause strain on structures above ground. And it is this strain that produces creaks and groans, drafts that blow out candles, pressures that open and close doors, and vibrations that knock over furniture.

Sometimes the strain upon a structure is so slight that it does not manifest itself in dramatic disturbances, yet it is sufficient to cause a vague feeling of uneasiness in a person or persons living within the disturbed structure. Lambert believes that this uneasy feeling, sometimes preceded by unaccountable noises, can make people dream or imagine they see all kinds of apparitions.

He told me of a London woman who was haunted by a coughing ghost. She called in her clergyman and together they drove the ghost away. At least that's what *they* thought. Lambert explained the ghost geologically. He checked back through records and learned that on the date of the ghostly intrusion, a sudden flood had disturbed the drainage system in the area. It was probably the drainage pipes, not a ghost, "coughing" under the sudden strain.

Londoners happen to be extremely fond of ghosts. Luckily for them, and for the London Society for Psychical Research, which has devoted itself diligently to this particular type of parapsychic phenomena, the city of London is situated in a hollow with the heights of Hampstead on the north and the heights of Clapham on the south; underneath the ground is London clay, impervious to water. When water travels underground in London, it can go no great distance. It just stays there, says Guy Lambert, making noises like ghosts.

Scotland, too, has underground forces that are responsible for its ghosts, he explained, but the forces aren't water forces; Scotland's an earthquake area. Add to this the Scots' love of ghosts, which is on a par with the Britishers', and the result is enough hair-raising ghost stories to fill many volumes.

Lambert is meticulous in his ghost research. Besides his ghost detection machine, he uses charts, graphs, maps, and meteorological data, and is adept at analyzing the relationships of streams, rivers, and underground creeks to, say, the houses on Upper Wimpole Street or Buckingham Palace. He has also made thorough studies of wet and dry years, rainy seasons and floods, in relation to ghosts, going back as far as 1868, and has found that the wetter it is, the more phantoms there are to create mischief. In London, the phantoms seem to prefer the drizzling autumn and winter months, though there is also a summer peak in July and August—the season of thunderstorms.

"The time has now come," says Lambert, "to look for further detailed observations in the most likely quarter, namely underground, and no longer to the conclusion that all (ghostly phenomena) is lying, trickery, or 'psychic' agency."

Nor does Lambert go along with the widely held theory that murder, suicide, or some other form of death by violence is most likely to leave a house haunted by ghosts. This is a theory that needs very careful examination, he stated, and that may melt away on close inspection.

One of London's most famous ghost stories, for example, has its setting in the Sir Christopher Wren house at Hampton Court on the Green, the site of an old courthouse. Sir Christopher built the house, which is near the Thames River, and according to the story, died an agonizing death there. On the night of his death, the women in the household heard noises downstairs, which they soon identified as coffins bouncing about. On the anniversary of his death the coffins start up again, and many persons have sworn that they have heard them.

"Rubbish!" says Guy Lambert. "First of all, Sir Christopher didn't even die in the house, but passed away peacefully in his carriage en route to downtown London. Secondly, the records show that on the night of his death terrible floods occurred all along the Thames, enough to place great strain on the big old drains in that house. Can't you just imagine the creaks and groans and straining on the staircase?"...

In ghost lore, despite the view held by Guy Lambert, the role of violence has been so emphasized that many people accept as gospel the frequently advance theory that all ghosts are those of persons who have met tragic ends.

The ghost of Abraham Lincoln in the White House has perhaps offered more in support of this theory than any other ghost. Mrs. Eleanor Roosevelt, whose bedroom was once Lincoln's bedroom, reported that she often felt the presence of another person standing behind her, but when she turned to look, no one was there. Former President Harry Truman sometimes heard ghostly rappings on his bedroom door in the dead of night. They were often loud enough to awaken him from a sound sleep, but when he answered the door, no one was there.

One afternoon in 1934, Mary Eban, a member of the White House household staff and an intelligent, level-headed girl, was sent on an errand to the second floor. Two minutes later her scream pierced the quiet atmosphere of the White House and brought other staff members running to her side. She was pale and trembling with fright. She had just seen Abraham Lincoln sitting on his bed pulling on his boots. Other White House maids and butlers have sworn they have seen Lincoln many times.

Lincoln is not the only president, however, whose ghost has returned to haunt the White House, though it is the one seen most often. Others are Andrew Jackson, Ulysses S. Grant, William Howard Taft, and Woodrow Wilson. Did the five presidents who still haunt the White House possess some special quality not shared by other ex-presidents? Possibly, according to a theory advanced back in 1893 by Thomas Jay Hudson, a doctor of philosophy and of letters, whose book, *The Law of Psychic Phenomena*, is still regarded as a classic in its field.

Dr. Hudson's explanation for ghosts includes three basic premises:

1. The power to create "phantasms" (the fancy word for ghosts) resides and is inherent in the subjective mind, or personality, of man.

2. The power becomes greater as the body approaches nearer the point of death.

3. At the moment of death, or when the functions of the body are entirely suspended, the power is greatest.

"Hence," he concludes succinctly, "ghosts."

In his further analysis of ghosts he states:

"It is not true that all ghosts are those of persons who have died violent deaths. On the contrary, many of the best authenticated ghosts are of persons who have died at a good old age and in the due course of nature. But it is true that those who have met death by violence far outnumber the others.

"... The first fact which seems to be universal and to possess significance, is that *all phantasms of the dead are of those who have died under circumstances of great mental stress of emotion.* [Italics are Dr. Hudson's.] No one whose death was peaceful and quiet, no one who left this life with no unsatisfied longing or desire present in the mind at the time of death, ever projected a phantasm upon the living objective world.

". . . The strength, persistency, and objectivity of the phantasm seem to be in exact proportion to the intensity of the emotion experienced at the moment of death."

Ghosts apparently come in a number of varieties, forms, shapes, and sizes. Guy Lambert in London, judging them on hearsay only—since he has never encountered a ghost—would lump them all into two types: those that are so life-like that they do not look like ghosts, and those who come dressed in the traditional flowing white robes. Arthur Conan Doyle, a great believer in all psi phenomena, organized ghosts into groups according to their capabilities: those who speak through mediums, those who write on slates (a talent referred to as automatic writing), those who operate Ouija boards, and those who can only bang around in the dark.

But judging from countless incidents on record, ghosts can take still another form: those that are produced by a sleepy mind and this kind of apparition can appear in the form of a cow, a deer, a house, or some common or familiar object that actually isn't there at all. More precisely, the word for it is hallucination, a strange mental phenomenon which, because it occurs in the transitory period between waking and sleeping, is called a hypnagogic dream. So real are these hallucinations that they have caused accidents on highways and mistakes in industrial plants.

In a report to the American Psychological Association, Alfred L. Moseley, of the Harvard School of Public Health, told of 33 long distance truck drivers who had experienced such hallucinations. One trucker overturned his vehicle trying to avoid a cow that wasn't there. Another saw herds of mules in shining harness crossing the road, while still another saw a large colonial mansion astraddle the road and veered his truck into a 20-foot-deep gully to avoid hitting it. Others saw cattle, deer, logs across the road, and millions of red spiders on the windshield.

The psychological explanation is that such hallucinations are spun from the driver's desire to stop because he's tired—so he sees things that make him stop.

There is another psychological explanation of ghosts, particularly those seen in childhood. It is called *eidetic imagery*— meaning mental images of unusual vividness which many children can project with a clarity approaching that of a visual hallucination. It is connected with the imagery of memory and imagination, and is comparatively rare in adults though quite common in children. Some adults, however, are firmly convinced of the reality of ghosts—as well as their own psychic rapport—because of apparitions they saw in childhood as a result of eidetic imagery.

A woman in Milwaukee, Wisconsin, for example, sent me a lengthy report on her psychic powers, which—as in the majority of cases—started in childhood. In her letter she wrote, "For about ten to fifteen years now, my mental receiving set has been tuned in clear and often . . . I saw my own ghost at the age of twelve after a tonsil operation and thought I had died. My ghost was hovering above the door to my hospital room and although my family came to the door while I was watching myself, I did not notice them. My mother asked, 'Edna, don't you know us?' . . . When I looked back my ghost had disappeared. From that time on nothing surprised me."

Chances are that in spite of sporadic scientific and pseudoscientific attempts to burden ghosts with earthly and logical explanations for their existence, nothing will destroy the phenomenal popularity of ghosts. The truth is that real scientists are—or at least should be—too busy to be bothered with investigating ghosts, and they are no closer now than they were 100 years ago to a rational explanation of these fascinating "phantasms." Ghosts have been blamed on everything from trickery, hysteria, credulity, and indigestion to mists, drafts, owls, and rats. But the true believer in ghosts finds no emotional fulfillment in such rationalizations. Nor will the true believer buy any hypothesis suggesting that ghosts may be nothing more than hallucinations, hypnagogic dreams, eidetic imagery, or flood pressure on underground drainage pipes.

Such theories will never replace a rousing good ghost story told before a flickering fire. One of the undeniably genuine powers of the human mind is its belief in its own delusions; and throughout all the millenniums, in man's eternal quest of the supernatural, ghosts have occupied a favorite spot and reigned supreme in the realm of wish over wisdom.

So popular are ghosts, in fact, that they have risen from the grave to heights of academic recognition in such seats of higher learning as Cambridge University in England, where psi researchers are investigating the "subtle psi factor" of those who believe in ghosts.

The uninitiated traveling in the world of psi must tread the alphabetical jungle slowly, a step at a time.

We know that ESP stands for extrasensory perception and PK for psychokinesis—the purported movement of objects by merely "willing" them or otherwise without physical means.

We now come to RSPK, meaning "recurrent spontaneous psychokinesis," a term synonymous with poltergeist in the minds of serious psi researchers. Poltergeists were much more fun before parapsychologists began calling them RSPK.

Webster's dictionaries still define poltergeist as a German word derived from *polter* (noise) and *geist* (ghost)—or, "a noisy ghost; a spirit assumed as the explanation of rappings and other unexplained noises."

A poltergeist is simply a racketing spirit that remains invisible but that manifests its presence by hurling objects about, turning things upside down, sending chandeliers, crockery, and coffins into orbit, and otherwise making a mischievous and delightful nuisance of itself.

Nothing brightens a dull night for a newspaper's night city editor more than a poltergeist story coming over the wires. And poltergeists are as popular in these modern times as they were 1600 years ago, when residents of the village of Bingenam-Rhein, Germany (in the year 355), were terrified by an eruption of stone throwings, raps, and physical blows by some "invisible force." Many reported being pulled from their beds at night by the "force."

The cause of the disturbance was never determined and was finally attributed to the devil and his followers. It is the world's oldest recorded case of RSPK, although in the year 355 it was still known as poltergeists.

In 1962, there was the widely publicized case of the flying objects in Portsmouth, Virginia, in the home of Mr. and Mrs. Charles Daughtery. A small vase on a mantle crashed against a wall in the hallway after rounding a corner apparently under its own power. Another vase, perched on a sewing machine in the hallway, fell to the floor three or four times, and a bottle of hair lotion sailed through the air and struck Mrs. Daughtery on the back of the head.

Parapsychological researchers were dispatched to investigate the phenomena and found them to be "typical of poltergeist activities"—with objects flitting about for no known reason, and the presence in the household of a teen-age boy (a grandson).

Poltergeists, like children, are mischievous and noisy, and RSPK almost always involves a teen-age boy or girl, although psychical researchers insist that RSPK is paranormal.

The poltergeist is no ordinary ghost. Within limits there is almost nothing this spirit entity can't do. It has a peculiar behavior pattern: fires are mysteriously lit, tunes rapped out, bells rung, windows broken, dishes smashed, furniture tumbled, bedclothes dragged from the bed; and there is much levitation.

Experts have even attributed Nijinski's dancing feats to RSPK levitation. Nijinski, the greatest male dancer in history, had the ability to fly through the air with the greatest of ease, and he also had the gift of appearing to remain longer in the air than any other dancer. The famous English historian Sacheverell Sitwell, whose book *Poltergeist* is one of the classics in the vast literature on the subject, cites Nijinski's feats as evidence of poltergeists. He points out that Nijinski seemed to hang motionless in mid-air for a fraction of a second at the summit of his leap, as though he were defying the laws of gravity, and then descend in a delayed, slow-motion trajectory. When questioned about this Nijinski's only comment was that it was simple. There is no evidence that Nijinski himself considered his act paranormal.

Recent reports of poltergeists include those of a Baltimore family that dodged flying sugar bowls and exploding bottles; an Iowa couple who found their davenport and refrigerator overturned; a Louisville family whose photo album sailed through the air; and a family in Wilmington, Illinois, whose daughter was hit by a flying cabbage.

In each case there was a teen-ager living in the house.

Dr. Nandor Fodor, a psychoanalyst and psychical researcher, defines the poltergeist as a "bundle of projected repressions." He has advanced a number of interesting theories regarding poltergeists. One is that the poltergeist differs from the true ghost in that the ghost haunts a house, and the poltergeist haunts a person—usually a girl or boy at the pubertal age. The why and how of this psychobiological disorder, Dr. Fodor admits, is as yet unknown, but he has labeled it "poltergeist psychosis" and considers it an "episodic mental disturbance of schizophrenic character."

Psychical researchers often cite the famous case of the Newark disturbances as "one of the best documented poltergeist cases in recent years." So important is the Newark case, in fact, that it has assumed a role as possible evidence of survival after death.

W. G. Roll, director of the Psychical Research Foundation, Inc., an organization devoted exclusively to research on postmortem survival and operating within Duke's Parapsychology Laboratory, has stated in his study of the Newark case: "Assuming that some of the disturbances were parapsychological, this study touches on two areas of survival research. The events are similar to the spontaneous PK occurrences which sometimes are associated with death."

The Newark disturbances were investigated by Roll and other researchers, and there is no doubt that they provided one of the "best documented" poltergeist cases in recent years. The case was so thoroughly investigated and well documented, in fact, that it would seem to settle once and for all the question of whether the poltergeist properly belongs under the heading of psychical or pathological phenomena.

The disturbances centered around Ernest Rivers, a fourteen-year-old Negro boy who lived with his grandmother, Mrs. Mabelle Clark, in a housing development in Newark, New Jersey. The case had a double significance for psychical researchers: it was the first time poltergeists had been reported from a housing development. Poltergeist activities are often explained as being caused by underground water currents, magnetic fields, seismological disturbances, or other natural unidentified causes. "Since the activity (in Newark) centers around only one small apartment in a large building, such an explanation seems to be automatically eliminated," said the psi researchers, who could not, however, automatically elim-inate the boy. There was no poltergeist activity when Ernest was not in the apartment.

The case erupted in May of 1961 and made front page headlines in many papers. Reporters covering the disturbances apparently were taken in either by the alleged poltergeists or their smashing manifestations.

Crockery careened through the apartment, bottles hurtled around corners, lightbulbs came unscrewed, lamps tipped to 45 degree angles, sugar bowls and salt shakers sailed about the room, and a jar of mustard spun past an investigator's head (barely missing it) and shattered against a wall.

Housing authorities, police, psychical experts, and psy-chiatrists came running to the scene of the poltergeists. For a whole week (May 6 to 12), the reading public had a field day. But even poltergeists, no matter how entrancing, must even-tually relinquish the front pages to other newsworthy items; so for the reading public, the Newark disturbances ended, like most poltergeist cases, just where they started—in the air. The mystery was "unsolved," but it had been great fun while it lasted.

The sequel to the story, which lacks the entertainment appeal of the original, can be found in the RSPK files at Duke.

The poltergeist-infested lad and his grandmother were brought to the Parapsychology Laboratory for further observation and testing. The disturbances followed them all the way to Durham, even into the hotel, where things began popping as soon as Ernest arrived. He went into the bathroom and soon a crash was heard. The light fixture had come off the wall. A water glass in the bathroom also levitated and smashed to bits. (The hotel now uses plastic glasses in the bathroom.) Even the Parapsychology Laboratory failed to inhibit the poltergeist manifestations.

Eventually, however, a test situation was arranged whereby psychical researchers could observe Ernest through a one-way mirror, and what they observed, in their words, were "events indicative of fraud." Ernest was observed hiding objects under his shirt and later throwing them at his grandmother.

In the light of this the parapsychological conclusion was that "the later phase of the events (in Durham) can be explained normally; the early ones (in Newark) remain difficult to account for." Psychiatric examination revealed an intense, underlying anger within the boy toward his grandmother; he was in a state of "mental dissociation" when he perpetrated the disturbances. The early phases of the Newark disturbances, however, are still regarded as important to survival research, since they were never explained.

Thus, it would seem, PK and RSPK can go on being their own frisky little selves, devilish, delightful, and delectable poltergeists, so long as no one spies on them through a one-way mirror.

CHAPTER 10

Ouija and Kindred Potpourri

In the procession of entertaining mental diversions, the vogue of the Ouija board is perennial. And though its ancestry goes back to the days when the mysterious was interpreted as an oracle of the gods, the cults of modern metaphysics and spiritualism have appropriated Ouija, as they have appropriated many other things, as a means of producing modern oracular information. But as usual, they garble their ads with obtuse double-talk.

Subconscious Mind or Spirit Voice? Which Speaks Through The MYSTIC OUIJA BOARD? Whatever it is, the answers are out of this world. Serious psychic investigators long ago recognized that the Ouija board provides amazing—almost unbelievable— true answers.

This is typical of ads appearing in psychically attuned journals, but the price of the Ouija board is only $5.25 ("Give one to a friend"), and its answers are indeed, as the ads say, out of this world. Are ouija's miracles produced by the subconscious mind or by spirit voices? Whether the psychical ad writers know it or not, this is the crux of the problem.

The real phenomenon of Ouija is something known in psychology as "automatism," or automatic physiological response under expectant attention. Automatism in the form of *involuntary movement* accounts for a great many of the phenomena usually attributed to psychic powers or to spirits of the dead. The principle behind Ouija is the same as that of the pendulum, and in fact in cases where fraud can be discounted, the effects produced by pendulum swinging, table-turning, and the Ouija board all depend on unconscious muscular movements. In psychology they are also known as *ideomotor movements*.

Anyone can test the existence of ideomotor movements for himself by suspending a ring or any other object of similar weight on the end of a fine piece of string about ten inches long. It will be impossible to keep the ring absolutely immobilized in this position. No matter how hard one may try, there will always remain a slight movement due to involuntary movements of the hand. Ideomotor movements are responsible for the "success" claimed in many experiments in telepathy and clairvoyance; and the popular trick of mind-reading is sometimes merely the highly skilled art of muscle-reading.

Although explainable in simple terms of modern psychology and physiology, the popularity of the Ouija-board-pendulum family, like most things mistaken as psychic forces, has its roots in the occult. The belief in the occult is the active starting point for the entire psychic adventure, whether ancient or modern. The prepossessed mind will always find out what it looks for on the way. When the mind creates a belief in a theory, the facts will then create themselves.

The Ouija board turned out to be a handy creation for those who believed in the theory of spirit communication. It was also much less cumbersome than a spirit-rapping table.

Men of the Fiji Island of Beqa prepare the *lovo*, or firepit, for their famous fire-walk. Fire-walking, or walking over glowing embers, is practiced in India and other countries, but only the Fijians are stone-walkers.

Here Fijians walk barefoot over the fire-pit of searing hot stones. Scientists attribute their immunity to burns to auto-suggestion or self-hypnosis induced by faith.

Norma Lee Browning in Western Arnhem Land, Australia, with a group of Aborigines who are painted for a *coroboree,* or ceremonial. The Aborigines are masters at the art of silent or non-verbal communication, and communicate by message sticks, finger talk, smoke signals and, apparently, telepathy.

Michael, a Kunapipi headman at Nourlangie, a buffalo camp on the Alligator River in Western Arnhem Land, Australia, carves a message stick for Norma Lee Browning to deliver to Michael's brother-in-law, Johnny, at Manangrida, 150 miles away.

Here Johnny reads the message stick brought to him from Michael by Norma Lee Browning. The message sticks mystify non-Aborigines, but the Aborigines themselves can read the lines and notches on them as though they were letters.

The Ouija board, or its pendulum godparent, has been around for a long time, and it has been in use from Europe to China through the ages. One of the earliest recorded references to the pendulum was by the Byzantine historian Marcellus. He records that in the time of the Emperor Valens, a number of men were condemned to death for attempting to divine the name of the Emperor's successor. The method they used was to set the letters of the alphabet out in a circle, as in a modern Ouija-board, and to suspend a ring over the center of the circle. The ring, by the direction of its swing, indicated in turn various letters of the alphabet. This method, used by the ancient Romans, was a very slow one and is seldom resorted to now. In spiritualist circles, a similar method popular at one time was to suspend a pendulum or ring in an empty glass and ask the spirits questions. One tap on the side of the glass meant no and two meant yes.

The claims made for the pendulum were as great and varied as those made for the magnet. In fact, the pendulum, in the modern garb of "radiesthesia," has far surpassed the Ouija board as an instrument of psychic significance.

Ouija's history, however, is a colorful one. From the slow swinging ring in the alphabet circle of the ancient Romans, Ouija progressed to Hydesville, New York, near Rochester, where the famous Fox sisters, Margaret, Katharine, and Leah, were then creating the new psychic wave—known as spiritualism—with their "rappings." The pranks of the Fox sisters not only inaugurated the great American movement of spiritualism (in1848), but they also started the raps that were heard around. Rapping soirees became fashionable in London and Paris, as well as America, and mediums thrived on rapping out code messages from departed spirits for credulous clients. The Fox sisters established a code of communication with the rapping spirit by rapping once for *no* and three times for *yes*. Forty years later, they publicly confessed that the raps were produced by dislocating toe and knee joints. History's most famous mediums upon inspection seem to follow a pattern, and the Fox sisters were no exception. Besides publicly confessing their fraudulence, Margaret Fox created a sensation by claiming to be the common-law wife of the Arctic explorer Elisha Kent Kane.

But they did create a market for Ouija boards.

In the marvelous pattern and tradition of the strange spirit world, it was an eminent scientist who fell under the spell of one of the Fox sisters and reduced spirit communication to a true Ouija by using an ingenious combination of table and dial. His name was Robert Hare, a professor of chemistry at the University of Pennsylvania, and he is generally credited with being the inventor of the first modern Ouija table. Professor Hare's simple credulity appears throughout his experiments in spirit communication. He referred to one communication as the most important experiment of his life.

Although Professor Hare was ridiculed by his friends and colleagues, he insisted that his experiments were made under "test" conditions. And his faith in mediums was never shaken. The Hare form of Ouija—a word derived from the French *oui* and the German *ja*, both meaning "yes"—went through several refinements. One of them was called a *spiritoscope*. Another is known as the *planchette*, still used widely in spirit circles for automatic writing.

Actually, there is nothing extraordinary nor psychically phenomenal about "automatic writing." The typist, for example, who concentrates all her attention on transcribing her notes, or on deciphering poor handwriting, operates her typewriter automatically. The pianist who plays a tune while singing or talking to someone else plays automatically.

The term automatic writing—which psychologists call *autonography*—implies the ability to write intelligibly without the direction of one's conscious attention. Some versatile automatists reportedly can engage in conversation at the same time they were writing prose, or even verse, and are apparently oblivious to what is being written.

Psychologists say that genuine psychological automatism is not uncommon and can in fact be developed by the majority of people who have the time and patience to practice. Tests made by Dr. Anita Muhl, a trained psychiatrist, proved, for example, that it is possible under proper conditions to train

the majority of normal well-balanced individuals to write automatically. Dr. Muhl used autonography as a form of therapy
for her mental patients, although her tests were not limited to
them. One of her patients even wrote music autonographically.

The relationship between autonography and the hypnotic
states of consciousness has been noted by most authorities in
the field of abnormal psychology.

In the same category and closely allied to autonography is
something the psychologists call verbal automatism and the
psychic experts call *glossolalia*—a word coined to denote the
phenomena of "speaking in many tongues," as purportedly
is done in a mediumistic trance, or sometimes in hysterical
persons. Uncontrollable verbal automatism is a common phenomenon among psychotics. In fact, the borderline between
so-called psychic phenomena and phenomena associated with
psychotics appears at times to be disconcertingly thin.

A case in point is the dual personality (or multiple personality as in *The Three Faces of Eve*), which has carved its niche
in current and popular abnormal psychology. In mediumship,
automatic writing, glossolalia, or what-have-you, the other
half of a "split personality" takes over in the form of a spirit
"control" or "guide"—a hangover from the days of demonia-
cal possession and witchcraft. The phenomenon has its modern psychological manifestations in hysteria, hallucinations,
and personality dissociations of the type frequently found in
mental institutions. It is no wonder that people are sometimes
confused in the worlds of psi and psychology.

The pendulum, which paved the way for a golden era of
supernatural phenomena, has advanced far further than has
the Ouija board in acceptance by twentieth century gullible, perhaps because of the many peculiar varieties of "scientific" theories and jargon now associated with it. After all,

who besides a Professor Hare would consider a Ouija board scientific? But when the pendulum turns up as *radiesthesia*, almost anything can happen. Radiesthesia is the pendulum-inspired modern version of ancient occult beliefs, and its cult is widespread and flourishing. Adherents claim to be able to divine practically anything by means of the pendulum, and their prognostications range from medical diagnosis to treasure hunting and crime solving. One school of radiesthetists ascribes oscillations of their pendulums and divining rods to a variety of mysterious "waves," "radiations," and "fields" emanating from the objects of divination. Another school of radiesthetists maintains that all such divinations are due to the exercise of psychic forces and faculties such as telepathy, clairvoyance, and prophecy. Most water-diviners cling to the physical theory of rays and emanations.

Of all the mystical kin in the Ouija clan, the divining rod has by far the largest representation in literature. The quaint superstition of water-witching, represented for centuries in the figure of a man with a charmed forked stick and supernatural powers, has persisted and is still widely practiced in an era that is commonly thought of as scientific and rational.

It was the distinguished French chemist Michel Eugene Chevreul who first discovered (1833) that the swing of the magic pendulum was dependent upon involuntary movements, and it was he who linked the pendulum, the divining rod, and table-turning under the same psychological law.

Carefully controlled experiments of reputed diviners have been almost uniformly negative, and their theories remain unsupported by modern physical science. Careful investigators have left little doubt that involuntary ideomotor movements are responsible for a wide realm of psychic wonders ranging from the dowsing rod to Clever Hans and Lady Wonder, the "telepathic" horses who reacted to involuntary (or voluntary?), unconscious (or conscious?) muscular movements and cues from their guides.

The principle of the magic pendulum, however, has formed the basis for countless numbers of gadgets and theories, all variations on the same theme and inspired by the urge to believe in the "special gift"—and ready-made for swindling the credulous public.

One of the most perfect examples of this in modern times was the incredible case of the Dutch dowsers and the deadly earthray epidemic in Holland, which got so out of hand that the Dutch government requested an investigation by the Royal Academy of Science of the Netherlands.

It started when a group of Dutch dowsers manufactured a brand of propaganda nonsense concerning the existence of mysterious earthrays. These earthrays, said the dowsers, were the cause of cancer, various kinds of rheumatic diseases, etc. The only way the earthrays could be detected was by means of a divining rod (a thin metal wire was used for the purpose), and if a man wanted to remain healthy the first thing to know was whether he was living on top of an earthray.

Naturally, this information could be obtained through a dowser only, who of course had to be heavily paid to go over the client's house with his rod. If earthrays were detected (and they were invariably found in the bedrooms under the beds, or under desk chairs where the clients spent several hours daily working—but never in the bathrooms), the potential victims could escape growing malignant cancers, etc., by buying ray-screening apparatuses, supplied by the dowsers themselves and costing up to one hundred dollars. (The dowser's cost was usually one dollar.)

The whole thing soon became a widespread racket and had such an influence on the general public and highly placed authorities that people *en masse* had their houses screened off in order not to run the risk of developing serious illnesses. Governmental buildings were having antiearthray apparatuses fitted at great cost, and even the Royal Family had dowsers over to run the damaging rays to earth and protect themselves by having the various apparatuses installed. Farmers, cattle-breeders, and bulb growers were paying out large sums of money to prevent crop failures and sickness of livestock, which the dowsers claimed could be caused by the earthrays. The Dutch public, threatened on all sides by the mysterious and deadly earthrays, began to panic. It was then that the Dutch government stepped in and asked the Royal Academy to appoint a committee to investigate the claims of the dowsers. The dowsers even claimed that they could tell what special kinds of diseases the rays produced by counting the turns of the rods. The committee's experiments gave nothing but negative results. The earthrays, in the committee's opinion, existed only in the dowsers' imaginations.

After this verdict, the earthray epidemic in Holland died down, leaving more than 5000 Dutch dowsers crying their eyes out for being deprived of a very lucrative business. But not for long. The principle of the divining rod, the pendulum, the doodlebug, and other devices dependent upon involuntary motor action could be put to use in other forms of radiesthesia (sometimes called radio detection and radio perception) for believers in the supernatural and the metaphysical.

On May 5, 1961, at the University Museum Lecture Hall in Oxford, England, George W. de la Warr read a paper to the Oxford University Scientific Society. The subject of his scientific treatise was "The Power of Thought." At the outset, he warned his audience, "It is quite evident that a whole new science, as yet without a name, is springing up but with nowhere to lay its head."

De la Warr proceeded to lay its head in the lap of "applied paraphysics," concluding with the speculation that this new branch of science would one day be known as "subatomic physics."

He explained in some detail how paraphysics was born from a mating of the dowsers' twig and the divining rod, with subsequent variations based on the electronic phenomena of one Dr. Albert Abrams.

De la Warr's little black boxes are famous all over Europe, and are the subject of Bulky Reports of psychical researchers and the American Medical Association. It somehow seems ludicrous that they should be so solidly and respectably entrenched at Oxford.

I had been hearing about the famous little black boxes in psychical-research circles throughout Europe. One report I heard was that the Russians had stolen one of the boxes to study its "radionics principles" for use in their experiments in long-distance telepathy. This intrigued me. I decided to go to Oxford and check on the rumor, as well as the boxes.

Sure enough, de la Warr and his wife told me, a Russian scientist had paid them a visit a while back, and shortly after his departure they had noticed that one of their black boxes was missing. If the Russians are using it in their telepathy experiments, it might take quite a while for them to make telepathic contact with astronauts or submarine commanders. For in 1957, U.S. customs confiscated a consignment of the de la Warr boxes and according to newspaper reports, the scientists who took them apart found them to be filled with sawdust.

Like some of their fellow practitioners in radiesthesia, dowsing, and psychic healing, Mr. and Mrs. de la Warr give an impression of sincerity, and many investigators have come away from their laboratory convinced that the de la Warrs really believe in their own black magic boxes. They were courteous and cordial to me, and perfectly willing to give me a guided tour of their laboratories, which are located on an estate at the edge of town. The laboratories are situated in four separate modern brick buildings, all neat, tastefully decorated, and well equipped with the boxes—literally hundreds of them.

From the moment I walked into the first laboratory, I felt right at home—after recovering from the initial shock. The walls were paneled with little black boxes, all tuned in with knobs and dials and beaming healing waves to people hundreds of miles away. I had hardly expected to come all the way to Oxford to find only that the famous little black box was nothing more than the famous Abrams-Drown machine, which in America has been denounced by both Government and AMA officials as being without therapeutic value. In my own investigations in Chicago, I have seen quite a few of the same little black boxes, but never in such abundance as at Oxford.

How the boxes made their way into paraphysics at Oxford may seem mystifying to some, but it doesn't require any sixth or seventh sense to figure it out. The magic password is that four-letter prefix—*para*. It means: *beside, alongside of, beyond, aside from, amiss,* according to Webster's, and with a choice like that, para-anything can include just about everything, and in the *meta*physical sense, usually does. The prefix *meta* means approximately the same thing (*beyond, transcending, higher*) but has gone out of style; and *para* is a tailor-made substitute for the cap-and-gown approach to mysticism. Hence, paraphysics et cetera.

When I visited the laboratories at Oxford, the boxes were indeed tuned in to patients all the way from Sweden to Tanganyika, and beaming treatments for everything from baldness to schizophrenia to "pain in the groin."

It was easy enough to see who was being treated for what, as the patient's name and ailment were written on a small card posted above each machine. I was somewhat startled, however, to find a card that read: "Tangy. Rheumatism in Hind Legs."

"Oh, we treat many dogs, horses, and cats," said Stanley Channon, the laboratory director. "With animals we have no interfering thought patterns."

Budgy, a parakeet, was being treated for droopiness. A dog, Angus, was getting healing waves in absentia for fits. Absent treatments were frequently beamed to sick elephants and tigers in zoos, I was told.

It is no secret that the black box, with only a blood spot, allegedly cured Lady Y's Pekinese of asthma; and that a racehorse belonging to a famous person had a reading on the box and was cured of liver trouble just in time to win two races. The owner admitted that every horse in the stable had been on the box getting long distance radionic therapy. In healing sick racehorses by his magic box, miracle healer de la Warr doesn't even need a blood spot. He can do it with a single hair from the horse's tail. These revelations were made at a black box fraud trial against de la Warr in 1960, which, according to newspaper reports, was dismissed because of the sincerity of the de la Warrs and 36 witnesses. One witness told how the black box had diagnosed "hypochondriasis affecting the visual psychic area of the brain of a racehorse." The horse had been running badly after winning a 5000-pound race, until given the box treatment.

That case began in October 1958, when the de la Warrs were sued by a woman alleging fraudulent misrepresentation. She was described as a spinster of slender means who, after paying 110 pounds for the box, and six guineas for two lessons, concluded that she had been bilked. She had hoped to set up a black-box practice with the "backward peoples of Europe and the Middle East," but she couldn't get the box to work. During the trial it was brought out that one woman in South Africa had bought seven boxes and was treating both humans and animals successfully. Another radionic practitioner from Oxford testified that she had broadcast treatments to a tiger and an elephant in a zoo, through hairs from their tails. The tiger, she admitted, died anyway, but the elephant recovered from lameness after the broadcasts—and after receiving veterinary treatment for two years.

The dismissal of the case against the de la Warrs, involving sincere people, is suggestive of trials in the United Stated involving the unauthorized practice of medicine. The success of the defendants is based on a combination of human gullibility and the genuinely miraculous phenomenon of suggestion. The power of suggestion is psychological. It can create and cure human maladies, and is the basis of psychosomatic medicine.

The real power of suggestion brings dramatic recoveries, so it probably matters little whether the magic, multiple-personality little black boxes are beaming their healing waves via radiesthesia, radionics, or plain telepathy, so long as the believing mind finds what it seeks.

CHAPTER 11

Fraud in the Dark

There are many reasons for the continued success and popularity of fraudulent spiritualists and fake mediums. One, of course, is the human urge to believe in communication with the dead. In most cases, the sitters who are continually fooled by the performances of mediums are usually characterized by a basic or subconscious desire to be deceived—which stems from their intense will to believe in survival after death.

For many people, spiritualism is an undeniable blessing. But the histrionics of the séance room should not be confused with genuine religious or Christian spiritualism. Religious spiritualism for many, transforms the facts of death and suffering into something that does not hurt quite so much, and that often helps the individual to adjust himself to the problems of life.

But this is a far cry from the spiritualistic swamp of deliberate fraud and trickery.

Some psychical researchers still argue that proof of fraud is not necessarily disproof of the supernatural or psi faculty. They would have us believe that although a medium is detected on numerous occasions practicing conjuring tricks, the supernatural powers may have been displayed on other occasions when the investigators failed to see how the phenomena were brought about. In other words, if a medium is good enough at her tricks to fool the psi-investigator, she has paranormal or psychic abilities.

It is little wonder that thousands of credulous minds continue to believe in the supernatural when some of the most intelligent of psychical researchers still indulge in wishful interpretations of mediumistic utterances.

The survival question, of which mediumship is an integral part, is still a subject of serious research within the precincts of modern universities. It has currently hit a snag, however, because of arguments among various factions of psychical researchers as to whether some of the phenomena suggesting survival might be explained by clairvoyance or telepathy.

It would seem to be obvious to anyone who has talked with the spirits of the Great Beyond that their level of intelligence is depressingly low. At least the one with whom I have chatted should provide any reasonable person with a good argument against suicide. Yet vast and scholarly volumes have been written trying to establish proof of their reality, and of survival. This fact—the bestowal of serious, scholarly attention—has probably contributed as much as anything else to the perpetuation and popularity of the séance room.

Although psychical researchers do not like to admit it, there is a strong parallel between modern spiritualism and medieval witchcraft. Witches were subject to delusions, hallucinations, and frenzied ecstasies, which later became known as the mediumistic trance. Witchcraft still flourishes in primitive societies, and its principal ingredient is still the belief in spirits and the supernatural. In the West Indies, the voodooman's biggest claim to fame lies in his purported ability to bring the dead back to life. The African witch doctor is also an adept at acquiring information from the spirits of the dead. The Australian aborigine—as we have said earlier—is particularly susceptible to the witch doctor's magic. All these practices have their roots in *shamanism,* a generic term covering many primitive cults that involve belief in spirits and in the power of certain individuals to influence them or communicate with them.

The term derives from *shaman,* a Siberian medicine-man or "mystery-man," noted for his mediumistic practices. Nowadays anthropologists use the word shaman to designate almost any class of tribal magician whose magic is in any way attributed to practices designed to control, placate, or otherwise influence discarnate spirits.

Apart from the fraudulent medium, there is another type of medium who is often sincere in the sense that her mediumistic trance is genuine. Such mediums are known generally as "hysterical mediums," and are found more in the annals of abnormal psychology than in the séance cabinet.

Many psychologists maintain that the hysterical medium is the true medium. That is, he or she is subject to states of consciousness in which her normal mental process break down, producing a state of mind known as "hysterical dissociation." In this state, disconnected and dreamlike delusions take over; the medium finds an outlet for fantasies and mental aberrations. These are also characteristics of mental patients diagnosed as schizophrenic. The hysterical medium is, in fact, mentally unbalanced and no more clairvoyant or psychic than a schizophrenic.

It might be argued that a great many nonhysterical mediums are also mentally unbalanced. But some are clever enough to know how to combine the dexterity and psychology of both the conjurer and the pickpocket in the subtle arts of fraud and deception; and many must now be tittering up their sleeves in the spirit world at the trail of immortality they carved for themselves by hoodwinking some of the brainiest men of their times.

Let's take, for example, D. D. Home, whose clientele included such luminaries as Napoleon III, the Empress Eugenie of France, and Alexander II of Russia.

Home claimed to have discovered his gift for dealing with spirits at the age of thirteen, and from 1850 until his death in 1886 he had a triumphant career as a medium. Although he is supposed never to have been *paid* in the commercial sense of the word, he managed to do well enough from the gifts showered on him by the great and near great of Europe and America. In his drawing room séances, furniture moved with no apparent cause, ghostly hands appeared, and the furniture and Home himself would rise in the air. There was much dispute about the validity of these highly physical manifestations of spirits.

The March 1930 "Proceedings of the Society for Psychical Research" in London are largely devoted to unmasking the trickery of Home, who for so long was known as the bulwark—the alpha and omega—of physical mediumship, with whom modern spiritualism must stand or fall. During Home's séances, usually in darkened rooms, members of his audience would sit around a table with their hands beneath it, and often with objects—such as handkerchiefs—in their hands. Soon one of them would feel the touch or a tug of another hand, assumed to be that of a departed spirit, grasping at the article he or she held. If the article was a handkerchief, the holder would often find that a knot had been tied in it during the séance.

At least two members of Empress Eugenie's staff detected Home using not only sleight-of-hand but sleight-of-feet. His trick was very simple. One signed record states: "Mr. Home wears thin shoes, easy to take off and put on; he also has cut socks which leave the toes free. At the appropriate moment he takes off one of his shoes and with his foot pulls a dress here, a dress there, rings a bell, knocks one way and another, and, the thing done, quickly puts his shoe on again."

Another who caught Home in the act recounted that he saw the medium open the sole of his right shoe, leave his naked foot for some time on the marble floor, then suddenly with a rapid and extraordinarily agile movement touch with his toes the hand of the Empress Eugenie, who cried out, "The hand of a dead child has touched me!"

It has never been made clear whether Home's handkerchief trick was done by sleight-of-hand, or feet. Giving him the benefit of the doubt, he may deserve some credit even for his trickery, for tying a handkerchief with the toes is not an easy trick.

Objective investigators also found that in Home's *modus operandi* he would have been able to admit an accomplice into the room if he had chosen to do so—and he probably did. The only phenomena he was able to produce without trickery or cheating were, perhaps, his performances with burning coals. But these can be explained on a physical basis similar to that involved in firewalking.

It is curious how the psychic adventures of history's most famous mediums follow a pattern.

It may be a long time before the world of psi fully recovers from the traumatic blow of the Sir William Crookes and Katie King scandal, which was rumored but not publicly exposed until 1962, with the publication of Trevor H. Hall's book, *The*

Spiritualists. This is a thoroughly documented and detailed account—as well as a shocking one—of the most celebrated and significant spiritualistic alliance of all times.

Materialization séances had become the rage in England, with full formed phantoms gliding about rooms in subdued lights. But it was Florence Cook, a lithe young lady from Hackney, who was destined to become the most famous materialization medium of them all, for she was supported and sponsored by Sir William Crookes himself, a brilliant and distinguished scientist who publicly and without qualification declared her phenomena to be genuine.

Florence Cook, true to the spiritualist tradition, started her career as a child medium, with table-tiltings and other amateurish phenomena. She soon developed into a materialization medium, first starting with "spirit faces"—which looked very much like Florence Cook—and eventually becoming able to "materialize" a full spirit form, which called itself Katie King.

Her Katie King seemed to have been as solid as a human being. It could emerge from the cabinet in which Florence lay entranced, and walk freely among those present at the séance. It was photographed on a number of occasions, and could converse with the sitters and even be embraced.

It was the active sponsorship of Florence Cook by Crookes that raised her to pinnacles of fame—just as it was Crookes' corroborative scientific testimony that had brought preeminence to D. D. Home as a medium.

In fact, by lending his name as a believer, Crookes probably contributed more than any other single person to belief in the supernatural. His doing so was a real *coup* for both spiritualists and disciples of psychic science. In the vast literature of psychical research it is recorded that Crookes, the celebrated physicist and chemist, was the first leading man of science to test the influence of the spirit world by experiment.

Alas, the crystal ball is shattered. Disillusioned psi believers are still trying to pick up the pieces and salvage what they can of a famous scientist's besmirched reputation. For it developed that Sir William, although a scientist, was also human, and so indeed was the spirit form of Katie King. She not only deluded but seduced him. He became her accomplice in fraud.

Psychical researchers, unwilling to believe the charges of collusion in fraud, or of sexual involvement, are still researching all the angles of the Crookes-Cook affair, trying somehow to retrieve the fallen idol. One apologist wrote, "Scientists are probably as liable to sexual delinquencies as other men. They are less likely to be hoodwinked by a fraudulent medium, but this also can happen . . ." (*The Journal of Parapsychology*, Volume 27, June 1963.)

There is no doubt that Sir William pulled one of the biggest psychic boo-boos in history by publicly endorsing a lovely young medium's phenomena as genuine.

There was also the marvelous Madame Blavatsky, who claimed to be a reincarnation of Pythagoras, and whose "astral" form purportedly floated around one country while she was in another. She has been called "the most monumental liar in all history." The London Society for Psychical Research concluded its 200page report on Madame Blavatsky with these words: "We think she has achieved a title to permanent remembrance as one of the most accomplished, ingenious and interesting imposters of history."

Madame's own confession is an indictment of human foibles: "What is one to do, when in order to rule men, it is necessary to deceive them? . . . For almost invariably the more simple, the more silly, and the more gross the phenomenon, the more likely it is to succeed."

Many regard an illiterate Neapolitan peasant, Eusapia Palladino, as the cleverest of all "physical" mediums. For many years the spectacular career of the great Palladino was viewed by spiritualists and psychical researchers as the test case for the existence of supernormal faculties. She was the object of investigation by eminent scientists and savants of Europe and America, and converted many to belief in her supernatural powers. She specialized in a piece of psychic furniture known as the levitating table, and its curious gyrations transcended the accredited behavior of other non-pedigreed tables. Palladino's famous levitating table act was unmasked as nothing more than fancy sleight-of-foot work. But thousands of faithful still regard Palladino as one of the great enigmas of the past.

There are many devious ways in which modern mediums obtain information from the "spirit world" to pass on to their clients in séances. Anyone who doubts this should read Harry Houdini's entertaining book, *A Magician Among the Spirits*. As we said earlier, Houdini was noted almost as much for his exposure of fraudulent mediums as for his magicianship. Houdini's real name was Erich Weiss. He took his stage name after the celebrated French conjurer and magician, Jean Eugene Robert Houdin, who was also famous for publicly proclaiming that his magic was based on natural instead of supernatural means.

Houdini was heartless in his exposure of mediums. He regarded them as "human vultures," "clairvoyant blackmailers," and far worse than payroll bandits. Among the more common methods he attributed to the psychic "fraud fraternity" were tapping telephone wires, searching court records and letter boxes (letters would be steamed open and copied), employing pickpockets and "plants" for all kinds of public gatherings—from funerals to a Turkish bath—where information might be obtained for use at séances, and bribing hotel clerks, switchboard girls, elevator boys, chauffeurs, and salesman to collect data on clients.

It may also come as a disillusionment to know that many of the spirit spooks that float around the séance rooms are born in a mail-order factory in Columbus, Ohio.

"The world wishes to be deceived, so I deceive it," said an obliging entrepreneur named Robert A. Nelson, whose made-to-order ghosts, spirit faces, ectoplasm, spirit knockers, et cetera are shipped all over the world. Among his best customers are spiritualist mediums and the famous fakirs of India.

Among Nelson's most successful creations is a floating and talking spirit face that has scared the psyche out of hundreds of sitters at séances. It is the spirit face of Don Pedrito, a famous medicine man known all over South America, who promised to come back after death. He not only came back, he talks, and he has even been known to wink an eye at a pretty girl, all for $16.50.

Nelson once sold a medium the ghost of a dead husband for one of her clients. He attended the séance himself, and later remarked to the widow that her dead husband's ghost looked a lot like luminous gauze.

"Well, of course," she murmured; "that's because *you're* not psychic."

Another time he slipped into a séance, sat through a medium's amateur hocus-pocus, then suddenly in the pitch-black room whisked out one of his own ghosts. The sitters screamed. The medium fainted. Soon thereafter she went out of business.

A few years ago Nelson visited the Lily Dale spiritualist camp in New York, made famous by the ghost rappings of a murdered peddler whose corpse was buried in a basement. A medium offered to bring back the peddler's spirit to knock for Nelson—for a fee.

Nelson paid and listened to the little knock, knock, knock, from the peddler. Suddenly there came a loud clatter of knocks all over the house.

"What's that?" screamed the terrified medium. "That's not the peddler."

"Certainly not," said Nelson. "That madam, is my Little Wonder Spirit Knocker, now retailing for $3.50. It is far superior to the knocks produced by the spirits." He sold her two Little Wonders, then proceeded on to his next customer.

It was the public's interest in the astral world that put Nelson in business. He invented his first ghost from an old sheet, when he was only nine years old, to get rid of a neighborhood bully. At the age of eleven, with his brother Larry, he was doing a professional mind-reading act. They had a secret code of communication between them; labeled "cosmic vibrations" and bulwarked by a few magic tricks, the code sometimes brought them $250 a night while they were still in their teens.

In the belief that their occult powers should be strengthened occasionally by new mechanical devices, they started their own manufacturing firm and promptly were deluged with orders from mediums for floating tables, self-writing slates, trumpet voices, ectoplasm, crystal balls, Adam and Eve root, and Ouija boards.

Nelson's brother left the business to go on the road as a swami, and he became a famous children's magician in California.

Robert Nelson also became one of America's outstanding magicians, and served for a while as president of both the American Mentalists Association and the Magic Dealers

Association. But his slickest trick was always in manufacturing ghosts to order.

Nelson ghosts range from a $15 dancing, swaying, unbreakable, instantaneous model—operated like a roll-up window shade—to an uncanny, life-sized luminous skeleton for $75—with a wide variety of disjointed zombies and scare masks in between.

You can buy a package ghost show for $165, but the really good ones cost as high as $2000 to $3000.

The items most in demand by mediums are ectoplasm at $3.00 a roll (merely a luminous wad of silk or papier-mâché); astral lights, $2.00 each; floating spirit faces, $15 to $20; and spirit voices, kisses, knockers, slates, and assorted other spook props at lesser prices.

Most of these spirit-world accoutrements Nelson invents or contrives himself, and they comprise the major part of his business. However, he also deals in crystal balls (made in Czechoslovakia), Ouija boards, fortune-telling cards, dream books, and magic gadgets—all of which the American public seems to require and demand.

Nelson, a tall, suave, distinguished looking man with graying hair and gimlet eyes, told me when I visited him that the American public spends approximately 125 million dollars a year trying to get inside tips on the future—from fortune tellers, mediums, palm readers, and other types of soothsayers. They're mainly interested in money, love, and health, in that order, he said, and for some reason they depend mainly on ghosts to give them the right answers. There are more mediums per square foot in Washington, D.C., the nation's capital, than anywhere else.

In recent years Nelson provided a "haunted-house service." The demand for this, he said, has probably arisen because of the shortage of real haunted houses and because of overcrowded conditions in our gregarious society. Most of his requests come from people who want to scare away their mothers-in-law or other unwelcome guests who have overstayed their visits.

Nelson prefers to haunt new houses, especially those that haven't been built yet and that are to be built as "haunted" houses. He goes over the house plans with an architect and decides on locations for the built-in ghosts, knockers, and strangled screams, some of which need mechanical devices to help them function. These secret devices are kept locked in safe places provided for this purpose in the house plans.

"The human mind," Nelson said, "is a funny thing. It'll believe in anything, even ghosts. And I guess real ghosts are pretty hard to find these days."

CHAPTER 12

How Much of It Is Trickery?

An unavoidable question, in any investigation of psychic phenomena, is this: To what extent can deliberate, conscious trickery account for the results?

A proper approach to the question entails an exhaustive search through the voluminous literature on all phases of psychic experience, for no one, amazingly enough, ever seems to have devoted an entire work to the techniques of psychic trickery. Anyone who attempts such a study immediately learns an inescapable fact: trickery is present to such extent that *special training* is required to detect it.

Time and again, experts have warned that intellectual competence, in itself, is not sufficient for the unerring detection of psychic fraud. Harry Houdini, modern history's greatest mystifier, put the idea in these words: "The scientific mind is usually helpless against a trained trickster. Because a man has mastered the intricacies of chemistry or physics is no qualification for him to deduce how the Chinese linking rings, for instance, seem to melt into each other, passing solid metal through solid metal. Only knowledge of the rings themselves can reveal the secret. The scientific mind is trained to search for truth which is hidden in the mysteries of nature—not by the ingenuity of another human brain."

John Mulholland, another magician and student of psychic phenomena, has stated: "It takes a large amount of knowledge and special training to observe correctly a mediumistic exhibition."

Edward Saint, another conjurer, once used a simple demonstration of "psychic" power to prove interested scientists that they were not qualified as psychic investigators. A set of precision scales was set on a table under a glass covering. Saint announced that through the power of his mind, he would cause the scales to unbalance (psychokinesis). After the scientists had examined the apparatus, Saint then concentrated—and sure enough, the scales suddenly went off balance. The scientists, impressed, thought of every possible solution: atmospheric pressure, vibrations, preset machinery, and so on. Finally, Saint explained: just before he placed the glass jar over the scales, he released *a number of fleas* into the space from the hollow head of a fake pencil. With the glass jar over the scales, one or more of the fleas, invisible at even a few feet, would land on one side of the scale and upset the balance while Saint was concentrating. Scientists who witnessed this demonstration went home a wiser and humbler lot.

Most psychic tricks used today actually grew from, and are variations of, tricks that were practiced 50, 100, 200, and even 1000 years ago. Every trick consists of two parts: the mechanics and the presentation. While the mechanics may remain the same, or change but slightly, the presentation can undergo an infinite variety of changes, completely altering the effect of the trick. As Julien Proskauer, a prominent magician and exposer of spirits, has said: "There are only about fifteen basic methods used by fortune tellers, fraudulent mediums, and spook crooks. But there are about a thousand or more variations."

The same trick can be done by a magician as a trick, by a spiritualist as proof of spirit communication, and by a 'sensitive" as proof of clairvoyance. Houdini's first conjuring effects, for example, were tricks he adapted from a book on spiritualism (*Revelations of a Spirit Medium*). These effects involved the rope-ties that were used as a method of controlling the medium, but which Houdini appropriated for some of his famous escapes.

It is interesting to note that spiritualist phenomena, always performed under cover of darkness or very dim light, have a more sensational character then those performed by sensitives in the light. Table-levitation, for instance, when performed by spirit mediums, involves violent lifting, often to reportedly astonishing heights, and sometimes a final jump to a new position. This same phenomenon, when performed by a sensitive in the light, takes the form of a table "floating" under the sensitive's outstretched hand. The difference is obvious. The darkness allows the medium to use more elaborate methods: the hand-foot clamp (toes under table leg, hands on table-top), special harnesses that grip the tabletop, false hands that cover for the real one under the table edge, leverage gimmicks that protrude under the table edge from the medium's sleeve, etc. The sensitive, on the other hand, working in the light, is restricted to simple and subtle apparatuses such as a small nail in the table-top—rising less than a sixteenth of an inch—that he grips by a small, almost unnoticeable notch in his ring. (And even at that, the sensitive can use this trick only under certain favorable conditions.)

Spiritualism, of course, utilizes other phenomena of a physical nature. These include the production of ectoplasmic bodies (everything from egg white to cheesecloth); spirit hands (the spirit dips its hand in melted paraffin, leaving a mysterious cast for all to see—except that the cast is most often made by an inflatable rubber glove); spirit lights (black cards with luminous insignia, mounted on reaching-rods), and so on. But all of this—literally *all*—has been shown at one time or another to be the result of trickery.

Out of voluminous testimony it will perhaps be sufficient to cite the following examples.

1. In 1887, The Seybert Commission, drawn from among scholarships at the University of Pennsylvania, reported that every medium who appeared for examination over a three-year period had to be rejected as fraudulent or ineffective (produced no phenomena). This was the first large-scale, objective attempt to evaluate spiritualism's claims, and it should be noted that before beginning its work, the commission studied *all* the available literature on the subject, as well as records of previous investigations.

2. Harry Price, a believer in psychic phenomena but an implacable exposer of frauds, concluded at the end of his 50 years of investigation: "The history of spiritualism was one long trail of fraud, folly, and credulity."

3. Julien Proskauer, another believer in psychic possibilities, but a trained magician, stated unequivocally: "To anyone who has made an exhaustive study of the science of deception, as I have, the production of so-called psychic manifestations of a psychical sort . . . simply constitute a degraded or misused form of parlor magic or sleight-of hand."

4. Francis Martinka, leading manufacturer and retailer of magical apparatus during the heyday of spiritualism, wrote as follows in a letter to Houdini: "How can I believe in such a thing as spiritualism when for more than two-score years as the prominent magical dealer and manufacturer of mysterious effects, I have supplied almost every known and thousands of unknown tricks or apparatus to the great majority of magicians and indirectly to well-known mediums . . . It has always amused me to see how easy it is to deceive human beings who delve into the mysteries of which they know nothing."

5. Harry Houdini, student and foe of spiritualism for three decades, and the first to challenge all mediums to showdown demonstrations, concluded that: "Spiritualism is nothing more than mental intoxication, the intoxication of words, of feelings, and of suggested beliefs . . . It ought to be stopped, it must be stopped, and it would seem that the multiplicity of exposures and the multitude of prosecutions that have followed rational investigation should be sufficient to justify, yes, demand legislation for the complete annihilation of a cult built on false pretense, flimsy hearsay evidence, and the absurdity of accepting an optical illusion as a fact."

On the evidence, there isn't a court in the world that would hesitate to condemn the physical phenomena of mediumistic spiritualism as almost entirely based on trickery. But what of the more modern version practiced by psychics and sensitives under the intriguing label of psychokinesis?

This concept has not been investigated as intensively as spiritualism from the point of view of fraud but enough has been done to make it rather apparent that much of what passes as psychokinesis is a lineal descendent of a discredited parent.

Harry Price, for example, has recorded his investigation of a sensitive claiming psychokinetic power. The man demonstrated his ability to influence a needle in a specialty constructed number board. The man did not touch the board, but Price noted that his hands touched the table. By placing a bowl of mercury on the table between the man's hands and the board, Price discovered that subtle but very physical vibrations were the motive force that moved the needle. The sensitive confessed that he had developed a technique of muscle-tension that transferred vibrations from his arms to the table and thence to the board.

A great amount of preparation and practice go into the production of physical phenomena. Houdini once reported that Mina Crandon—the Boston medium known as "Margery"—practiced her effects for hours every day, just as though she were a professional magician. Such a thing is understandable when it is remembered that Margery was probably the most versatile medium in history. The seeming complexity or elaborateness of phenomena should never be accepted as supporting their authenticity. The ordinary person would never go to such trouble to perfect a "trick," but the psychic fraud will practice month after month and year after year to learn his trade. In fact, he is doing no more, in his own way, than any good doctor, lawyer, or athlete.

In psychical circles today, mental phenomena are much more important than physical phenomena. In a way, mental phenomena are easier to arrange than their physical counterparts, and through all forms of mental phenomena runs a common thread. This thread is the production of "psychic information." A working definition of this might be: facts, specific or general, that seemingly could not be known to the sensitive through ordinary means, and that fit a designated individual to a more or less degree.

How and where does the psychic trickster come into possession of his nonsensory or extrasensory information?

Here are some of the more common sources, gathered from reports on investigations of psychic fraud:

1. *Newspapers.* If a medium or psychic is "working" a town, he will tabulate such things as births, deaths, engagements, and marriages over a considerable period of time, in addition to sifting the news columns themselves for pertinent information. Back files of newspapers in the libraries constitute gold mines of usable information. The medium will record and index the information he wants.

2. *Court records* of property and mortgages, businesses and lawsuits, etc. These are open by law to the public or to lawyers. Sensitives have been known to have the clerks of courts and other such institutions in their pay. This type of thing holds true for all branches of public records systems.

3. *Confederates.* Young men, for instance, are sent to social affairs to mingle with guests, especially women. Older women—"nice old lady" types—are sent to sit for hours in reception rooms, carefully noting all that passes. Such unsuspected confederates might also question children in the street, or even enter houses under some pretext. A "mourner" at a funeral might be more interested in what the relatives are saying about the deceased than in grieving over the dead. Newspaper proofreaders relay the next day's news to a "psychic," allowing him to score a brilliant "prediction." The logical extension of this type of opera-

tion is obvious: restaurants, clubs, beauty parlors, and so on. Some sensitives have found beauty parlors and turkish baths so productive of usable information that they have opened their own establishments.

4. *Correspondence.* Letters are not as inaccessible as the public thinks. Hotel servants and house servants can easily investigate the contents of envelopes by steaming them open and making copies. Old letters by the baleful are sold as waste paper by large concerns; these can find their ways into the hands of sensitives and mediums.

5. *Elevator boys, superintendents, and servants* see and hear much that can be of value to a medium. Money often can shake loose this information from these people, especially if they do not know where it is going, why it is wanted, or what it will be used for.

6. *Telephone taps and hidden dictaphones* are obvious.

7. *Permanent personal collections* of old city directories, yearbooks, maps, and other compendiums are standard equipment with some mediums and psychics.

8. *The Blue Book.* This is ostensibly an index of people who frequent spirit mediums and psychic advisers. Supposedly, it assures the professional psychic that he is dealing with reliable and sincere persons. The book can usually be obtained only by those on the inside of the profession.

9. *Personal papers.* Everyone carries on his person a large amount of information about himself. To a professional pick-pocket, it is child's play to obtain these documents, make a record of them (miniature camera?), and return them without the "mark" being aware of the transaction.

The items detailed above are sufficient to indicate the number and variety of possible sources. The information gathered from them constitutes the "raw material." The skill with which it is used spells the difference between success or failure. All such information is carefully recorded, indexed, and even cross-indexed. It is painstakingly put together to produce a picture or an effect. From the combination of facts, rumors, suppositions, and probabilities that have thus been gathered, amazing and ingenious inferences can often be made by the experienced trickster.

To the above should be added two generally recognized psychological truths: (1) most people, if they talk long enough, unknowingly reveal a great deal about themselves; (2) most people say and do things in the course of a day that they will not remember a week later. After the passage of a few years they might even deny saying or doing those things—thus, seeds of "psychic" information are carelessly planted in forgotten places.

One of the most ingenious developments in psychic fraud is something known as the "cold reading." The cold reading is a subtle and practical art based on a close study of human nature and human affairs. People may differ in many ways but the fundamentals of life remain the same for everyone. In giving a cold reading, the medium will feel his way through a dozen preset categories with such skill that the client will be led to believe it is all spontaneous and that the medium is "receiving" the information through some psychic power. Though each medium necessarily develops his own system, most of them work through ten or a dozen major categories, such as: time and its relationships, personal magnetism, investments, partnerships and business associations, best friends, obstacles, sickness to be wary of, enemies, marriages, money conditions, change in affairs, trips, surprises, warning.

The medium "prospecting" within these categories will change and arrange the details according to the age, sex, and appearance of the dupe. They become extremely sensitive to "hits" and "misses." No matter how hard the customer tries to conceal his reaction to the reading, the experienced medium can detect subtle signs that tell him when he is on the track or off it.

As Julien Proskauer points out in *The Dead Don't Talk*, "The cold reader can detect right and wrong guesses in time to remedy or capitalize them, talk his way out of tight spots, reverse himself entirely at times, and in the end convince even hard-headed businessmen and well-informed women that 'there is something to it!'"

Then potential of the cold reading in the hands of a wily practitioner, especially if it can be combined with some bits of real knowledge, is limitless. And after the cold reading, when the client is hooked, there is ample time to gather a dossier before a second meeting.

An integral part of psychic business and stage magic for well over 200 years have been talking and silent codes. Through the use of codes, information can be passed from one person to another before the very eyes and ears of an unsuspecting audience. They are almost impossible to detect because they are arbitrary and are capable of unbounded variation.

In a talking code, words or syllables in a sentence stand for numbers or letters of the alphabet, objects, colors, metals, phrases, symbols, or anything the users desire. The skill involved consists in fitting the tell-tale words or syllables into a simple, innocent-sounding sentence. Ease of operation is the essential element, and this can be acquired only after long training.

A code, in brief, might look something like this:

```
Please ............. metal
hand............... paper
hold............... leather
holding............ wood
have............... watch
waiting........... dollar bill
tell ................. box, small
tell me............. box, large
now ................ scarf
quickly ............ red
without .......... white
touch ............. hat
```

Thus, the sentence: "Tell me, without hesitation, what object I touch," would stand for "a large white hatbox."

This is a simplified example. In practice, the codes become very involved and often depend to a great extent on sequence, pronunciation, and emphasis.

The silent codes are only a version of the talking codes, and depend on such things as bodily signals, practiced and rehearsed to the point where they are invisible to the audience, or seem unquestionably natural. Silent codes also make use of objects. A small trick sometimes used by "psychics" might go like this:

Two people claim telepathic powers. The first person leaves the room and the second invites anyone to pick a number from one to 10,000. He writes the chosen number on a card and places it facedown on a table. The second person reenters the room and correctly announces the number.

The secret: The two performers have *visualized* on the tabletop a numbered board divided into twelve squares. According to the square in which the card is placed and the angle at which it rests, the psychic can read the number. For very high numbers, the placement of the pencil is also a signal.

Imagination obviously can supply endless variations on just this one trick.

The "psychic" reading of sealed (or burned or destroyed) messages is one of the oldest tricks of the trade. The procedure varies, but basically the client is invited to write a question or statement on a piece of paper, which is then sealed in an envelope and kept by the client, or torn up and burned, torn up and blown away, crumpled and held in the medium's hand, etc. The medium then proceeds to correctly state the question, or nearly so, and make some appropriate comment.

There are many known ways by which sealed messages can be read. Some are available in ordinary books on magic; others can be gathered from the confessions of various mediums and stage mentalists, as well as from psychic literature in general. Here are some samples:

1. A message is written on a slip of paper. The medium folds it, tears it, then burns it or throws it away. What he has done is to fold and tear the paper (two folds, four tears) in such a way that he can retain (palm) the small folded corner on which the message appears. Momentary misdirection of the attention of his audience will allow him to read it.

2. A message is written, crumpled up, and placed in an envelope. The medium places the envelope in a fire tongs and holds it in a fire until it is entirely consumed. What he has done is to make sure the crumpled message fell into

one corner of the envelope, and that corner is the part by which the tongs hold the envelope. Thus the message does not burn but the envelope does. It is read during a bit of momentary misdirection.

3. A message is written on a piece of paper and immediately placed in the client's pocket or destroyed by the client. In this case the surface on which the client wrote was a prepared surface, containing disguised carbon paper. This could have been a desk, clipboard, arm of a chair, etc. The carbon copy is retrieved and read later.

4. A simple but daring technique that can be used only under certain conditions is the "one-ahead" method. A number of messages written by an audience are placed in envelopes and put before the sensitive. He picks one up, holds it to his head to get the "vibrations," then correctly quotes the question on the card inside. The question is identified by a member of the audience; the sensitive extracts the card and quotes it aloud so that the audience may check the closeness of his guess. He then answers the question and proceeds to the next question, repeating the procedure.

What he had done is to announce a fictitious question with the first envelope which is identified by a shill (confederate) in the audience. He then extracts the message and actually *reads* it mentally while he is supposedly quoting his first question aloud. When he picks up the second envelope, he announces the question that really appeared in the first envelope. Thus, he can proceed through the entire stack of envelopes, no matter how large. The last envelope (marked) contains the fictitious question of the confederate.

Only one conclusion seems possible from a survey of sealed-message reading: whenever a client is required to write, *no matter what is done with the message afterward,* a trick is involved.

Sometimes psychic power takes the form of an ability to find hidden objects or to distinguish one designated object from among many. One medium, for instance, may be able to name correctly a card known only to the investigators. Another may find unerringly an object carefully hidden in a room by investigators. These demonstrations are variously billed as telepathy, clairvoyance, etc. Depending on the methods used, the answer to all these effects is usually hyperaesthesia or muscle reading.

Hyperaesthesia has been established by investigators to be an abnormally developed awareness in the sense of touch or in visual observation. A psychic with this ability can stroke a playing card in the dark—he is supposedly magnetizing it—then identify the same card in the light either by touch or sight. He may also be able to uncover the hidden object, a trick performed through his ability to "read" the unconscious or subconscious reactions of the people who have hidden it.

If the method includes touching the arm or wrist of someone, then the psychic is probably in reality a muscle-reader, able to follow the almost imperceptible and unconscious volition of a person who is thinking of some action he wishes performed.

From all of this it can be seen that fraudulent psychic information is really made up of two parts: information that the medium *actually* possesses, and information that he only *appears* to possess.

The credulous mind never lacks for good company. William James, Aldous Huxley, Maurice Maeterlinck, and scores of others believed in various forms of mental magic and psychic powers. Thomas Edison believed in prophetic dreams. Mark Twain believed in telepathy. Carl Jung, the great Swiss psychoanalyst, even believed in ghosts. And Sir Arthur Conan Doyle, whose gullible mind would believe almost anything, was so convinced of the genuineness of "spirit" photographs that he founded the S.S.S.P.—Society for the Study of Supernormal Photographs, and even accepted "spirit" pictures as proof of the flesh-and-blood reality of fairies. That both the fairies and the photographs were fraudulently produced was abundantly demonstrated later by Dr. W. F. Prince, research officer for the American Society for Psychical Research. But the evidence made no impact on Sir Arthur, who credulously looked upon his contributions to knowledge of the reality of the "beyond" as the crowning achievement of his memorable life.

Considering the thoroughness with which spirit photography has been exposed during the last century, it seems incredible that today, in this era of alleged enlightenment, spirit photography has made a comeback and is being taken seriously in psychic circles in many parts of the United States and Canada. The resurgent interest in this hocus-pocus is largely the result of recent widely publicized claims. So-called "spirit" or "thought" photographs have mystified people of sophisticated intelligence, who have been fooled into believing that some psychics can point a camera at their heads and come up with pictures of far way places.

Some of the nation's leading and most respectable metropolitan newspapers have devoted a great deal of space to such "psychic" photographs, apparently unaware of the amount of fakery there has been in the long history of spirit photography.

The literature on the subject contains detailed explanations of dozens of methods and indicates that the total number of trickery techniques probably reaches into the hundreds.

An arbitrary grouping of past techniques would include such divisions as substitution of plates, doctoring of plates, and various kinds of double exposure. Harry Price has pointed out (in his *Confessions of a Ghost-Hunter*) that unless a person possesses the knowledge of a chemist, photographer, optician, electrician, anatomist, physicist, and conjurer, "he stands no chance whatever against a photographic medium." He makes the following very strong categorical statement: "Every spirit photograph I have investigated is a fake, and the history of photographic mediumship all over the world is a sorry story of imposture, fraud, exposure, imprisonment, and amazing credulity."

As with all psychic trickery, spirit photography has spawned its share of offspring. During World War II, spirit photography branched off into what were called "skotographs." This was a neat trick in which the medium gazed at a blank piece of paper and caused the picture of some client's deceased relative to appear. When investigated, this turned out to be a clever use of, believe it or not, a children's toy. "Futurescopes" had been on the market for sale to children for years; they revealed a picture when a drop of hypo was allowed to fall on them. In using this principle, the mediums had procured some actual photos, doctored sensitive paper and presented their spirit pictures with appropriate hocus-pocus.

Other techniques have included the deliberate fogging of unexposed plates while still in the original package, preparation of the camera with a wax-paper substitute of the "spirit extra," and the use of microphotographs. These are minute photos, less than a millimeter square, which cannot be seen except through a lens or magnifier of some kind. These could be placed within the components of the lens or affixed to a pinhole in the bellows. Still another possibility is that these microphotographs could be attached to the photographer himself, allowing him to use any camera provided.

After gathering information on the techniques of spirit photography, my husband, who is a professional photographer, decided to try his hand at "psychic" photos, and came up with one on his very first try. He used no theatrics. He does not claim to have "psychic" powers. He merely practiced titling the camera to various angles and aiming his tilts to pick up reflections from various objects in the room. In only one hour he scored several hits, including "psychic" photos of himself, St. Basil's Cathedral in Moscow, and our French poodle Gogi.

Obviously, with a little practice at sleight-of-hand trickery, almost anyone could become an accomplished "psychic" photographer.

PART IV

Interlude:
Let Your Mind Reach Out

by W. Clement Stone

CHAPTER 13

Mind Power, You, and the Future

What you have read in the first three parts of this book—fascinating, exciting, and informative as it may be—can be more meaningful if you relate and assimilate the underlying principles as well as the stark facts. Which of these principles, if any, can you use in a practical way? Only *you* can answer these questions fully for yourself, but here are some ideas that occurred to me.

The Door to the Inner Mind

Emil Coué and Sigmund Freud each started with the use of hypnosis to cure mental and physical illnesses. Each abandoned hypnosis but used techniques employed by the hypnotist, especially the use of *suggestion*. Their new method was to use suggestion and self-suggestion, *not* hypnosis.

But it was hypnosis that opened the door to the inner mind. And until some dedicated psychiatrists begin to devote their entire efforts to a scientific exploration of the unconscious mind in depth through hypnosis, many of the unseen forces of the mind will not be revealed.

But we don't need to wait for these discoveries. We can use suggestion and *self-suggestion* in our daily living. In fact, we do. Yet not everyone knows how to use them advantageously. But before we discuss their practical application, let's clarify the term *suggestion.*

Motivate Others Through Suggestion

Every stimulus that affects any of your five senses (sight, hearing, smell, taste, and touch) is a form of suggestion. It is often, but not necessarily, communicated to your subconscious by way of your conscious mind. *Verbal suggestion* is a word or statement such as "Pay attention." Self-suggestion, in simple language, is a conscious thought in any form. It, too, affects the subconscious. It's the most powerful form of suggestion.

Self-suggestion can be in the form of word symbols, ideas, pictures, sounds, odors, or physical contacts that you envision in your mind. The use of your imagination is one of your greatest powers. The average person thinks in word symbols more than any other form. Yet picture symbols are most frequently used by some creative thinkers such as inventors and artists, and there is also a more highly developed use of sound symbols by a composer, poet or blind person than by the average individual.

The Practical Application of Suggestion

You motivate others to action through suggestion. The quickest and most effective form of verbal suggestion is to give a command . . . start with an action word such as: stop, think, try, go.

Also, use *positive* statements with desirable key or trigger words if you want positive, rather than negative, results. Take for example the positive statement: "You *can* learn" as contrasted with "You *can't* learn."

Now here are a few illustrations of everyday positive or negative suggestions. The key or trigger words that propel one to action are underlined:

Mother: You're a good child. Each day you're trying to be better.
Mother: You're a naughty child! You can't keep out of trouble!
Wife: The Browns are coming for dinner, dear . . . try hard to get home by six.
Wife: The Smiths are coming for dinner . . . I suppose you'll be late as usual.
Teacher: What a wonderful day to be inside! Now we're going to take up a thrilling, exciting subject . . . the story of the electric light.
Teacher: What a miserable, depressing, rainy day!
Friend: You look so much better than the last time I saw you! You do feel better, don't you?
Friend: I don't think you look so well today. How do you feel?

Again, these illustrations of suggestion are simple. But remember, *universal truths are simple.* You'll soon see how the practical application of such verbal symbols is used to motivate large masses of people, as well as the individual, for good or evil. Then you will more readily understand why the Communists have successfully motivated good people to adopt a philosophy contrary to their best interests—even to become criminals and traitors to their nations. But more important, you will see how we can use the power of suggestion to help our own people as well as those in other nations to win the Cold War more effectively.

But before you can be motivated to use positive suggestions purposefully, and to avoid negative approaches, you must consider what you have just read to be believable, desirable, and attainable. Therefore, before continuing, let's again refer to hypnosis.

The hypnotist places his subject in a state of hypnosis through the use of word symbols. He may first condition the mind of the subject so that he wants, expects, or even fears to be hypnotized. The hypnotist will then use common *trigger words*: relax, peaceful, serene, drowsy, sleep; he will use *positive statements*: now your eyelids are becoming heavy . . . you feel drowsy . . . you are going to sleep. . . . you will listen to my voice . . . you won't be aware of anyone else in the room; he will use *repetition* of these positive statements or even repetition of words: sleep . . . sleep . . . sleep. And, at the proper time, he gives direct *commands*. The subject, in a state of hypnosis, *literally* responds to the commands. He acts upon statements whether they are true or false. But in a state of hypnosis, he will not act on a command that is below his inviolable standards unless he is *deceived* into doing so. And fortunately, even though you may be a person of great suggestibility, no one can hypnotize you if you don't want to be hypnotized—and provided you know how to neutralize the attempt. For you have a power that affects and controls your subconscious mind—*the power of self-suggestion.*

The Practical Application of Self-Suggestion

I first realized how to apply self-suggestion in a wholesome, beneficial manner when I read Emil Coué's *Self-Mastery Through Conscious Autosuggestion.* I was able to relate and assimilate the principles discovered by this great doctor. He found the answer to two important questions:

Question No. 1: Is it the suggestion of the doctor, or is it the suggestion in the mind of the patient, that affects physical cure?

Answer: Coué proved conclusively that it was the mind of the patient that consciously or subconsciously made the suggestion to which his own mind and body reacted. Without either (unconscious) autosuggestion or conscious autosuggestion (self-suggestion), external suggestions are not effective. In other words, if your mind does not accept an external suggestion, it will not motivate you to do something against your will.

Question No. 2: If the suggestion of the doctor stimulates internal suggestion of the patient, why can't the patient use healthful, positive suggestions on himself? And why can't he refrain from harmful negative suggestion?

Answer: Anyone, even a child, can be taught the proper use of suggestion and self-suggestion. One effective method is to repeat positive affirmations—which I call self-motivators—such as: *Day by day, in every way, through the grace of God, I am getting better and better.*

And here are important statements to be remembered: *Suggestion is not hypnotism. Self-suggestion is not self-hypnosis.* But suggestion and self-suggestion are necessary to bring about a state of hypnosis or self-hypnosis. And you are constantly receiving suggestions in one form or another by what you see, read, hear, taste, and smell. In essence, your *environment*—anything outside yourself that creates any stimulus within—is rich with suggestions to you. Also, you are constantly making suggestions to yourself—every thought you think is a suggestion, for example.

This knowledge is important because you can use it to your advantage. You can select your environment or neutralize its effect through the power of thought.

And that's where the conscious mind comes in. Now let me repeat here a conclusion I have reached:

You are the product of your heredity, environment, physical body, conscious and subconscious minds, experiences, and particular position and direction in time and space—and something more, including powers known and unknown. You have the power to affect, use, control, or harmonize with all of these aspects of being. And you can direct your thoughts, control your emotions, and ordain your destiny. For you are a mind with a body. And your mind consists of dual, invisible, gigantic powers: the conscious and subconscious. When the two work in harmony, they can affect, use, control, or harmonize with all known and unknown powers.

The Masters of Deceit

In psychological warfare against the Communists, we can all play a part. I have tried, in a small way, to do mine by pointing out, both here and in foreign countries, that the power of suggestion, like all power, can be used for good or evil. The Communists use deception and operate on the premise that the end justifies the means regardless of how unscrupulous the means may be. One of the astonishing phenomena of our age is that through propaganda (verbal and written suggestion), they have deceived good men and women—often idealists—into zealously dedicating themselves to an ideology contrary to their religious beliefs, moral principles, and patriotic instincts. They insidiously steal the minds and souls of men.

I earnestly believe that we could prosecute the Cold War more effectively if the government employed the marketing, sales, and advertising techniques of American businessmen. They are, after all, the experts in *motivation*. But what kind of salesmen are we if we can't sell something as good as God, love of family or individual freedom?

And it was in reading about experiments in telepathy with a hypnotized subject in Vasiliev's *Long Distance Suggestion* that I was reminded that we could train our American youth to increase their resistance to brainwashing. We could teach them how to use the power of suggestion and self-suggestion to repel the harmful suggestions of an enemy—potential or otherwise.

To motivate a person one must appeal to his imagination, emotions, and reason. There is always a fallacy in reasoning by logic when you reason *only by what you know*. One must always reckon with the unknown. It wasn't many years ago when it seemed impossible that the atom would be broken, or that manmade satellites would orbit the earth. But the scientific idea that very little, if anything, is impossible even though it may seem improbable, brought these achievements into reality. The unknown is an important element in reasoning correctly through logic. Therefore, in reasoning, always consider the *possibility of the improbable*; search for the facts; search for the truth. When you find them, have the courage to accept them.

The Challenge of Soviet Human Resources

Norma Lee Browning and I have learned things that many do not like to hear. We have learned that the research going on behind the Iron Curtain is a major challenge to America—and, unfortunately, few Americans are even aware that they are being challenged.

Throughout the U.S.S.R., in dozens of centers, the problem of human telepathy is being tackled by scientists of the

198 The Other Side of the Mind

highest caliber. Some of our own government people know this and are trying to get the message across—but who wants to be told that the Russians are ahead of us in anything?

We were having dinner in Washington with Oliver J. Caldwell, Acting Commissioner for International Education of the Department of Health, Education and Welfare. He is one of the most knowledgeable men in our government about what is going on behind the Iron Curtain, and he and his associates have made many trips to the U.S.S.R. and are specialists in matters of Soviet education and science.

Oliver Caldwell said: "I am amazed at the skepticism and sometimes hostility which I encounter when I try to tell Americans about some of the experimentation which is taking place in the U.S.S.R. in parapsychology and related fields. I find this strange because there is an available documentation in translation which substantiates most of the things I saw in the U.S.S.R. I am really disturbed, because if the United States does not make a serious effort to move forward on this new frontier, in another ten years it may be too late."

He confirmed our impression that while it is impossible for an outsider to see clearly what is happening within a secretive, closed, Communist society, there are sound reasons to believe that the Soviet Union is engaged in some important experiments in developing and exploiting the human mind. And, he said:

"It is imperative that Americans try to understand what is happening in cybernetics, in psychology and neurology, and in education today in the U.S.S.R., for these are the tools with which Communism is shaping its human resources to meet the challenge of tomorrow. If Americans today are unwilling to make the necessary sacrifices for the safety of our children tomorrow, the time may come when the next generation of Americans will curse our indifference and stupidity.

"Personally, I consider it a national tragedy if this indifference continues much longer."

Now we come to the subject of cybernetics. We have a whole chapter on cybernetics in the next section of this book. But Oliver Caldwell also confirmed our findings of how important cybernetics is in Soviet science. "Cybernetics is today almost a religion to some distinguished Soviet scientists," he said, "but it seems to be regarded with suspicion by certain Communist Party leaders.

"Berg is the high priest of the Soviet followers of cybernetics; he has said that the process whereby the State will wither away into a truly communist society is in itself a cybernetic process. He is also said to have predicted that cybernetics will make the teacher obsolete; this statement was greeted in the U.S.S.R. with wrath similar to the reaction of American teachers to a similar prediction by an American educator.

"When Norbert Wiener's book on cybernetics first appeared in the U.S., the Communist leadership in Moscow denounced Wiener's theories as a bourgeois aberration. Two years later, the Communists reversed themselves, and both cybernetics and Wiener have an extraordinary prestige today in the Soviet Union.

"The term itself seems to have a broader connotation in the U.S.S.R. than it does in the United States. Cybernetics seems to include in the U.S.S.R. any machine that will respond to a given stimulation with an appropriate feedback.

"Thus the term seems to encompass things as diverse as vending machines, programmed-learning devices, dial telephones, automation in industry, and a great deal of speculative thinking concerning the relationship between man and machine." Caldwell said.

Oliver Caldwell has talked with many of the leading Soviet scientists—linguists, mathematicians, biologists, neurologists, and physicists—and he has been fortunate enough to be invited into many of their institutes and laboratories, including the Institute of Energetics.

I was amazed when he told us that there are 18,000 students at the Institute of Energetics—most of whom are working on programs connected with cybernetics. It was also interesting to learn that so many young Russian students are studying the English language. How many of our American students are studying Russian?

Do We Use All Our Brain Cells?

Perhaps the most disturbing thing we learned from Oliver Caldwell was the affirmation of Soviet research into the human mind.

"The normal individual does not use more than 10 percent of his brain cells during his lifetime. Scientists are agreed on this. The important and unique function of the human mind, they agree, is to *create;* and the basic difference between the human mind and a machine is *creativity,"* he told us.

Therefore, Oliver Caldwell told us, the Soviet solution to the problem lies in the development of a small electronic device about the size of a transistor radio that could be used to store the facts needed by a creative mind. This machine would be used by the creator in any field of human endeavor, much as an engineer today uses a slide rule. The machine could be programmed with the basic facts needed by the creator, who could then free his mind from the burden of having to memorize facts. The creative person would draw upon the machine for his chemical formulas or his counterpoint or his historical or economic data, or whatever other facts he needed to enable him to develop and to implement creative new theories.

A model of such a machine has already been built by Soviet scientists. And another use for it would be in the training of children in school, where it would be used in drilling them in their homework and other lessons. One big and remaining problem is to reduce the machine to portable dimensions.

A specialist in neurological research also told Oliver Caldwell that there is another approach to the problem, which is to free the human brain from whatever physical barrier it is that prevents it from using its full capacity. He said that a "defense mechanism" has been identified in the brain, and that Soviet scientists are now making models of the brain in an effort to find a way in which the mind of the individual could surmount this barrier, and make full use of his intellectual capabilities.

When Oliver Caldwell asked why they did not remove the barrier if they had identified it, scientists explained that if the defense mechanism is cut out of the human brain, the individual will live an immensely full and perceptive life for 24 hours, at the end of which all of the brain cells will have been utilized. From that time forth the individual will be able neither to forget anything from his past nor to learn anything new from his future.

But there is a third way to increase the capacity of the individual to use his intellectual potential, and this is through the development of extrasensory perception, a field in which top Soviet scientists are now working, whether they call it by ESP or some other name. As one of the Soviet Union's top physicists, Landau, told Oliver Caldwell:

"It is now apparent that every living mind broadcasts on various short radio waves, and that someday it may be possible for an individual to control his own cerebral-radio wavelengths and to tune them in on other minds. When this happens, the teacher can teach a student beyond the normal capacity of his mind by broadcasting over the defense mechanism into the normally empty 90 percent of the brain."

It is so far-fetched, then, to believe that there may soon be a breakthrough in the area of mental telepathy?

Can we ignore the Soviet research in this direction?

Are we naïve to point out that the Russians are doing some exciting and daring experiments in the development of their human resources?

The American people must accept the fact that the United States and the U.S.S.R. are today engaged in competition in the development of their respective human resources. We could lose this competition if we do not face facts and rededicate ourselves and our material resources to the development of the total intellectual and spiritual capacities of our children.

Science Moves Slowly

Science often seems callously indifferent to some of the most profound and basic experiences of mankind. As William James once said, nothing has been treated with more contemptuous scientific disregard than the mass of phenomena generally called *mystical*—or psychical—experiences. Orthodox psychology, physiology, medicine—all have turned their backs on these phenomena that are all around us—sparks of creativity, inspirations, our precognitive and telepathic dreams, and miraculous healings.

Some scientists have been intolerant of psychic phenomena. They deny the existence and significance of many human experiences that are universal and meaningful.

As the patriarch of parapsychology, Dr. J. B. Rhine, once said:

Science moves slowly, creeping on from point to point . . .
Those who are acquainted with the halting, handicapped
way in which radical scientific advances have been made in
the past will understand the difficulties and delays . . .

It is my belief that the objection of many scientists to the
acceptance of telepathy and other areas of extrasensory perception is emotional rather than rational. But the Russians are
broadening the frontiers of the mind, and we should do no less.

When Dr. Rhine's first starling reports appeared in the
early 1930's and attracted widespread public attention to ESP,
the reports were criticized by other psychologists. But still the
evidence for ESP has been convincing to a large group of people, including prominent philosophers in both America and
England. Anyone who pioneers in a new branch of science is
open to attack by those "rigorously scientific" disbelievers; but
the truth itself cannot be overthrown just because orthodox
science disowns it.

It takes a man of great courage and dedication to continue
working at something he believes in despite the criticism of
skeptics, and no one will question that it is to Dr. J. B. Rhine's
credit that he has taken a disputed subject matter out of the
realm of the taboo and into the experimental laboratory for a
scientific approach.

The scientific world, which once had settled down to the
assumption that extrasensory perception was impossible, has
been shaken by the reports of the Russian research program.

Perhaps this will be the turning point for parapsychologists—for those patient researchers who have kept at the
problem in spite of the intolerance of some outsiders. Ignorance is as commonplace in science as in other areas of human
endeavor.

When you start thinking about new theories, new facts, new truths, it is inevitable that you will find yourself immersed in controversies, for men are constantly getting their egos tied up with their theories and their facts. But controversy can also be healthy and constructive.

How American Parapsychology Began

While ESP (extrasensory perception) has become a very familiar expression, the field to which it belongs, parapsychology, is not so well known. For one thing, it is a comparatively new branch of study. While ESP and the related abilities investigated in parapsychology had been known throughout recorded history, under one heading or another, it was not until the mid-1930's, at Duke University, that a report was published that offered an organized account of the field of odd phenomena. While earlier work had been done, it had been scattered and for the most part unconnected. The publications from the Department of Psychology at Duke University by Dr. J. B. Rhine, then an assistant professor of psychology, introduced the term "parapsychology," as well as the term "extrasensory perception," and pulled together into a lawful pattern the various types of related ability that parapsychology would cover in its studies.

Dr. Rhine's book, *Extrasensory Perception*, created a stir in the world of academic psychology such as no publication on this problem area had ever done.

The book on ESP was an account of seven years of experiments on telepathy and clairvoyance, conducted by Dr. Rhine and his colleagues and students in the Duke department and presenting the case for the occurrence of ESP, especially of the clairvoyant type. The profession most concerned with these experimental findings was that of psychology, and psychologists rose to the challenge with vigorous clinical attacks. Slight modifications of method were, in some cases, needed to meet them, and these were made. The first point of attack was the statistical methods used in evaluating the successes.

In December 1937, the Institute of Mathematical Statistics at Indianapolis issued a release stating: "If the Rhine experiments are to be criticized, it will have to be on other than mathematical grounds."

On the whole, as Dr. Rhine says, "We have paid no attention to criticism unless it was presented by writers with some scientific pretensions."

By 1950, the laboratory at Duke was attracting visiting scholars from other parts of the country and from foreign lands.

One aspect of the laboratory program has been the financial support of outstanding workers in cases where such support has been needed. Generally the effort is made to bring research workers to Duke if their work is outstanding, but it is not always possible or desirable to do so. Workers have been maintained in their own localities in countries such as India and Czechoslovakia. Research grants-in-aid have been made in many cases.

It has been possible for the Duke laboratory to undertake many projects that could not have been handled by lone workers in isolated centers. One of these was the investigation of the claims of mediumship. A team of workers was necessary to investigate the performances of mediums, under proper control, and a number of years were spent during the mid-1930's in investigations of mediums' claims, leading to clarifications in that problem area. In an important investigation in this series, it was found that although the medium under investigation contributed relevant information to sitters who were not even in the same room or within earshot, the information conveyed was not greater than the information the medium was able to get from target cards and senders, also in the adjoining room, in the routine ESP tests to which she was subjected. The problem of mediumship was left as not at present interpretable except in terms of ESP. The question of the source of the information, whether discarnate or living, could not be answered.

Another important branch of inquiry was the search for ESP in animals. Cats, dogs, and pigeons were subjected to investigation for this type of ability following the collection of large numbers of case records that strongly indicated the presence of that ability.

The laboratory's investigation of the possible connection of psi capacity with mental disorders has been handled mainly at Duke, but in a combination of investigations. Mental hospitals were visited for research material, and neurotic inventories (mental-health evaluations) were used in connection with the ESP investigations with college students. Psi was given a complete bill of health.

Dr. Louisa E. Rhine, from her study of spontaneous cases, has identified the more familiar channels of ESP messages as: first—dreams, both of the realistic or photographic type and the more symbolic or phantasy type; second—hallucinations in the waking state; and third—intuition or the simple knowledge without any identifying means indicated. Most subjects in ESP tests use simple intuition. The subject will call the symbol he has a hunch is correct. Or some will simply guess without any distinctive reason for choosing one target or another.

The financial support of the Parapsychology Laboratory at Duke must be credited mainly to Duke University. The maintenance of the laboratory, secretarial staff, and the salary of the director have been borne by Duke University over the years. Support for other staff members and some of the additional operating expenses have come from contributions from certain foundations such as the Rockefeller Foundation; the Parapsychology Foundation, Inc., New York; the W. Clement and Jessie V. Stone Foundation of Chicago, and a few others. The late Charles E. Ozanne, Mrs. Frances P. Bolton, and Alfred P. Sloan, Jr., have been the main private donors. And there have been a few who remain anonymous.

There is, in both Western Europe and the U.S.A., a decline of readiness on the part of the university world to recognize the field, largely because of the slow recognition of it by professional and academic psychology. Thus, while the research advances and in many ways gains in status, it meets with a cold reception from the larger universities, rather making its headway in new institutions or the more modest ones.

A new foundation, the Foundation for Research on the Nature of Man, has been founded to carry on, on a more advanced scale, the kind of coordination that has been exercised to some extent by the smaller unit within Duke University. Now, with expanded staff, resources, and a bolder program, parapsychology can be given aid on a scale it has never known, and many of the difficulties that have dogged its efforts over the years will quickly be overcome.

They Mislead, Deceive, Delude and Beguile

It's not uncommon for everyone, at some time or another, to be misled, deceived, and even deluded or beguiled by a person in whom he has placed his confidence. For you assume that another person is honest until you have reason to believe otherwise. Because the majority of people are fundamentally honest, it's difficult for them to believe that others would deliberately try to deceive.

But now it's time to remember:

Truth will be truth regardless of any person's belief, ignorance, negligence, or misunderstanding, or the failure of scientific proof. Don't lose faith in mankind because of those who deceive. And don't lose faith in psychic experiences that do occur.

Let's have the maturity to extract the truth even though the truth may be enmeshed in undesirable surroundings. For the "sensitive" may be morally corrupt. And in his greed for money, he may become a trickster. But this is no reason to assume that all sensitives are cheats.

Norma Lee Browning and I both agree that when you read accounts of supposedly legitimate psychic phenomena, you should check for the classic errors common to this type of literature. You can ask yourself the following:

+ Does the author indicate primary authority?
+ Is his acceptance of source material uncritical?
+ Does he indicate knowledge concerning fraud and trickery?
+ Are his stories based on unsubstantiated secondhand or third-hand accounts from persons who are prejudiced or biased?
+ Is the truth hidden in his art of writing?
+ What are his motives?

Some Ideas Regarding Physical and Psychical Experiences

With the development of technology, science has been able to detect what were previously some of the unseen and unknown physical forces. Yet instruments have not yet been invented to record many of the waves of different lengths that are passing through you and the room in which you are now reading this book. Each wave carries energy and *information*. But even when a wave is recorded, it is also necessary to interpret properly the information it contains. It must be transcribed or converted to become meaningful.

It takes a recorder or phonograph to convert the message on magnetic tape, in the one instance, and on a record in the other. Also a radio or television set is necessary to convert the information received from waves that affect them. Because no instrument has been invented to convert the information contained in the brain wave itself, we have no assurance that a brain wave and a thought wave are one and the same thing.

A brain wave can, however, be amplified, carried by a telephone wire, and relayed by radio around the world. On April 25, 1963, brain waves were sent from the Burden Neurological Institute in Bristol, England, by land line to the British transmission station at Goodhilly Downs, and then radioed by communications satellite to the United States receiving station at Nutley, New Jersey, from where they were sent by telephone line to Minneapolis.

The brain waves were too weak (although their frequency was low enough) to travel the distance on their own power, so they were tacked onto a carrier signal of 1750 cycles per second. And at Minneapolis they were separated from the carrier wave and transmitted to a graph.

Now why couldn't a thought wave (even if it's of a different frequency from a brain wave) be carried on some other wave? Humans, animals, and plants are affected by waves from *outer space*. The distance between one individual and another on each is thus relatively small. Also, waves are carried *through* the earth. Some day this fact may be of importance in long-distance communication.

It isn't difficult to conceive that there are waves carrying a new form of energy of which science is not now aware, and that there are unseen, unknown forces that affect the mind in a manner not known to us and with energies that may not act as stimuli to the five senses but yet do affect the subconscious mind; and because the subconscious transmits to the conscious mind an awareness of an image of an idea, picture, sound, taste, or physical feeling, such an image may seem as clear to the individual as if stimuli from the physical environment had affected one of the five senses.

Another thought: isn't it logical to assume that psychical experiences must be caused by some sort of external or internal influences, or both? And if this is true, isn't it doubtful that a person who has always been blind would have the physical experience of *seeing* an apparition? Why? Because even if the energies for the apparition existed, the blind person's past experience would not give him the ability to visualize it in his mind, for *seeing* is a learned skill. Again: to be meaningful, information must be converted into something that can be interpreted.

Telepathy . . . Yes or No?

If someone should ask me, "Do you believe in telepathy?" my answer would be, "Definitely yes!"

I believe in telepathy. I don't need scientific proof of its existence. I don't need proof of the powers I use or the experiences I have. And if a given cause has a given effect repeatedly, that's good enough for me—even though I may not have the scientific explanation of the means. Every scientist I have talked to on the matter has indicated a belief in the existence of the phenomenon of *spontaneous* telepathy, even though he is unable to prove controlled telepathy in his laboratory. But then, there are many scientists of renown who have found that a given cause produced a given effect, yet who have come to the wrong conclusions as to what brought this about. So while I am not a scientist, at least I find myself in good company.

I don't know if telepathy is a physical or a psychic phenomenon. My feeling is that it can be both. But now here are a few simple suggestions that you yourself can use to investigate the existence of the phenomenon of thought transference.

Try to recall any personal experiences that you feel were of the nature of thought transference.

In conversation with friends, try an experiment that always gets results for me. If you wish, you can lead up to it easily by saying, "I'm reading a book—*The Other Side of the Mind.*" Then ask a question such as, "Have you ever had any experiences in telepathy or any form of ESP? Or has anyone in your family had such experience?" You'll be amazed—truly amazed. For many will tell you stories they wouldn't have dared to mention if you had not introduced the subject. You yourself can evaluate the reliability of the persons involved.

The best way to test anything is to try it. You have everything to gain and nothing to lose by experimenting in thought transference if you are sufficiently interested. But keep in mind that spontaneous experiences will most often occur when either you, or the other person involved, is highly emotionalized. Therefore, in your experiment, don't be facetious. Be certain that the thoughts you send or the information you are seeking is of great importance to you. It may concern a loved one, for example.

You may prefer concentrating your thoughts on meeting some particular person or having him communicate with you. You may not have learned or been taught the art of concentration. If you find it difficult to concentrate, then take the easy route—just use your imagination: think of the person or the event you want to take place. Try this throughout the day for a few days and see what happens. Let the results speak for themselves.

The way you can use telepathy most advantageously is to think good thoughts. And these thoughts can affect others. Conversely, unkind or evil thoughts harm you and the other persons involved. Now I have found in my interviews with many persons that many husbands and wives state they often have experiences of thought transference. And I have wondered if in many instances where there is discord between a husband and wife, the unkind thoughts of one have affected the mental and physical health of the other. It's something to think about.

It Just Happened

Earl Forte, one of my sales representatives, told of an unusual experience. He told the story at a sales meeting a few days after he had the experience. He said:

"I was selling at California, Missouri. I sold an accident policy to a woman prospect. As I was writing down her answers to the questions on the application, she touched my arm nervously, and when I looked up I saw that she was alarmed. She looked pale and a little frightened.

"'Do you know what you just did, young man?' she asked.

"'No,' I responded.

"'You filled in the name and relationship of my beneficiary. I didn't give you the information. How did you know it?'

"I looked at the application and saw that I had written the name and relationship of the beneficiary. I was particularly puzzled because the name was different from hers. The relationship was her brother. I didn't even know she had a brother. So in answer to her question I said, 'I don't know . . . it just happened.'"

After telling of this experience, he gave the following explanation: "I believe that my prospect was reading the application as I was filling it out. And when she saw the words 'beneficiary' and 'relationship,' she thought of her brother. For some reason I don't understand, I picked up her thought at the instant when I got to that particular question in the application."

I know from experience in selling that I often grasp the thought of a prospect during the course of a sale just before he expresses it—it just happens. But now let me tell you of an experiment in communicating thoughts over a distance in excess of 3400 miles.

Thoughts Through Space

Norma Lee Browning and I spent an entire day interviewing Mr. and Mrs. Harold Sherman. Harold is the author of many books. *TNT, The Power Within You* is one of his self-help books that I have recommended to my salesmen and others for many years. But our interview was on another matter. It concerned telepathy and other forms of ESP.

"Tell us about your experiences in telepathy," I asked.

With enthusiasm, he told the amazing story of how thoughts were successfully communicated over a distance in excess of 3400 miles. Later I read his book *Thoughts Through Space*, which is devoted to the 68 tests in thought transference between himself and the Arctic explorer Sir Hubert Wilkins. Here, briefly, is what he told us.

In 1937, Sigismund Levanevsky and five companions set out by plane from Moscow to the United States by way of Fairbanks, Alaska. Near the North Pole their plane was forced down. The Russian government commissioned Sir Hubert Wilkins to search for the missing men and plane.

Before Sir Hubert left New York City for the Arctic, he and Harold Sherman arranged to try to communicate through thought transference with regularity at set times during the expedition.

"How successful were you in your experiments?" I asked.

"Over 70 percent," he replied. And then he gave illustration after illustration. One was of particular interest.

"On Armistice Day, 1937, I recorded an impression of Sir Hubert's plane being forced down in a blizzard, and I saw Sir Hubert attending a ball attired in a full-dress suit."

Harold went into further details of what he saw and continued with: "My conscious mind told me that Sir Hubert wouldn't take a full-dress suit with him on a serious rescue mission of this kind. Nonetheless I recorded exactly what I saw."

And what Harold visualized was correct in practically every detail. The dress suit had been loaned to Sir Hubert so he could attend an important function in the city of Regina.

"Tell us how you receive these impressions," I inquired.

Harold tried to explain exactly what happened. "I concentrated. In this period of concentration I saw pictures moving quickly just as you would see them on a large movie screen. The pictures crossed the screen of my mind so rapidly that I often had difficulty keeping pace as I recorded them."

I am personally convinced that such experiences are more common than many of us realize. In any case, regardless of what has or has not been scientifically established or accepted, *never* underestimate the real hidden powers of the human mind.

CHAPTER 14

Your Greatest Powers

黃大仙 is pronounced Wong Tai Shim, which is the name of a famous Buddhist temple in Hong Kong. As I entered the gates of the courtyard leading to the temple, I looked around me. To my right, not far from the walk, was an open building, which may, for want of a better term, be described as a one-story pagoda. I saw a crowd of Chinese hovering around a Buddhist priest. It was easy to see him, for his head and shoulders were above the crowd.

On my left, at an equal distance, was a good-sized tree with many branches. It drew my attention. For instead of leaves, hundreds of little objects which I didn't recognize were hanging from its branches. A few coolies appeared to be tying these objects to the tree. I was close enough to observe that their faces indicated great sorrow or concern.

I hastened to join the crowd on my right. The Buddhist priest was on a platform raised about two feet above the ground. He was busy turning an instrument that looked like a large wooden spool, or cylinder, with sides thirty inches in diameter and a horizontal length of five feet. The instrument turned out to be a series of wooden wheels, each less than one inch in thickness, and each of which could revolve independently on its own axis.

Tightly rolled pieces of parchment protruded from holes on the rim of each wheel. These little pockets were separated at equal distances of about one-half inch; thus the instrument must have contained hundreds of such parchments.

I found a native in the crowd who spoke English, and I asked, "Can you explain what this means?" "Yes," he replied. "I'll be glad to. You can have your fortune told. If you don't like it, you can go over to that tree and attach your fortune to a branch. Then the prediction will *not* come true."

I thanked him, walked back to the Buddhist priest, and paid the necessary yen. The priest turned the wheels of fortune. Soon he picked out a tightly rolled parchment, and handed it to me. And here's what I read: "You'll be successful. You will experience happiness, wealth, good health, and good luck." That was good enough for me; I didn't tie my parchment to the tree. Nor did I at that time think it strange that the message was printed in English. For I like to be superstitious; but I believe this about superstition: if you are superstitious, be practical—make it pay off. And it has paid off for me.

It was in my high school days that I came to the conclusion that good luck or bad luck depended on how you think. I wanted good luck. So I determined not to insult my intelligence by believing in symbols of bad luck. In fact, if other persons had negative mental attitudes toward a specific object or event, I would deliberately turn this superstition from negative to positive and make it good luck for me. Thus, thirteen is a lucky number for me. Friday the thirteenth is a terrific day.

And I don't hesitate to walk under a ladder, if I can see there isn't a can of paint at the top of it. If I accidentally break a mirror, I know I'm in for seven years of good luck.

And furthermore, in selling, I turn the superstitions of others to our mutual advantage. For example: there are persons who purchased accident insurance from me in the early days of my career because of the seed of thought sown with my statement: "The president of our company says that as long as you carry this policy, you'll never have one of these accidents." (I was the president, but the prospect didn't know this.) Then I'd laugh. He'd laugh. We'd both laugh together, and I would continue: "In fact, we make a cash guarantee. If he's wrong, we'll pay you in cash."

To this day there are policyholders who, when competitors try to twist our policy, will say: "Many years ago, a young salesman told me that as long as I carried his policy I would never be in an accident. I never have been. So I'll just keep his policy. I'll never give it up."

Yes, it pays to be superstitious, if you are practical and make your superstitions pay off for you. Also, it's a good way to learn how to overcome fear. So attract good luck—not bad luck; use superstition to your advantage in a wholesome manner.

We Believe What We Want to Believe

Now this story reminds me that *we believe what we want to believe.* And what we believe affects our subconscious and conscious minds, our actions, and our everyday living. Also our beliefs have a decided effect on our environments, particularly the reactions of other persons. When you reread this book, you will see how apparent this is in each and every chapter. Here are a few examples:

The Russians believed the false report about the *Nautilus,* and they took action. We in the United States, as well as persons in high positions in other Western powers, believed reports coming from Russia to the effect that they were engaging in serious research into telepathy, and we found these reports to be true. I was especially interested in knowing the extent, if any, of the United States government's participation in research into telepathy.

After Norma Lee Browning's eight weekly articles concerning her trip around the world in search of mind phenomena appeared in *The Chicago Sunday Tribune*, beginning June 2, 1963, she received numerous letters and telephone calls that gave us specific leads. One of these she asked me to trace down. The story pertained to the locating of enemy submarines through the use of ESP. In reading the story, which I shall relate here, you will observe how far-fetched ideas originate in the minds of certain types of people who don't keep their feet on the ground when they get mixed up with psychic phenomena.

Can We Locate Enemy Submarines with ESP?

I was eventually able to locate Capt. Harry A. Adams, Jr., U.S.N., now retired. At the time this incident occurred, Capt. Adams was Assistant Chief of Staff for Intelligence on the staff of the Commander of the Western Sea Frontier. He received orders from Washington to investigate a report concerning an individual in Los Angeles who claimed to have the ability to locate submarines by the simple process of moving a special sensitive instrument over a map of a given body of water. This instrument was said to have properties similar to those of a divining rod or doodle bug, except that it was to be used on a map instead of over the actual terrain.

Arrangements were made for a demonstration at the Naval Air Station in San Diego. Large maps of a part of the Pacific were laid out. The so-called psychic sensitive, in the presence of Capt. Adams and other naval officers and some civilian research experts, moved his instrument carefully over every inch of the map. He indicated the location of a very large number of submarines. Furthermore, he gave the nationality of each.

This person had amazed many laymen with demonstrations of what some termed psychic powers and others termed magic or trickery. Capt. Adams and those watching him locate submarines were also amazed—but for another reason. For they knew that the number of submarines he located just couldn't be—there could not have been that many submarines in the Pacific at that time. Furthermore, many of the submarines were identified with countries that had no navies.

Captain Adams told me, "At that time our submarines in the Pacific had been instructed to keep minute-by-minute logs to indicate times and locations. Later, when we received their reports, we compared them with the time of the demonstration and the locations indicated by the so-called psychic sensitive. We found that he was 100 percent wrong."

Now it isn't uncommon for sensitives to claim to be able to locate gold mines and oil wells by just passing their hands over maps of given territories. Yet Norma Lee Browning and I have found no instance where any of them acquired wealth through such efforts, although they have gotten sizable fees for their services. One individual told me that he had lost $20,000 by following a psychic sensitive's advice concerning a gold mine.

And now the time has come to leave the negative and take a positive approach. Let's look into some of the wonderful, inspirational, meaningful experiences of *mind* phenomena, always remembering that *man is a mind with a body*—he lives by more than bread alone. We are all interested in developing and maintaining physical, mental, moral, and spiritual health, and we know that we approach them by the use of our imagination and *creative thinking*.

The writing of great music has always seemed to me to be among the most exalted examples of creativity. It is done without words and the mind is open to intuition and inspiration in its purest form. What mysterious process takes place in the minds of great composers?

Creative Thinking of Great Composers

In the opening paragraph of the foreword to *Talks with Great Composers*,* Arthur Abell says:

> During my long residence in Europe, from 1890 to 1918, it was my privilege at various times to discuss the subject of Inspiration with Brahms, Strauss, Puccini, Humperdinck, Bruch and Grieg. These pages contain detailed accounts of the disclosures made to me by those famous composers concerning their intellectual, psychic and spiritual experiences while composing and the manner in which they were moved by the soul forces within when they felt the creative urge.

Later he states: "In interviewing great men I have always made it a rule immediately to put on paper their actual words so as to have a verbatim account of what they said." And here's what they did say:

JOHANNES BRAHMS

. . . To realize that we are one with the Creator, as Beethoven did, is a wonderful and awe-inspiring expe-

---

* Philosophical Library, N.Y., 1955

rience . . . When I feel the urge I begin by appealing directly to my Maker and I first ask Him the three most important questions pertaining to our life here in this world—whence, wherefore, whither (woher, warum, wohin)?

I immediately feel vibrations that thrill my whole being. These are the Spirit illuminating the soul-power within, and in this exalted state, I see clearly what is obscure in my ordinary moods, then I feel capable of drawing inspiration from above . . .

RICHARD STRAUSS

. . . When the inspiration comes, it is something of so subtle, tenuous, will-o-the-wisp-like nature (von solch Scharfsinnigkeit, Feinheit-wie-ein-Irrlicht) that it almost defies definition. When in my most inspiring moods, I have definite compelling visions, involving a higher selfhood. I feel at such moments that I am tapping the source of Infinite and Eternal energy from which you and I and all things proceed. Religion calls it God . . .

GIACOMO PUCCINI

. . . I know from my own experience when composing that it is a supernatural influence which qualifies me to receive Divine truths, and to communicate them to the public through my operas . . .

I first grasp the full power of the Ego within me. Then I feel the burning desire and the intense resolve to create something worthwhile. This desire, this longing, implies in itself the knowledge that I can attain my goal. Then I make a fervent demand for and from the

Power that created me. This demand, or prayer, must be coupled with full expectation that this higher aid will be granted me. This perfect faith opens the way for vibration to pass from the dynamo, which the soul-center is, into my consciousness, and the inspired ideas are born . . .

RICHARD WAGNER

I am convinced that there are universal currents of Divine Thought vibrating the ether everywhere and that anyone who can feel those vibrations is inspired, provided he is conscious of the process and possesses the knowledge and skill to present them in a convincing manner, be he composer, architect, painter, sculptor, or inventor . . .

. . . No atheist (composer) has ever created anything of great and lasting value . . .

MAX BRUCH

. . . The composer while creating any work of lasting value stands face to face with this Eternal Energy from which all life flows, and he draws on that infinite power.

But I have discovered that to contact it, one must conform to certain laws, and two of the most important are solitude and concentration. Brahms was right in declaring that he had to be absolutely alone and undisturbed. The composer must sit in the silence and wait for the direction from a force that is superior to the intellect. If he knows how to contact that power, he becomes the projector of the infinite invisible into visibility, or rather into audibility . . .

EDVARD GRIEG

. . . I composed as the spirit moved me, without comprehending clearly that I was working with great cosmic laws. Whereas Brahms realized, just as Beethoven did, that he was being aided by Omnipotence. It is only a supreme creative genius who can rise to such heights.

These composers were geniuses in the field of music, and they unanimously attributed their great works to the action of Divine Power. Whether or not you are a genius, you can use common sense. And it's common sense to recognize that Divine Power is creative at *all* levels of endeavor.

You Are a Mind with a Body

I was amazed and inspired when I recently read the papers presented at a symposium consisting of outstanding theologians, ministers, medical doctors, and psychiatrists on the subject, *Body and Soul in Illness and Health*. I was amazed to learn that practically all Christian denominations are now making a study in depth of physical and mental cures through the media of prayer, singing of hymns, confession, pleading for forgiveness, repentance, laying on of hands, and faith in God; I was inspired because I realized that now the great masses of people will receive the benefits of powers of healing heretofore experienced by only a few.

The interest of Catholic, Christian Science, and Pentacostal churches wasn't at all surprising, but the knowledge that divine healing was being studied in depth by the Presbyterians, Baptists, Episcopalians (Anglicans), Methodists, Lutherans, and others was definitely surprising to me. It may be news to you too, for these studies are not yet being publicized.

Perhaps this information shouldn't be surprising after all. For the modern internal reformation of the church is one of the great historical movements of our time; also the enlightenment of the medical practitioner on the spiritual nature of man as it relates to physical and mental health is becoming more common than many of us realize.

Because the papers I read were marked "Not for publication in part or whole," I am not permitted to quote from them. Instead I will tell you about a doctor friend of mine and what he has to say on the subject.

Now when you read his story, ask yourself, "Wouldn't it be wonderful if all doctors had his outlook?" You, as I, may desire to see the day when those concerned with the physical, mental, moral, and spiritual health of the people will work together in harmony—the day when man will be helped through religion, science, and modern therapy.

Remember, one of the fallacies of logic is in the concept that something is "either—or"—a conclusion reached without reckoning with the unknown.* The doctor who would exclude psychiatry, religion, or chiropractic is just as wrong as the religious person who closes his mind to the benefits of modern science. Each discipline has its specific benefits. Each has its special place. Each affects the whole man—the mind and the body.

> . . . the blind receive their sight, and the lame walk, the lepers are cleansed, and the deaf hear . . . and the poor have the gospel preached to them. Matt. 11:5

---

* And speaking of logic, many persons criticize what they feel is an erroneous concept of the Christian Scientists. Yet, if they would first study a book on semantics, like S.I. Hayakawa's *Language in Thought and Action,* they would be less critical—that is, if before criticizing, they read the Christian Science definitions or the words used. These definitions can be found in either *Science and Health with Key to the Scriptures,* by Mary Baker Eddy, or in *Webster's New Collegiate Dictionary.*

Howard F. Moffett, M.D., was born in Pyengyang, Korea, the son of pioneer Presbyterian missionaries. Most of his life has been spent in the Orient. Today he is superintendent of The Presbyterian Hospital in Taegu, Korea; also he is superintendent of the leprosarium under the American Leprosy Mission, Inc., and of a children's hospital unit caring primarily for orphans. These three institutions, together with large outpatient clinics, treat more than 100,000 patients annually.

Not long ago he was on a leave of absence in the United States. Like the dedicated man that he is, he spent most of his time in raising much-needed funds for the expansion of his hospital facilities. We had several talks together, and among other things this is what he had to say:

"This is the proud age of science, and the tendency is to accept nothing until it has been established by mathematical law or the all-heralded scientific approach. Yet here is a paradox. For even in this age when we think we accept only proven statements, actually practically all of us accept the claims of science through faith."

"Have you read any books on faith healing?" I asked.

"Yes," he responded. "One little book written by A. J. Gordon in 1882—*The Ministry of Healing*—was especially helpful to me."

I asked him to tell me of his own concept of divine healing.

"Let us establish, for the sake of clarity, that there are two classifications of divine healing. One is indirect, in which God effects healing through the medicines and skill of consecrated personnel. The other is direct, in which He Himself, in a miraculous way, more or less instantly and completely heals illness in answer to prayer of faith. Indirect divine healing is widely accepted today. The direct, supernatural manifestation of healing is not, and moreover, is seldom seen. People today shrink from unduly emphasizing it, for fear of being called fanatical, yet there may be a greater danger in ignoring it."

"What about miracles?" I asked.

"Only a small minority support the view that miracles are possible in all ages and that they have appeared in every period of the church's history. Many doctors can testify to miracles we have known either at first or second hand. But strong popular opinion, even in church circles, fails to give credence to miraculous healing by the Holy Spirit."

"Why is this?" I inquired.

"If mighty works are not now seen, might it not be because of unbelief, just as it was in Capernaum?" he asked. "How else shall we account for the way in which a drunkard is cured in a moment of enslaving appetite, through the prayer of faith; or for the way the opium addict who has resisted every effort of physicians to help him for years is instantly delivered from his curse through the same prayer of faith? Is this not also the work of the Holy Spirit? I believe so, and many are the accounts of such cures in our own day."

Dr. Moffett had obviously made a thorough study of the subject. He quoted from the Scriptures: "In the 16th chapter of Mark we read: "These signs shall follow them that believe: In my name shall they cast out devils; . . . they shall lay their hands on the sick and they shall recover." And then he said further: "It is important to observe that this rich cluster of miraculous promises all hangs by a single stem—*faith*. And there doesn't seem to be any basis for limiting this promise to apostolic times and apostolic men . . . Miracles of external nature, like the turning of water into wine, and the multiplying of the loaves, belong exclusively to the Lord; we do not find them perpetuated beyond His own ministry either in fact or in promise. Miracles of cure, on the contrary, were more directly connected with the Lord's redemptive work, and we find them frequently in the ministry of the disciples as well as in the ministry of our Lord Himself."

And then Dr. Moffett discussed what he called the "testimony of reason," and in the course of our conversation proceeded on to historical evidence. He referred to the book *Conflict of Christianity with Heathenism,* by Dr. Gerhard Uhlhorn, which states that "witnesses who are above suspicion leave no room for doubt that the miraculous powers of the apostolic age continued to operate at least into the third century."

"We find," said Dr. Moffett, "testimony of miraculous healing in the writings of Justin Martyr and Irenaeus in the second century, and of Clement in the third century. While in his earlier writings, Augustine (fourth century) apparently doubted the existence of miraculous interpositions in that day, in his later work *De Civitate Dei,* he cites specific instances of miraculous healing which occurred in his own day in answer to prayer. Martin Luther's prayers for the healing of the body are among the most powerful on record. Other pastors of note in more modern history—Knox, Wishart, Livingston, Welch, Baillie, and Craig—all testified to the occurrence of miraculous healings through faith during the course of their ministries. And we find this testimony not only throughout the history of the church down to the present day, but all around the world: Boston, Philadelphia, Greenland, South Africa, Sumatra, Burma—everywhere.

"And isn't it interesting to note that wherever we find a revival of primitive faith and apostolic simplicity, it is there that we find a profession of the evangelical miracles of healing which characterized the apostolic age? We find them with every spiritual reformation."

Today, of course, we hear stories of faith healing and claims for such faith-healing abilities on all sides. While it is true that many of these are frauds, it is also true that daily, in our own times, there are many examples of miraculous healing in answer to prayer that can be attested to by doctors and clergy alike. The next chapter will present one of the most astonishing of modern instances.

Professor Hans Bender, head of the psychology department at the University of Freiburg, one of Germany's outstanding psychologists and parapsychologists, told Norma Lee Browning: "We have made scientific investigations of sleep, dreams, and memory functions. Why not telepathy? I think the experiments in telepathy behind the Iron Curtain may be more significant than we realize."

Dr. W. Grey Walter (*left*) and an assistant at the Burden Neurological Institute, Bristol, England, studying an electronic apparatus that analyzes brain waves. Dr. Grey Walter is a world recognized authority on brain physiology and electroencephalography, and was a pioneer in the new medical development of ESB, electrical stimulation of the brain.

Dr. Grey Walter (*right*) with his famous electronic tortoise, which behaves like a live tortoise. Dr. Grey Walter says that the synthetic tortois is really a "crystallized idea"—the idea being that there is a chance of developing "thinking" machines which one day may be able to reason as effectively as the human mind.

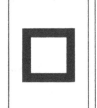

The famous Zener cards for testing extrasensory perception originated in the Parapsychology Laboratory at Duke University by Dr. J. B. Rhine. A deck consists of twenty-five cards, with each of the five symbols above repeated five times. Results of tests with these cards are judged on the basis of complex mathematics.

CHAPTER 15

I Went to Lourdes

I plan a trip to Lourdes—I'd like to see about the miracles for myself," I told Dr. Smiley Blanton.

"I'm glad to hear it," he said. "I don't know if you know it or not, but I made quite a study of Lourdes when I was over there. Medical science has no explanation for the cures. It's the only place in the world where complete case histories of the patient—including medical records, X-ray pictures, and scientific data—are available showing the condition of the patient before and after a cure through alleged divine healing." Then he continued.

"Margaret [Smiley Blanton's wife] wrote a book, *The Miracle of Bernadette*. Have you read it?" he asked.

"No, I haven't but I'd like to."

"You're in a hurry to catch your plane, but I'll send you one. And then, when you come to New York again, we can discuss it."

And we did discuss the book the next time I was in New York. But this was months later, after my trip to Lourdes. In fact, I had several visits with Smiley and Margaret Blanton for the purpose of verifying the material I had gathered. For I found, as you will see, that the name Dr. Smiley Blanton plays an important part and is mentioned more than once in the *Miracle of Lourdes* by Ruth Cranston—another book you will read about later.

Dr. Smiley Blanton, who studied under Freud, is the chief psychiatrist of the American Foundation of Religion and Psychiatry, which has its headquarters in New York City. And this foundation was established by Dr. Norman Vincent Peale and Dr. Blanton in the years of great depression—a period when those in need crowded the churches seeking help and guidance. Today the foundation is reaching out into all lands through churches of all denominations. It shares its knowledge, experience, and financial aid in its efforts to get the clergy, psychiatrists, and members of the medical profession to work together simultaneously and harmoniously for the purpose of avoiding mental illness, maintaining mental health, and administering to the physical, mental, moral, and spiritual needs of individuals.

Smiley Blanton sent *The Miracle of Bernadette*, and I read it. And it increased my desire to check into the miracles of Lourdes for myself—particularly since the doctor and his wife are Protestants and the book was written without any signs of religious prejudice or bias. This seemed significance to me, because the miracles of Lourdes were previously associated in my mind with Catholic belief. Later I saw how wrong I really was.

Do Miracles Really Happen?

Now in my lectures and writings, I have often used the statements: "I believe in miracles—I believe in the miracles of the Bible—I believe that miracles are being performed today as they have been in the past. For a miracle to me is merely the achievement of that which others do not believe or do not understand."

As you see, the word *miracle* was used with the loose definition used by so many of us and in this respect is defined by Webster as: ". . . an event or effect in the physical world deviating from the known laws of nature or transcending our knowledge of these laws."

But from here on in this chapter, my use of the word miracle will be the more technical one: ". . . an extraordinary, anomalous or abnormal event brought about by a superhuman agency." By this definition *a miracle is a direct intervention of the Divinity in human affairs. It is always accompanied by suspension of the laws of nature.* Only in this sense will the miracles of Lourdes be discussed unless otherwise indicated. Now it is significant to state that in my investigation of *mind phenomena,* all paths finally led me to the primary source of all power—God.

"But do miracles really happen?" you may ask. To this question you will find your own answer as you continue to read this book. Also I'll let you know mine. But first let me tell a little about the persons I met, some of my experiences, and particularly how I thought and felt at Lourdes. For there, what one thinks, feels, and experiences is more important than what he sees, even though what he sees is most inspiring.

We Met the Woman Who Knows

On arriving at the Lourdes airport, I noticed an airline bus but no taxicabs. As I preferred a cab, I inquired in the terminal building how I might obtain one. Jan Bruning, who was an employee of one of the airlines, offered to take Mrs. Stone and me, in his Mercedes Benz, to the Bethany Hotel, where we had reservations. During the ride, when I'd ask Jan Bruning questions about Lourdes, he would answer enthusiastically.

Now I had a problem—a serious problem. And I had left its solution until my arrival. As we approached the city, I realized a friendliness had developed between Jan Bruning and Mrs. Stone and me, so I said to him, slowly and in a serious manner:

"I have a real problem. I'm working on a book about mind phenomena. I came to Lourdes to check on the miracles. My time is limited; therefore, I need to locate the right person who can be of assistance—a person who speaks English—who knows from actual experience what has, and is taking place—someone who can help me make arrangements to interview individuals who have been cured—preferably a person who has been cured himself. I'm looking for someone who can be of maximum assistance in the shortest space of time. That's my problem. Can you help me solve it?"

"The one person who can help you is an English woman—Mrs. Winifred Feely," Jan Bruning said. "Mrs. Feely had an instantaneous cure of cancer some years ago. Since then she—in gratitude for her healing, like so many who have been cured—devotes her time each summer to helping others who come to Lourdes. Mrs. Feely holds interviews for Americans from two to three every afternoon at the Medical Bureau. When we get to the hotel, I'll tell you exactly how to find her office."

We arrived at the hotel at noon. It wasn't necessary to remind Jan Bruning of his promise. On the back of his personal card he wrote a short note of introduction to Mrs. Feely and gave us the necessary directions on how we could find her office in the Medical Bureau building.

At two o'clock, Mrs. Stone and I met with Mrs. Winifred Feely. Someone had pointed her out to me at my request. "Are you the Mrs. Feely who had the miraculous cure from cancer?" I asked.

I later found that she was a smiling, happy person, but this question brought about what seemed to be righteous indignation. "I'm Mrs. Feely," she replied, "but I didn't have cancer, and it wasn't a miracle. I had a large tumor which was instantaneously healed, but that is not a miracle. There are thousands of cures at Lourdes, but they don't all come under the category of miracles. Are you a doctor?"

"No." I explained my project and told her that I was searching for facts regarding the miracles of Lourdes. From the type of personal questions she asked, I could sense that before she would make a decision about how much she would cooperate, she would try to be certain that I would adhere 100 percent to the truth in what I would later write. After about ten minutes, it became obvious that she would be happy to help me. And later it developed that she gave me much more information than I might have hoped for.

"Have you read any books or done any outside research on this subject?" she asked.

"I read Margaret Gray Blanton's *The Miracle of Bernadette*."

"That's fine, but the most recent book is *The Miracle of Lourdes* by Ruth Cranston. Ruth Cranston is a Protestant and she was most thorough in her investigation while here. She spent a lot of time with me. I know it will be difficult for you to obtain a copy of her book, so I'll give you mine." And she gave me the last copy she had. Also she recommended *Miracles Still Happen* by Sanford and *Our Lady of Lourdes* by Deery. She suggested that we sit down in the warm sunshine just outside the door of the Medical Bureau, where we could continue our conversation. Within 45 minutes she told me enough to fill a book.

But before continuing, let me mention now that although Mrs. Feely and others told me the stories of the apparition of

the Blessed Virgin related in 1858 by the peasant girl Bernadette Soubirous, my comments here will be directed to what
happens at Lourdes—what it meant to me—what it can mean
to you.

Let me tell you now what Mrs. Feely told me when we were
seated outside.

"I asked if you were a doctor," she said. "If you were, you
could register and get a permit. Any properly certified medical doctor can check the Medical Bureau records, observe any
examination, and actually take part in the proceedings when
there is an investigation into an alleged cure. We welcome
such participation.

"Any doctor, of any race or faith, is granted the right to
examine the records and raise questions. During the existence of the Medical Bureau, over 40,000 doctors have partic-
ipated: Catholics, Protestants, Jews, Buddhists, agnostics, and
atheists. The Medical Bureau is run entirely by doctors and
receives its financial support entirely from doctors in all parts
of the world."

Thus a very high proportion of the medical signatures on
the records of examinations belong to non-Catholics. This
doesn't necessarily imply belief in miracles on the part of these
men; it merely signifies the *truth* of the medical facts observed.

At that moment Mrs. Richard J. Hughes, the wife of
the Governor of New Jersey, and two women companions
approached, and Mrs. Feely interrupted her talk for a few
minutes while she gave directions to them in response to a
question they asked. As they were leaving, Mrs. Feely encour-
aged them to return later in the day. And then she continued
her conversation with us.

First she told about the thousands of pilgrimages that
come each year. "There are often several pilgrimages at the

same time," she said. "Each pilgrimage is accompanied by one or more medical men, and no sick person is accepted without a medical certificate from his home physician, stating his disease, present condition, and the progress of the disease at the time he left home.

"Right now you will observe a pilgrimage from Dublin. And then tomorrow, the first official pilgrimage in history from The Anglican Church (The Church of England) will arrive. I'm anxious to meet them." She seemed to be anticipating a pleasant experience as she apparently pictured the arrival of this new group in her mind's eye, for she hesitated for several seconds. Mrs. Stone and I were listening eagerly for everything Mrs. Feely had to say, and I didn't want to interrupt her thoughts with a question.

But she did answer a question I had in mind when she continued: "You may see as many as 40,000 people at The Procession of the Blessed Sacrament this afternoon, or at the Torchlight Procession tonight. There were eight million visitors to Lourdes in 1958—the Centennial of the Apparition. And most of the people who come here do so with hopes of cures for themselves or loved ones. There are many cures here at Lourdes, but I remind you once again—few miracles," she said.

The Medical Bureau Needs Scientific Proof

And she continued: "The Medical Bureau needs scientific proof.

"When some cure that appears to be a miracle occurs, the patient is quietly and immediately taken to the Medical Bureau for examination. This avoids undue commotion. The patient is thoroughly examined.

"Keep in mind," she said, "no hysterical or neurotic cases are considered for study by the bureau or the Church. There must be some organic change with medical documents to prove it. It is only then that the alleged cure will be examined.

"After the first examination the patient is to return in a year. In the meantime, the bureau starts accumulating all the patient's past medical history and building up a file. They keep in touch with the patient and receive copies of any medical examinations he has by his own doctors after he returns home. The file becomes very voluminous, with reports, X rays, and every bit of available information pertaining to the patient.

"It's important to remember that the Medical Bureau can, from the viewpoint of science, proclaim a cure. But it's up to the Church alone to determine whether the cure is a miracle. As a matter of fact," she said, "the Church is more strict than the Medical Bureau, and many doctors have privately stated that they felt a patient experienced a miracle in spite of the fact that the Church did not recognize his cure as such."

But again she impressed upon us the thoroughness of the bureau's investigations. "For," she said, "the doctors of the Medical Bureau check into five special characteristics that distinguish miraculous cures from natural cures. These are:

- Those were medical treatment has completely failed and the patient does not use any medicine or other therapeutic treatments.
- Those where the restoration is immediate—for example, a dying person is immediately restored to full health.
- Those where the patient is made entirely whole at once and does not regain his health through a period of gradual improvement. In other words, there is an absence of convalescence.
- Those where there is a variation in the method of healing. At Lourdes the cures display a wonderful irregu-

larity; they are completely unpredictable, patternless, and almost haphazard.

+ Those where functional restoration takes place without organic restoration. A sick person with a diseased organ, such as an eye, lung, brain, or heart, finds the function working perfectly although the organ itself remains unchanged and biologically incapable of performing its function. Take for example the cases at Lourdes where the blind see without the faculty of seeing, and not only on one occasion, but regularly during a year or more until the eye itself returns to a healthy condition."

What Makes the Water at Lourdes Different?

Let me now tell you of the high points of our conversation as we discussed the physical qualities of the water at Lourdes, the places and occasions on which miracles have occurred, and the procedure for the Church's authentication of a miracle.

"Every time the water has been analyzed by scientists," Mrs. Feely said, "it was found that it contained nothing remarkable. The water of Lourdes chemically contains no curative or medical properties whatsoever. It's similar to any other mountain water where the soil is rich in calcium. It isn't radioactive. And it contains no active chemical substance that has healing properties.

"The baths are changed twice daily. Only a small percentage of the sick who take the baths are cured, but no one has ever suffered harm or been infected after immersion in the baths. For one of the peculiar things about Lourdes water is that even when polluted at the end of the day because of the immersion of persons with all types of illness, the water remains perfectly harmless.

"A bacteriological study of the water after the last bath at the end of the day indicated that billions of bacilli were present—but they were inert.

"Six months after guinea pigs were inoculated with this water in a scientific experiment, all were living and normal and in a healthy condition. Yet guinea pigs inoculated with water from another source containing the same bacilli died.

"It's not a pleasant thought," she said, "but it's not an uncommon experience for a stretcher-bearer or a nurse to drink a glass of water scooped up from the baths at the end of the day as an act of faith—yet there has never been a single instance where there has been an ill effect."

And then Mrs. Feely mentioned the names of some of those who have experienced miracles, and she described the occasions. She urged us to read about them in *The Miracle of Lourdes*—the book she had given us. She particularly referred to Pierre de Rudder and Edelthraud Faulda.

We were told that miraculous cures have occurred at the grotto, at the piscine (baths) while the sick persons were in the water or immediately thereafter, at the Procession of the Blessed Sacrament, in the hospital, on the return trip from Lourdes and, at Holy Communion. Sometimes they have come on the person's first pilgrimage, sometimes they have come after several pilgrimages. Sometimes they have come after the first bath, and they have come after as many as nine baths.

Also miracles have occurred away from Lourdes—at home when a person has been lotioned with Lourdes water; after novenas by those who have never been to Lourdes but have called upon the name of Notre Dame de Lourdes (Our Lady of Lourdes); at shrines or replicas of the Lourdes grotto. Of special interest are the miraculous cures of unbelievers, when relatives who were believers prayer for them.

The Church Makes the Final Decision

Again and again during our conversation, Mrs. Feely repeated, "There are many cures at Lourdes—but very few miracles. It takes a minimum of two years and more often four or five before a cure is termed a miracle." She told us of the diligent investigation of the Canonical Commission and about the Church's reluctance to proclaim a miracle. She said in a very serious tone of voice:

"When the few cases that pass the stringent rules and investigations of the Medical Bureau and the International Medical Committee warrant a study by the Church, indicating that the patient is truly cured and his cure cannot be explained by laws of nature, there are seven characteristics that must apply before the event can be declared a miracle by the church. They are (1) that the disease shall have been grave and either impossible or difficult to cure; (2) that the disease shall not have been in decline; (3) that no medicaments shall have been employed, or if employed, shall certainly have been without effect; (4) that the cure shall have been sudden and instantaneous; (5) that the cure shall have been complete; (6) that the cure shall not have been preceded by any noteworthy decrease or crisis occurring in due natural course; (7) that the disease shall not have returned—in other words, that the cure be permanent."

In the early part of our interview I had informed Mrs. Feely that we had just arrived at Lourdes. Now she told us how to get to the grotto and the piscine; also she took us out on the Esplanade and pointed out the best vantage points for viewing the Procession of the Blessed Sacrament that was to start at 4:30.

It was only a few minutes after three o'clock when she said, "I have a very important meeting that I must attend, but I do want you both to come back after the procession. You'll be on your feet for a long time so . . ." she said, as she stood up and turned to walk toward the door leading into the Medical Bureau, "I'll get you two folding camp chairs which you can return when you come back." And she went into the building and brought us the chairs without giving us an opportunity to say "no."

Have you ever met a person with whom you developed a bond of friendship quickly and who seemed momentarily to be steering the course of your destiny in his efforts to help you? I had just that feeling with Mrs. Feely. I felt that she would be directing our activities while we were at Lourdes for the purpose of helping me learn as much as we could in the shortest space of time—it was a good feeling. And that is what actually happened, as you will soon see.

Mrs. Stone and I walked across the Esplanade and on to the grotto. Then to the piscine. On returning to the Esplanade to view the procession, we once again stopped at the grotto. Also, for the first time, we drank the Lourdes water from the new water taps on the side of the old baths. We viewed the Procession of the Blessed Sacrament. And it was almost 6:30 when we returned the camp chairs to Mrs. Feely at the Medical Bureau office.

Because I have not given a detailed description, I feel it advisable to mention that my discussion of Lourdes must be confined to one chapter. Furthermore, it is my hope that you will be motivated to read at least one of the very interesting books I have referred to here, which will give you the description of the entire *Domain*—the water, the ceremonies, the baths, and the cures—in greater detail. Later I will express what I experienced, felt, and thought while at the grotto and the piscine and while watching the procession—for these things are more important than what I saw. It is the effect that Lourdes has upon the individual that is important to him— more so than what he sees, however inspiring that may be.

The Torchlight Procession

Mrs. Feely was pleased with our enthusiasm. And because she didn't want us to miss a thing she said, "The torchlight procession starts at 7:30. You will want to get your candles and join in. It's an experience you'll never forget. You might like to go to your hotel now to have dinner, for you won't have much time. I'll see you tomorrow morning at 8:30."

It had been a long day, and we were tired. Instead of rushing, we took time to relax before going into the dining room of the Bethany. This hotel is on a hill, above the bend in the River Gave. From our table in the dining room we could see the entrance to the Domain below, part of the Esplanade that wasn't hidden by trees, and in the distance the piscine.

Thus we could see the thousands of lighted candles as the marchers moved in the procession—over 40,000 in all. It was my intent to join the procession the following evening, so we didn't hurry. But the ceremony lasted for over two hours that evening, and we were able to join the marchers towards the end of the procession.

Mrs. Feely was right. It was an experience I'll never forget, and we joined the procession again the following evening. And the chorus sung by the marching throngs—*Avé, Avé, Avé Maria . . . Avé, Avé, Avé, Maria*, reminded me of Margaret Gray Blanton's book, *The Miracle of Bernadette*, in which she describes this beautiful *Song of Bernadette*.

At every sales meeting and public lecture, and in almost everything I write, I try to motivate those who hear or read what I have to say to read inspirational self-help books. But

I doubt if I ever did a better job than Mrs. Feely did in motivating me to read *The Miracle of Lourdes* by Ruth Cranston. After the procession, we returned to the Bethany, and I read this exciting book until three in the morning. Now I'll share a portion with you.

In reading I was surprised to meet my friend, Dr. Smiley Blanton, at eight different places in the book. The first such meeting was on page 67, where Ruth Cranston wrote: "Often the President (of the Medical Bureau) will invite one of the visiting physicians to preside over the examination. An American physician, Dr. Smiley Blanton, directed the examination of one of the most famous cures—Charles McDonald . . ." She tells the story of Charles McDonald in detail, and on page 73 (paperback edition) she again refers to Smiley Blanton:

. . . On September 16, 1937 he returned to Lourdes, where Dr. Blanton and other physicians examined him on September 17.

Thirty-two doctors were present at the Medical Bureau during McDonald's examination. In their concluding remarks they made the following statement:

"Charles McDonald has been afflicted with (1) tuberculosis of the left shoulder with three fistulas; (2) tuberculosis of the dorsal spine with two fistulas; (3) chronic nephritis characterized by the presence of pus, blood, albumin. These three conditions were in full evolution at the moment of the pilgrimage to Lourdes, the five fistulas giving off pus.

"They were abruptly halted in their evolution on September 7. An immediate functional healing after a bath in the piscine was followed in less than four days by a definite cicatrization of the five fistulas, of return to normal urinary secretion rid of its infectious germs; cessation of pain, return of partial movements of the left arm and lumbar region.

"This healing, obtained without the use of medicaments or of any therapeutic agent whatever is confirmed by one year of excellent health and work . . . No medical explanation, in the present state of science, can be given; considering the extraordinary rapidity of the healing of these tuberculous affections, judged incurable by the specialists called in to treat him, and whose beginning was noted by general infection, later by bony localizations. This healing is written down as on the margin of the laws of biology."

The signatures of the thirty-two doctors end this statement.

In his report to his American confreres Dr. Blanton concludes:

To summarize, we have a man who seems certainly to have had tuberculosis of the lungs. He also had an infection of the twelfth thoracic vertebra which had destroyed it, and an infection of the shoulder which had practically destroyed the bony structure of the joint. In bed fifteen months, he had to have his wounds dressed twice daily. After the second bath in the piscine he was able to move without pain; he was able to walk that day; within three weeks he was able to walk several miles a day; his sinuses were practically healed in a period of two weeks. What is the explanation of this healing?—for that it is a healing I am myself convinced. The records seem adequate to support this conclusion, and they were made by well-trained and reputable physicians. Furthermore this is not an isolated case but one of approximately ten or twelve that occur at Lourdes yearly, in which the records seem well and honestly made.

We must lay aside as untenable the accusation that these cases are in any way 'fixed' or the histories 'doctored.' There does appear to be at this shrine . . . a sudden quickening of the healing processes, a removal of symptoms and a feeling of well-being. The percentages of such cures . . . are certainly too great to be laid to coincidence, nor do the details of the cures conform to the laws of recovery as we know them. Even coincidental cures in our hospitals do not, in the space of two or three days, get up and walk without pain after fifteen months of life in bed with continual pain . . .

The basis of the cures seems to lie in some aspect which has to do with the psychology of the situation . . . It is my feeling that in this case and in similar cases at Lourdes there is a quickening of the healing process.

I feel that we are justified by what we saw at Lourdes in stating our tentative belief that processes leading in the direction of death were not only halted but reversed, and the libido liberated in this way was put to the use of the individual in the restoration of health. I believe that something does occur which is, as Dr. Vallet has remarked, on the margin of the laws of nature.

And Ruth Cranston adds in a footnote: "Charles McDonald is in excellent health today—a robust man of forty-nine. He comes to Lourdes frequently, and was there with his daughter shortly before my own visit."

And I met Smiley Blanton again, on page 141, where he says: "One thing you quickly notice: the difference in attitude of the rationalist physician *before* he has seen a cure, and *after*."

I Had a Guilt Feeling

At 8:30 the next morning, Mrs. Stone and I were greeted by Mrs. Feely on our arrival at the Medical Bureau. We had a pleasant surprise.

"Would you like to take the baths?" she asked.

This was the same question she had asked me the day before. I had told her that we would—if we could get permission. I desperately wanted this experience, but I didn't ask for her help. For there is something about Lourdes that keeps one from being overly aggressive or asking for anything that might violate the rules or customs.

The surprise: two cards—one for each of us, with the official stamp of the Secretariat Bureau Medical Lourdes, which granted special permission for baths for five days.

I can still see the gleam of happiness in Mrs. Feely's eyes when she handed us the cards. She was like a mother watching the delight of her young children when they catch their first glimpse of the tree on Christmas morning.

"I'll take you over to the piscine myself," she said. And as we walked to the baths, she prepared us for what we might experience. "First, you will be taken almost immediately. After the baths, you aren't to dry yourself. Just put your clothes on— you'll find you will be dry very quickly. Meet me back at the Medical Bureau and don't wait for each other as one of you will be through first." Then she directed her conversation to the spiritual aspects:

"You may wish to pray for the sick . . . some worthy desire of your own or . . . the health of a loved one." We arrived at the piscine. "Mrs. Stone, you wait her while I take Mr. Stone over to the men's section," she said. I was conducted close to the front of a long line of men waiting to take the baths. And then she left to help Mrs. Stone at the women's section.

I had a guilt feeling—for I had been passed ahead of several hundreds of the sick who would have to wait, some a few hours, before they would have their turns. "But," I rationalized, "I may say or write something in the future that will inspire many of the sick to come to Lourdes for help. And if they should experience cures this special personal attention will have been warranted." I may have been wrong, but I had a feeling that Mrs. Feely felt perhaps through me she would be able to help others. For I was certainly sincere in my search for the truth about the miracles of Lourdes for this book. She was helping me learn as much as I could within the shortest possible time.

As I stood in line, I could hear a priest praying aloud and many voices responding. But I was thinking. I was praying in my own way. I was getting keyed up as I do in preparation for a sale or a speech. But this time it was different. For instead of getting keyed up to do something, I was becoming emotionalized to prepare myself to receive something. My prayers were continuous—for the sick—for some worthy desires of my own, and for help for my loved ones. For I am a great believer in prayer and believe that man's greatest power lies in the power of prayer.

I was ready for a great emotional experience. For I had been to the grotto and the Procession of the Blessed Sacrament, and at these times too I had prayed for enlightenment in atmospheres generated by thousands of souls searching for Divine guidance and help.

And when I was directed to the anteroom, which is separated from the bathing compartment by a curtain, I and five others sat on a bench to await our turn. Again I prayed continuously, until I entered the bathing compartment.

Three men who had been immersed were getting dressed; three others were getting undressed; another was being immersed in the piscine and was being assisted by two attendants.

When my turn came, everything happened quickly. I stood in the water. The attendants found that I spoke English.

A large card was placed in front of me on which was a short prayer. The attendants and I said it aloud. I was erect and rigid while they lowered me backward into the water until I was completely immersed. The water was cold. Throughout the ceremony I felt in a highly emotionalized state of a nature I had never experienced before. The inspiration of that moment created an impact within me that made me feel from then on I was to be a better person. I dressed hurriedly. And as I walked back to the Medical Bureau, I kept thinking of this experience. I realized that only time would tell whether I would fulfill that moment of inspiration.

Mrs. Stone arrived outside that Medical Bureau a few minutes after I did. We could see that Mrs. Feely was busily engaged in conversation with one of the doctors. But she excused herself, walked over to greet us, and said, "I'd like very much to take you to see the Sept Douleurs and the other hospitals, the home of Bernadette at the prison, and other places I know will interest you. I'm not in a position to do so now, but I'll ask one of the nurses if she has time." She stopped one who was passing by, and the nurse seemed most pleased to help us. As we left, Mrs. Feely said, "I'll see you again when you return. I am anxious to take you through the Museum of the Medical Bureau myself."

A Gallery of Miracles—Before and After Evidence

To me the Museum of the Medical Bureau was a gallery of miracles—before and after evidence. For there you see pictures of evidence and photographic copies of written evidence of miraculous cures to many persons about whom you read in any book on Lourdes. Now let me tell you of just one.

When we came to the pictures of Pierre de Rudder, Mrs. Feely translated the French inscriptions into English. She pointed out the section of new bone in his leg as she told us this story.

"There are cures away from Lourdes also," she said. "Take Pierre de Rudder, for example. His leg was broken . . . the two sections of the bone in his leg were separated about an inch . . . the lower part of the leg could be turned around. As time went on his leg became worse; pus and blood flowed from it continually. The doctors advised that the leg be amputated, but de Rudder refused even though he suffered great pain and had to dress the wounds twice a day.

"After eight years he went on a pilgrimage to Oostacker, near Ghent, where a grotto had been erected in honor of Our Lady of Lourdes. When taking the public carriage from the railroad station to the grotto his leg discharged so much blood and pus that it soiled the seat on which he was resting it. The driver created quite a commotion and in an angry voice shouted, 'You'll have to pay for this!'

"With the aid of his crutches Pierre walked from the carriage to the grotto and sat down and prayed. He asked forgiveness for all of his sins, and sought grace to able to work and take care of his children and no longer live on charity. He prayed and prayed. And suddenly a sharp trembling shook his whole frame, and in a few moments he rose . . . cured.

"He walked around the grotto three times without his crutches. He walked to the carriage that was to return him to the station. At his home town he got off the train without any help.

"Pierre didn't report his cure to his doctor, but the doctor (who was an agnostic) heard the news and went to see him. He found Pierre digging in the garden.

"Pierre de Rudder died at the age of 75 of pneumonia, and after his burial Dr. Van Hoestenberghe (the family physician who had been converted from unbelief by this cure) caused the body to be exhumed. From it he extracted the bones which had knitted and had them photographed. The bones themselves are preserved at the University of Louvain. But a model can be seen right here at the Medical Bureau."

Then Mrs. Feely directed our attention to the pictures. She specifically pointed to the section of bone that had united the two separate parts and then gave the medical explanation for the lighter appearance of the new bone tissue. "Also note, in this picture both legs are of the same length," she said.

We left the museum and tireless Mrs. Feely took us to the St. Pius X Basilica. From there we returned to the Medical Bureau for tea. Mrs. Hughes and her companions joined us. We had a delightful hour of conversation.

Mrs. Feely showed us snapshots she had taken of famous persons. We talked about many things. Everything she had to say was of particular interest to me. She told about her experiences in her yearly trip to America to raise funds for Notre Dame de Lourdes, of her many friends, of the annual international pilgrimage of gypsies, of pilgrims from India, Africa, and all parts of the world. But of special interest were such statements as:

"It seems to be the poor and simple people who are blessed by miracles. One of the 'miracles' of Lourdes is the spirit here. You just feel it: the doctors, nurses, hospitalers, brancardiers—in spite of long hours they are always cheerful and eager to help. The sick seem to be more interested in another's welfare than their own. You never hear complaints, unkind words. Everyone seems to be considerate . . . Everyone here is equal—poor or rich. A lady of royalty is working in the laundry. A wealthy woman is scrubbing floors in the hospital." (She was here using the term *miracle* loosely, as many of us do.)

And then she described her home in England. ". . . my country cottage, a truly quiet and bucolic life, but restful and peaceful. I like it."

We invited Mrs. Feely to dinner that evening, but she smiled as she said, "I have work to do."

PART V

From Psi to Science

by Norma Lee Browning

CHAPTER 16

The Mind's Unfolding Secrets

The human mind is today undergoing the most exciting and intensive probing in the history of mankind. Science has conquered space; the goal now is to conquer the mind. And just as space shrinks under the onslaught of rocket ships, so the gulf between physical man and the human psyche is shrinking in brain-research laboratories.

The race to harness mind power has already exploded many myths and opened new vistas in the dim half-world bordering the physical brain. It may also open a Pandora's Box of problems, for who knows what strange and hidden powers lie behind the curtained secrets of the mind—and how they will be used when science finally enables man to bring them under control? Already science has established that human behavior can be predicted, controlled, and engineered by electronic and chemical stimulation of certain areas of the brain.

The metaphysical concept of ESP is giving way in many areas to a scientific technique known as ESB—electrical stimulation of the brain. ESB is rapidly replacing fantasies with facts, foremost of which is that "brain power" is a form of electrical power, and that most genuine psychic, mystical, or mental experiences and emotions are the results of highly intensified *sensory* perceptions (*not* extrasensory) produced by electrochemical processes in the physical brain. Ironically, too, ESB is responsible for increased scientific interest in one area of ESP—telepathy.

This interest is the direct result of the Russian claims of successful experiments in mind-to-mind communication. In fact, reports of the Soviet experiments in long-distance telepathic communications have stirred up the biggest controversy since flying saucers, and many of their claims sound more like science fiction than facts. But this is true of many of the achievements of modern science. Scientists have already told us that our enlightened nuclear age may soon relegate atomic energy to the junk heap. Who knows but what they may even be able to harness brain power to communicate telepathically with astronauts or submarine commanders?

A French scientist has demonstrated that it is possible to turn a lamp on or off by "will power"—merely by thinking about it, with the aid of electronic amplification of the brain's electrical waves. Early in 1963, newspapers around the world carried a report that signals from a woman's brain had been successfully bounced off a satellite across the Atlantic from the Burden Neurological Institute in Bristol, England, to the Mayo Clinic in Rochester, Minnesota. The woman wore electrodes on her head, and electronic signals from her brain were transmitted across the Atlantic, analyzed at the Mayo Clinic, and the interpretation flashed back to Bristol within minutes. Brain waves, however, are not the same as "thought waves," and the borderline between them is one of the million inscrutable mysteries in the scientific riddle of mind power.

Soviet scientists are hoping to discover and determine the exact nature of brain-mind energy that could produce the phenomena called telepathy. How close they will come to it remains to be seen, but in the scientific revolution going on for control of the human mind, science has already solved many of the awesome problems involved and is well on the way toward solving more of them in the near future.

Is the mind itself a specific entity—or merely a convenient fiction? The real mystery of mental activity is that the mechanism of the brain is accompanied by the phenomenon of consciousness. But what is consciousness? In what area of the brain is it located? And where is the line between the conscious and subconscious minds?

Such problems, involving both the physiology and psychology of brain-mind mysteries, were once thought to be beyond the grasp of science. But studies of the brain's electrical discharges and electrochemical makeup have changed this concept. Scientists have found that every brain activity is accompanied by minute electrical impulses. By amplifying these brain currents electronically and investigating their patterns, and by using ESB, scientists are coming closer each day to discovering the missing link in mind power—the link between physical brain activity and nonphysical mind, thought, and behavior processes.

One of the most challenging areas of research is *memory*. How does memory function? How and where are memories stored in the brain? Is there such a thing as a genetic memory that can dredge up dreams and events from an unrecorded past, or from some form of preexistence? Science already has part of the answer: through psychochemistry—the use of LSD or other vision-producing drugs—it is indeed possible to revive long-buried memories and even dreams from childhood. The drugs, sometimes called "chemical mind-changers," can take a person backward through time in a form of "age regression" similar to that sometimes produced by hypnosis. The controversial *Bridey Murphy* may have been a mesmeric flop so far as it was an attempt to prove reincarnation, but as a case of subconscious memory released under hypnosis, Bridey now has some basis of scientific fact, supported or reaffirmed by pharmaceuticals. In fact, Dr. Glenn T. Seaborg, nuclear chemist and chairman of the Atomic Energy Commission, has stated his belief that in the next few decades we may have "pharmaceuticals which can change and maintain human personality at any desired level." The implications of this are enormous.

Science, too, is taking a new look at hypnosis as a research tool for exploring the hidden channels of mind power. Hypnosis had fallen into disrepute largely because of its guilt-by-association with stage entertainers and quack healers, but it has made a comeback in the laboratories of neurophysiologists and psychologists who recognize its role in brain-mind research. Again, one of the principal reasons for the change of heart on hypnosis is the report of Russia's flurry of interest in the subject.

Among the most incredible miracles of brain-mind research are developments in the comparatively new fields of bionics and cybernetics. Through the study of sensory and motor mechanisms in both animals and humans, cyberneticians have constructed mechanical robots and brain-simulating machines that could conceivably replace people.

The most fabulous and highly organized apparatus in the universe is a physiological machine, the human brain—an enigmatic, three-pound, pinkish mass of nerve tissue, cells, and fibers, which, together with its attached spinal cord, is the physical center of human behavior. Within this human machine is a vast ten-billion-watt communications network of nerve cells and fibers flashing millions of signals and messages to and from and within the brain. The network has its own complex but orderly system of filtering, condensing, and correlating information, and shuttling the messages—or "nerve impulses"—along the right channels.

The force that keeps this intricate human machine operating is electricity, or more properly, electrochemical energy, for the electricity itself is created by chemical reactions in the nerve cells. It is this electrical key that has unlocked many of the mysteries of brain physiology and brought fresh realms of knowledge on human thought, behavior, and personality. And with this key, scientists are now able to construct machines patterned after the human brain and capable of performing many of the brain's jobs as well or better than the real thing.

There are machines that have been "taught" to think, and to recognize faces, patterns, and objects more accurately than the human eye can. There are "memory" machines that can store memories and release them in response to certain stimuli in much the same manner as the human brain does. There are electronic ears to speed up language-learning, electronic eyes for landing unmanned vehicles on the moon, electronic brain-wave analyzers that record and decode brain patterns on stacks of hole-punched cards like those used in IBM machines.

Many of the machines that flash and click in science laboratories today are, in fact, various forms of the extension of the living brain. The future of the brain becomes more intriguing daily as more and more of its intellectual processes are analyzed and imitated electronically.

Fear of the unknown is as deep in some people as the lure of the unknown is in others, and there are some who are repelled at any scientific meddling in the mind. "Leave the mind alone," they say. "You are tampering with a world you know nothing about."

But, like it or not, the scientific revolution for the conquest of mental secrets that up to now have eluded scientists is underway. And many eminent scientists agree that the results may exceed their wildest dreams. Dr. Frederic A. Gibbs, one of the world's leading brain authorities, and head of the Brain Research Foundation in Chicago, said recently:

> People who said we would never learn to understand the brain did not realize the technological advances that would be made. There is a scientific revolution going on in brain research today, and there is no question in my mind that our technology is going to give us a breakthrough in the mental sciences.

Will the breakthrough shed light on psychic phenomena— such as telepathy? After all, science has already invented radio telescopes that can tune in galaxies a billion light-years away. Could a sufficiently sensitive device, for example, read Khrushchev's mind? Dr. Gibbs, who like most scientists is cautious of anything hinting of the supernormal or metaphysical, says:

"To date we cannot read the thoughts in another person's mind. The brain waves do not show thought processes in the mind. They merely show the energy which the brain is using in thought. They do not tell what the messages are."

But he added that if technology advances at its present rate, it is "very probable" that scientists one day will be able to look into our minds and not only read our thoughts but control them. This does not mean, however, that all of us will become suddenly clairvoyant or attuned to other-worldly cosmic vibrations. It means that some things previously thought to be supernatural or "psychic" have a physiological substructure that can be electronically detected, computed, and controlled.

Whether telepathy falls into this category has become a subject of scientific debate because of the claims of Soviet scientists. Some say the prospect is no more inconceivable than rocket control, manmade satellites, jet power, or the splitting of the atom seemed only a few years back.

Science fiction has become fact in many areas. The same can happen in others.

CHAPTER 17

Cybernetics: Key to the Brain's Secrets

One conspicuous point of omission in the writings of Russia's Vasiliev: there is no mention of the kind of research going on since he opened his laboratory in 1960. This could be an intentional shrugging off—or it might mean that current experiments are following the same pattern as those of 30 years ago. The early experiments are presented in a way that easily misleads the reader into believing that they are current; and there seems to be no doubt that Vasiliev's own experimental approach is still through hypnosis. But his associates told me something that I was to hear again and again during my stay in Russia: "The real answers are going to come through cybernetics."

"Cybernetics" is a word that comes at you from every direction in Russia. Taxi drivers and Intourist guides speak as glibly of cybernetics as Americans do of baseball scores. Front-page articles on cybernetics are featured almost daily in the Soviet press.

What role, if any, can cybernetics play in explaining or controlling telepathy? In order to answer this question it is first necessary to have some grasp of the newly created and complex science of cybernetics—which bridges the gap between mathematics and physiology.

Cybernetics has many definitions—or, more precisely— many interpretations and applications. Perhaps the easiest to understand is its role in automation. One of the jobs of cybernetics is the development of machines that imitate human or animal behavior. In America, cybernetics is closely identified with the new teaching and learning machines. In Russia it is almost synonymous with the totalitarian concept of automation.

In Western countries, cybernetically constructed machines have proved valuable in education and industry, from the practical standpoint of relieving men of menial chores; they have proved even more valuable in medical and space research programs, from the standpoint of proving new knowledge about brain physiology, human behavior, and signal communications.

But Russia has taken cybernetics a step further and applied it to society.

The Soviet definition of cybernetics, according to academician V. Trapeznikov, director of the Institute of Automation and Telemechanics, is, "The science of control, the organization of purposeful action—in living organisms, in man-made automatic machines, and in the society in which we live." The Soviet cybernetical point of view is that all control processes, whether they take place in the nervous system of an animal or man, in a computer, in automatic controllers, or in the economic structures of modern society, are governed by common laws of physics, mathematics, engineering, and biology. And their scientists in these fields are now engaged in a large-scale automation program as part of the Soviets' overall space-research studies.

There seems to be little doubt that with cybernetics—"the science of control"—the Russians are reaching for the ultimate, whether it is with men or machines. They are confidently training machines to relieve man of "at least part of his intellectual burden," although one scientist, writing in *Izvestia*, has conceded that "it would be wrong to think that the main objective is to oust man completely." As Professor Vasiliev has pointed out in his appraisal of Russian research into telepathy, perhaps cybernetics will eventually solve the problem.

One of the major objectives of Soviet cyberneticians is to construct a "thinking" machine that can perform feats of telepathy so they can decipher how telepathy operates in humans. The Russians claim to have already perfected fantastic "thinking" machines. It has been reported that at the biocybernetics laboratory of Moscow's Institute of Surgery, scientists have developed a cybernetic machine that can even "predict" the course of healing in burns.

According to *Izvestia*, the Soviet cybernetics machines are alleged to be "acquiring and assimilating new knowledge" all the time, so it is assumed that it will be possible to design a cybernetics apparatus that "will produce all phenomena of mental suggestion with all their characteristics and drawbacks." Other reports describe the proposed machine as one that can generate artificial brain waves "designed to have a direct influence on the mental activity of people."

It is not clear exactly what is meant by this—whether the artificial brain waves will merely stimulate various types of mental activity within the human brain, or whether the "thinking" machine is going to beam a telepathic "thought" from its own artificial brain to a real one. Perhaps someone will simultaneously invent a mind shield.

Cybernetics, a comparatively new field of applied science, has a fascinating origin. And it started not in Russia, as anyone might be led to think from the emphasis that is given it there, but in America. The term "cybernetics," in its modern connotation, dates back to only 1947, when Dr. Norbert Wiener, world-renowned mathematician at the Massachusetts Institute of Technology, adopted the word to cover the entire field of control and communication theory, whether in machines or in animals.

Webster's defines cybernetics as "comparative study of the control system formed by the nervous system and brain and mechanical-electrical communications systems, such as computing machines." The literal derivation is from the Greek word *kybernétés*, meaning steersman or governor. The word was chosen by Wiener, as he has said, because it expresses adequately the idea of command and control. Moreover, from the same root, by way of the Latin *gubenator*, a corruption of the Greek word, Watt derived the name of "governor" for the control part of his steam engine.

The great French physicist and mathematician, Andre Ampere, used the word *cybernétique* more than a century ago for "science of government." The word was even used, with the meaning "science of piloting," by Plato, who put it in the mouth of Socrates: "Cybernetics saves souls, bodies and material possessions from the gravest dangers" (*Gorgias*, 511). Gordon Pask, one of Britain's leading cyberneticians, defines cybernetics as the "science of self-organizing systems." His definition emphasizes the study of how systems regulate themselves, reproduce themselves, evolve, and learn. "As an applied science, cybernetics aims to create the instruments of a new industrial revolution—control mechanisms that lay their own plans and make decisions." Pask says.

Whether cybernetics has to do with the governor of a steam engine; the steering engine of a ship; or the command-and-control mechanisms in men, machines, or society, the word is particularly apt—for the principles of steersmanship or government, as embodied in the original Greek meaning, are now being applied to machines that govern.

More intriguing is the physiological basis for this mechanical technology. It all starts from the basic idea that life—if it cannot be explained—can at least be approximated by mathematical reasoning and experiment.

As a science destined to bring mechanics and physiology into a common field of research, cybernetics was conceived and born during World War II. Actually, its birth certificate was an article published in 1943 by Wiener, Dr. Arturo Rosenblueth, then professor at the Harvard medical school, and Julian H. Bigelow, a mathematician and fellow researcher of Wiener. The article, published in the journal *Philosophy of Science*, carried the title "Behavior, Purpose and Teleology," but the word cybernetics did not appear in it.

This paper was the offshoot of study directly resulting from a series of dinner meetings held monthly at Harvard's Vanderbilt Hall in the years immediately preceding the war. At these meetings a nucleus of scientists, predominantly from Harvard, would hold round-table discussions on various scientific techniques, with specialists from various fields exchanging views. Wiener was invited to this round-table discussion group and there met Rosenblueth, and through him Dr. Warren McCulloch, a University of Illinois psychiatrist who was to become one of the leaders in cybernetics, and Walter Pitts, a mathematician who came to work with Wiener at M.I.T.

These conferences began to develop cybernetics when Wiener and Bigelow were called upon during World War II to research the possibilities of a machine to control antiair-craft fire, incorporating two nervous systems in a mechanical design. This involved what servomechanism engineers call "feedback." A feedback mechanism is a device that makes an effect act back on one of its own causes, enabling this effect to carry out its given aim. According to Pierre De Latil in *Thinking By Machine, A Study of Cybernetics*, a feedback mechanism can also be defined in practical terms as a self-correcting device that enables a machine to regulate its operation by adapting the drift of its own deviations. The steering engines of a ship, for example, are one of the earliest and best-developed forms of feedback mechanisms.

But the oldest and most highly developed feedback system is that contained in the human body. The human body automatically adapts itself to an assigned task by feedback—that is, when a person picks up a pencil a constant correction of movement occurs (steersmanship), governed by unconscious muscular movement resulting from messages sent to the nervous system and relayed back from the cortex of the brain. In fact, the principle of steersmanship by feedback undoubtedly played an important evolutionary role in the first stages of animal life, and was commonplace to the physiologist long before it became wedded to cybernetics.

As Dr. W. Grey Walter, one of the world's greatest living brain physiologists, explains it:

We have to visualize an elementary system of control by which the forward part of an organism can obtain information and feed it back internally for guidance of its operative motor-nerve centers . . . Our hypothesis is that the first nervous system evolved in this way from undifferentiated nerve-net. Some distant cousin of jellyfish or starfish, spawned with a deformity of its nerve-net, steered its way a little more safely through the crowded primordial sea.

In the years 1943 and 1944, Wiener's feedback theories played an important role in the war effort through the construction of giant calculating machines; it also was found at this time that there was a common basis of interest between neurophysiologists and calculating-machine experts.

Wiener wrote a book about his theories called *Cybernetics, or Control and Communication of the Animal and the Machine,* published in 1948 by the M.I.T. Press. This book, which sold 21,000 copies throughout the world, marked the first time the word cybernetics had been scientifically designated.

An American review of the book (*Business Week,* February 19, 1949) said in part: "In one respect Wiener's book resembles the Kinsey Report; the public response to it is at least as significant as the content of the book itself." Wiener, who is acknowledged to be a pioneer and leader in the rapidly developing field of the communication sciences, has concentrated much of his study in recent years on biological and neurological problems, particularly in matters dealing with brain waves and genetics.

A very important function of the nervous system, Wiener points out, and one equally in demand for computing machines, is that of *memory*—the ability to preserve the results of past operations for use in the future.

The important difference between the way we use the brain and the machine, he explains, is that the machine is intended for many successive runs, either with no reference to one another or with a minimal, limited reference, and that it can be cleared between such runs, whereas the brain, in the course of nature, never even approximately clears out its past records.

But with new discoveries and techniques, Wiener says, "We are already in a position to construct artificial machines of almost any degree of elaborateness of performance . . . "

Can man make the machines that he had created do his thinking for him? He already has come close enough to make himself stop and think.

For example, at Michigan State University, in East Lansing, a machine known as 3600 is writing a book. Here is a bit of history turned out by 3600: "The Soviet and pro-Western alliances have lost strength to the neutralists and to a growing African independence alliance."

The punch-card activated electronic brain is fed UN roll-call votes from all 111 nations. It grades each nation's variance from the total vote and tries to establish the nation's overall position on broad issues. Dr. Charles Wrigley, who heads the MSU Computer Institute for Social Science Research, believes there is a possibility that machines like 3600 can aim for day-by-day predictions of UN behavior, based on voting trends. Wrigley will do the actual writing, based on the generalities made by 3600, for a volume to be called "Statistical History of United Nations General Assembly Voting."

The young science of cybernetics, which had its theoretical and intellectual beginning in the U.S.A., evolved swiftly in Europe on a practical basis, and took concrete form with the creation of the famous electronic tortoises of Dr. W. Grey Walter and the homeostat of W. Ross Ashby, a psychiatrist from Gloucester.

Grey Walter (he is always called by the two names) and Ashby were Britain's counterparts to Wiener and McCulloch in America. They are generally acknowledged as the four pioneers of cybernetics, although a Frenchman, Louis Couffignal, now considered a world authority on calculating machines, was writing about machines that could reason as early as 1938.

Dr. Grey Walter, head of the Burden Neurological Institute at Bristol, England, is a pioneer in the new medical development of ESB (electrical stimulation of the brain) and a world-recognized authority on brain physiology and electroencephalography. He did his postgraduate work in nerve physiology and conditioned reflexes and was closely associated in his early years with both the great Russian physiologist Pavlov and with Hans Berger, the inventor of the EEG machine for investigating the electrical activity of the brain.

It was Grey Walter who tried to impress upon Pavlov that he who studies the nervous system cannot forget the brain, and vice versa. He opened new frontiers in brain physiology with his studies of the "alpha," "theta," and "delta" rhythms.

With this background it is not surprising that Grey Walter should be one of the first to come up with a working model to demonstrate the relationship between physiology and electronics in the new science of cybernetics. His electronic tortoises have cast shadows of doubt over the traditional assumption that only living creatures have independent, complex, unpredictable behavior.

Anyone who has seen a Grey Walter tortoise can testify that it has ten times more intelligence than the creature that crawls in the back garden. Though made of coils and electronic valves, it behaves like a real tortoise, only better. It can sit up and beg or come scooting at the sound of a human voice. It dislikes cold, damp weather, great heat, and bright lights. It moans in 40-degree temperature and runs toward any source of normal warmth. It likes company, recognizes voices, but can be easily frightened. It will nestle against your leg and purr at silk stockings. It likes women, dislikes men. It likes to be fed regularly and dislikes interruptions at meals. It can be temperamental, and it will be neurotic or sulky for days if teased or given too many contradictory instructions. "The tortoise," Dr. Grey Walter told me, "is really a crystallized idea." And the idea is that there is a chance of "thinking" machines being able to reason as effectively as the human mind.

Ironically, the Grey Walter tortoise was once rejected for entrance in the British Festival Exhibit on the grounds that the theory of conditioned reflexes was not British, but Russian.

The cybernetic tortoise, of course, has undergone various refinements and there have been many models of the electromechanical animals. The two best known ones were named by Grey Walter under zoological rules as the species *machina speculatrix*, with the pet names of Elmer (Electro-Mechanical Robot) and Elsie (Electro-Light-Sensitive-Internal-External). They were constructed in 1948 by Grey Walter and his wife Vivian, his assistant at the Burden Institute.

These tortoises live an artificial existence, "feeding" on light, which they seek out and transform into electrical currents, which in turn charge an accumulator. When their accumulators are charged—or their "stomachs filled"—they undergo a change in behavior patterns; no longer seeking a bright light on which to feed, they seek a quiet, dark corner where they "digest" their meal and rest until their batteries run down, when they again become "hungry" and again hunt for "food"—a bright light.

Each animal is equipped with a photoelectric cell and a steering motor and driving motor. The motors are mounted on a three-wheel base, and the photoelectric cell, like a head, swivels continually around exploring the surroundings, seeking a light. Grey Walter, using a flashlight, is able to make the tortoises move back and forth like animals. He had arranged, on the floor in a corner of the room, a sort of hutch in a portable box illuminated within by a very strong lamp. The tortoises, if not blocked by such obstacles as rugs or pieces of furniture, were able to scoot across the floor, enter the hutch, and plug themselves into the mains beside the bright light, thus recharging their batteries.

Still better than Elmer or Elsie, who only knows how to react to light, are some of their tortoise progeny who have learned to answer to the whistle of their master; that is, they have literally "learned," like Pavlov's dogs who salivated at the sound of the dinner bell. Another was taught to halt as soon as its master warned it by clapping his hands at the proximity of an obstacle.

There is a gigantic cybernetical step between Grey Walter's robot tortoises and "thinking" machines of the future.

Can man make a machine that experiences heights of elation at success or depths of depression at failure? Can he make a machine with an insatiable ambition to *learn*—or one that will play truant from school? Can he make one that even begins to approximate the human brain as a storage box of subconscious information, memories, and latent emotions? Can he make one that mimics that most mysterious of all life functions—reproduction? Can the *machina speculatrix* or the *machina docilis* give birth to a baby robot? Will the time come when humans, obeying some primitive command for preservation of the species, simply place their order with the appropriate bureau and wait for delivery?

Already cyberneticians are working on machines that they hope will be able to imitate the whole process of evolution. To the uninitiated the prospect is awesome, even frightening.

It is no wonder that the Russians are depending on cybernetics to solve their telepathy problems for them. One significant factor, however, is that nowhere in all the literature on cybernetics is the word telepathy even mentioned. Apparently, nowhere but in Russia are cyberneticians concerned with the mental phenomenon known as telepathy.

A British scientist, John H. Cutten, has summed up the status of telepathy in this way:

> If telepathy occurs, whether entirely psychic or not, something *causes it to occur*. What is required is not a continued search for the elusive occurrence, but an investigation of what causes it. Orthodox science will not be attracted by unverifiable reports of telepathic experiences, nor by the scores of an occasional good guesser whose prowess cannot be demonstrated with certainty at a chosen time. On the other hand, if it were possible to *cause telepathy to occur*, it would only require one type of experiment to set up an enthusiastic response from the scientific world. Unless and until this can be done the subject will remain the province of the enthusiastic amateur.

The Soviet goal in cybernetical research on telepathy is to create a machine that can reproduce the mental phenomenon of telepathy.

It seems, however, that although cybernetics has successfully accomplished with machines many things that the human mind can do, it still has not been able to duplicate telepathic communication. But hope springs eternal, and there is no telling what cybernetics may produce next.

CHAPTER 18

Wide and Deep Is the Mind

Within the last ten years, research in brain physiology and the sciences of human behavior has brought dramatic developments, and scientists are on the threshold of even more starling discoveries, some of them frightening to contemplate.

We were told that some day we may be able to shop for genetically pure babies in germ-cell banks, and that a child can be electrically socketed a few months after birth to develop into any kind of a mechanical robot a master controller wants him to be. We read that omniscient computers patterned after the human brain may take over the ordering of human life and affairs; that the human psyche, human behavior, and in fact whole societies or cities can be engineered, constructed—or wiped out, by manipulation of the normal electrochemistry of the brain and nervous system.

Using electricity and drugs, scientists are learning why our brain makes us feel pain, enjoy pleasure, love our friends, and hate our enemies; know fear, jealousy, anger, and envy; seek truth, honesty, and knowledge—and get seasick on a rolling ship. Of even greater importance, scientists have learned that many of these processes can be *reversed* by electrical or chemical stimulation of certain areas of the brain.

Emotions can be shifted quickly from love to hate, from bliss to anger, from pleasure to pain by electronic or chemical stimulators in the brain—just as they sometimes shift in human relationships without artificial stimulation. Scientists are moving closer to solving the mystery of why the human brain sometimes goes berserk, causing aberrations such as intense rage, hallucinations, deep depression, unwarranted fears, and feelings of dissociation.

Once scientists know *why* our brain makes us behave and react as we do, the next logical question is: can we then control the brain? Can we, with well-calculated doses of electrical stimulants and drugs, cure mental illnesses? Improve our behavior? Change our personalities? Prolong the useful years of our lives? Find a common meeting ground on which our thoughts and reactions—even our politics—can be synchronized?

Already scientists know that:

+ The force that keeps the brain working is electrical, and an adult-sized brain operates on about 20 watts of electrical energy.
+ With a new medical art called "electrosurgery," Parkinson's disease, epilepsy, and other diseases of the brain and nervous system can be arrested.
+ Tiny capsules of radioactive gas implanted in the brain can treat deeply seated tumors and cancers. Other medications can be inserted through tubes directly into diseased areas of the brain.
+ Tricks of the mind, such as visions, hallucinations, the feeling of "having been there before" (known as *déja vu*),

a sensation of dissociation, and a loss of sense of direction, have been traced to such easily remedied causes as fatigue, improper diet, and prolonged fasting—and they can be produced by electrochemical stimulation of certain areas of the brain.

+ Different areas of the brain play different roles in shaping our emotions. For example, the thalamus, a small "inner" brain about the size of a finger, governs our sensations of pain. A small region identified as the amygdala regulates our feelings of rage and fear. When we feel pleasure it's because several areas of the brain have been stimulated, but chiefly the hypothalamus, a tiny, rectangular piece of the brain located near the thalamus. (Other hypothalamic duties include thirst, appetite, sleep, and sex.)

+ Each of these emotions—pain, rage, fear, pleasure, thirst, hunger, drowsiness, sexual desire—can be deliberately produced in experimental animals by inserting electrodes into their brains and electrically stimulating the areas responsible for the sought-after emotions.

+ Humans undergoing brain surgery have experienced both visible and auditory hallucinations, accompanied by such emotional involvements as fear, awe, revulsion, and sadness, when certain areas of the brain, particularly in the temporal lobes, have been electrically stimulated.

+ Electrical records can be made of the events going on inside a patient's brain during surgery to show the effects of electrical stimulation on various regions. When these are compared with the patient's speech and actions during surgery, additional evidence is obtained of the workings of the brain.

+ Schizophrenia has been correlated with an abnormal amount of electrical activity in three areas of the brain known as the amygdala, the septal region, and the hippocampus.

+ Certain drugs, known as hallucinogenic drugs (the best known is LSD) cause symptoms of schizophrenia and other mental illnesses, and if an antidote can be found for these drugs, this could conceivably become an antidote for some mental illnesses.

+ Strong electrical stimulation or the administration of drugs immediately after an event can *prevent* the registering of the event on a person's memory. This discovery alone is an exciting step toward finding the answer to one of the brain's biggest puzzles: where are memories stored and how can they be summoned and put to use and integrated for conscious thought?

The history of brain research is a relatively short one. Before World War II, comparatively little brain research was done. The war, and the need for emergency care for brain damage, gave impetus to further research, but as recently as ten years ago not much was being done compared with what is going on now. The most dramatic developments undoubtedly have come from ESB—electrical stimulation of the brain as well as chemical stimulation. The two methods of brain stimulation—electrical and chemical—are interrelated.

The reason for this is basic. In the first place, though it is electrical energy that flows through the ten billion or more nerve cells for the brain as we think and act as we do, the electricity itself is created by chemical reactions inside the cells. Furthermore, when impulses travel from cell to cell, their behavior all along the route is governed by chemical reactions at the many synapses, or "decision points" of the nervous system. And finally, when impulses arrive at their destination, the activity that results is due to the release of certain chemicals, or neurohormones. For example, it is actually a chemical called acetylcholine that stimulates a muscle and makes it move. The whole process has been referred to as an electrochemical one.

Of the two methods beings used to stimulate the brain artificially, work with electrical stimulation has been developing, under controlled laboratory conditions, for a longer period of time.

An English physician, R. Caton, discovered in 1875 that the brain produces electric currents, but no one endeavored to measure or record these currents until Hans Berger devised his EEG machine in 1928. It was a simple, crude, almost primitive apparatus, as compared with those in use today, but with it scientists were able to determine that there were definite rhythms in the activity of the brain, and furthermore that these tended to stop when the subject opened his eyes or solved some problem in mental arithmetic.

This was a giant step—a means of "seeing" inside the brain and electrically recording what was seen.

But merely recording the frequency and amplitude of brain rhythms is not enough. It is the *pattern* of these rhythms that is significant. So began the laborious task of determining pattern from the wobbly lines.

In 1946, Dr. Grey Walter and his colleagues found that they could augment the information contained in EEG records by subjecting the brain to rhythmic stimulation, particularly by flickering a light in view of the subject's eyes, open or closed. At the end of the war they perfected the technique by using an electronic stroboscope that could be calibrated in fractions of a cycle per second, giving a very short brilliant flash, the duration of which did not vary with the frequency. It was found that each flash of light evoked in the brain a characteristic electrical response. Thus, with the flickering of controlled light on a subject's eyes, new and strange patterns of brain rhythms were recorded by the pens leading from every EEG channel.

Appropriate frequencies of flicker could even produce epileptic seizures. (This discovery showed that epileptic seizures were not the exclusive property of the clinically epileptic brain, and went a long way toward dispelling feelings of religious awe, professional diffidence, and revulsion with which some people regarded epilepsy.)

Perfectly normal people, subjected to flicker, described strange feelings of swaying, jumping, spinning, and dizziness. Their limbs jerked in rhythm to the flashes of light. Some experienced hallucinations, as well as emotions of fatigue, confusion, fear, disgust, anger, and pleasure. Sometimes the sense of time was lost or disturbed.

The number of normal subjects who regularly and repeatedly gave epileptic responses was large enough to indicate that "epileptic" phenomena can be evoked in normal people by physiological stimulation of a certain type.

But the important feature of the stroboscope, or flicker, was that it could stimulate the brain into producing brain-wave patterns identical to those recorded by the EEG machine. In one sense, it was as important a step in brain research as planting electrodes in a monkey's head, because the objective was the same: to stimulate the brain and observe the resultant behavior and emotional response. One major difference, of course, is that the electrode can be more nearly pinpointed to produce a desired experimental situation.

In addition to the EEG machine, another even more elaborate apparatus, called the toposcope, was devised for measuring and analyzing the brain rhythms, and much of what is known today about the relationship of the brain to human behavior is the result of toposcope studies of various types of brain wave or rhythms.

The alpha rhythms, for example, are associated with forms of ideas, and with the nations of images set up by the thinking brain. Theta rhythms are correlated with pleasure—and also with bad temper and psychopathic behavior. Beta rhythms are common in tension and chronic anxiety. Delta waves are large, slow rhythms found in infants, also in adults with organic disease or injury of the brain, and in epileptics between seizures and during attacks when there are no convulsions but only loss of consciousness.

It is hoped that one practical application of all this knowledge will be in the treatment of mental diseases. By combining what is known of the brain's rhythms with ESB, some treatment centers are already using frontal leucotomy—or implanting of electrodes in the brain—on their patients, on a limited scale.

The Burden Neurological Institute, at Bristol, England, headed by Grey Walter, was one of the first to experiment with frontal leucotomy. In this approach, a large number of very small electrodes are implanted in the frontal lobes and left in place for periods up to seven months. Electrocoagulation of tissue is performed, in progressive steps, by passing direct current through selected electrodes. The method does not inflict pain on the patient, as most parts of the brain are not able to feel pain. The patient moves about freely; his source of electricity is a transistorized supply that he carries around with him.

When I visited the Burden Institute in early 1963, there were patients walking around with dozens of electrodes in the brain.

"It's merely a matter of producing small lesions in the right place to reduce the impact of tensions," Dr. Grey Walter said. "The brain is constantly receiving enormous jets of information and hundreds of sensory signals from the outside world and from the rest of the body. The normal brain somehow manages to perform its own process of selection, but when the machinery breaks down we can help by planting the electrodes inside the brain to reduce the stress. It's just a thinning out process."

This new area of brain science, however, has potentials far beyond its use in treating the mentally ill.

As Grey Walter pointed out, with the current knowledge of brain-rhythm patterns, particularly those identified with psychopathic and abnormal behavior, it is not only conceivable but very possible that the time may come when juvenile delinquency and crime *can be prevented* merely by painless implantation of electrodes in the brains of children whose brain rhythms indicate impending criminality. It is not inconceivable that society could devise a rhythm-print system, much like the personal-fingerprint system, which could be applied to anyone suspected of violent tendencies.

This, of course, gets into a highly controversial area involving human rights and the powers of the state. Its possible application might be infinitely more involved than, for instance, the ideal of legally imposed sterilization. However, theoretically, it could provide society with an answer to crime prevention.

And many scientists have already advanced the intriguing theory that some day humans may wander around with electrodes in their heads attached to push-button control panels, small enough to fit into their pockets. Then if a person feels tired, he simply pushes a button marked "Drive." If he feels tense, he can tune into "Relax." He might even electrically control his urge to have another piece of chocolate pie. And if he is possessed of the desire to hit his neighbor over the head with a baseball bat, he could, by pressing the right button, offer to lend him money instead.

Fantastic? No more so than some of the miracles that modern science has already achieved. And no more so than the miracles that the human brain itself performs every second of its existence.

The brain as a whole is an organ of selection and storage, constantly sifting information from the senses, rejecting some of it and storing some. How does it decide what is important and unimportant? How does it select out of the enormous universe the impressions and information necessary for the process of learning? How and where does it store this information and by what electrochemical process does it know how to summon forth information when it is needed? These are the crucial questions that still need answering, but modern scientists are coming closer, bit by bit, to the answers.

As Dr. Grey Walter explained it, "The brain is a mighty good gambler. From all the hundreds of sensory signals and stimuli, how does it know what to pick? How does it know what chances to take? And in the long run it makes very few misses." One of the brain's deepest mysteries is how and where it stores memories. Scientists in both Europe and America are working feverishly to find a direct experimental approach to the nature and location of the elusive memory trace or "engram."

One of the most promising developments in recent years has been the discovery of a technique for confining the memory trace to only one side of the brain. Experimenters at Indiana University have used this principle to investigate how memory can move from place to place within the brain. Split-brain experiments with monkeys, cats and humans also have shed new light on the enigma of man's psychic machinery and opened up a wealth of possibilities for investigating many of the mind's mysteries, including memory. Current research on that aspect is much concerned with possible chemical processes that could store information in the form of "coded" nucleic acid or proteins.

Dr. E. Roy John of the University of Rochester in New York believes there are two distinct phases to the process of committing something to memory. He discussed the idea in a paper given at the International Congress of Psychology in Washington, D. C., August 26, 1963.

During the initial phase, he says, the storage of a memory in the brain is "susceptible to interference." For example, an electrical stimulus or administration of drugs immediately following an event can prevent the brain from "registering" any memory of the event. If enough time elapses before the interference takes place, however, the memory no longer seems to be susceptible to erasure. It has "acquired stability." How long it takes for a memory to enter safe storage varies with individuals and circumstances, but it is a comparatively short period of time—that is, minutes rather than hours. Dr. John believes it is reasonable to attribute permanent memory storage to a "modification of neural structure"—which means an actual physical change in the brain cells. In other words, the popular phrase about an event being "engraved" in memory may be a fairly accurate description of what actually happens.

According to Dr. John, there is evidence that ribonucleic acid plays a part in the modification of brain cells, or the "engraving." Many psychologists believe that during the initial phase of memory storage, the memory is held in the brain by some kind of reverberating electrical activity. It is this temporary "circuit" that is susceptible to interruption by shock.

One curious and fascinating aspect of memory, which has been discovered only recently as a result of hypothermia in heart surgery, is that after the body has been clinically "dead" or "frozen" in the operating room for an hour, memory *goes on* as usual after the brain cells are "unfrozen." Hypothermia is a medical term which means a "cooling down" or "freezing" of body temperature. The process is used especially in heart surgery and in other types of surgery in which a patient is unable to tolerate more conventional types of anesthesia. After this period of "frozen sleep" or "clinical death," as it is often called—memory continues to function normally, indicating that the chilling or "freezing" of the brain cells has very little, if any, effect on the memories stored in the deep recesses of the human brain.

The important question is: Does memory operate independently of life? Or is it dependent on the dynamic life processes?

This leads to more questions. If a child inherits *physical* features from his parents, could he not also inherit memory "engravings" from a long-distant past?

Many of the answers to the mysteries of the brain may lie within the animal world. Much has been written about the research on the bottle-nosed dolphin, for example. Dr. John C. Lilly, the well-known neurophysiologist who has directed most of the dolphin research, has discovered that the dolphin's brain is much like man's, that the dolphin can produce sounds of human speech, and that interspecies communications between dolphin and man may be possible. Dolphins are now being used in ESB experiments. Who knows what exciting developments will turn up from electrical stimulation of the dolphin's brain? Already dolphin brain research has led to the conclusion that dolphins are certainly the most intelligent of all nonhuman creatures—and that they are probably as intelligent as a good many human ones. Scientists hope they provide a means for communication with species that may be encountered in outer space.

Almost as intriguing as the dolphin research is the work now being done in animal hibernation. Research has resulted in contradictions of some popular conceptions about hibernation, including the finding that many states of sleep that are called hibernation are not truly hibernation. For example, bears are not hibernators, but merely winter sleepers. Hibernation is not simple sleep, nor is it continuous sleep, but proceeds in a bio-rhythm of the same sort that causes man to sleep and awaken at regular intervals regardless of his whereabouts. The measurable processes of animals are profoundly slowed down during hibernation; body temperature falls sharply, glands function differently, and food and oxygen needs of the animal are only one-hundredth of what they are during the animal's waking state.

The study of hibernation in animals contributed to the technique of hypothermia. But more awesome to contemplate is the possibility that true hibernation may possibly be induced in man to expand his life—that is, literally to add years to his life span.

Scientists engaged in research on hibernation believe there is a possibility of inducing true hibernation in man—which would be of considerable value in space travel.

The theory is that if hibernating bats can live 20 times longer than nonhibernating mammals of the same weight—

which they do—then hibernating man might live 1400 years! Considering that one year on Jupiter is approximately twelve years on earth, these extra years might come in handy for the man who plans to spend his winter vacations planet-hopping. Science will no doubt also come up with a computer machine to figure out how old he will be when he returns to earth.

How do animals tell time? Scientists are attempting to solve the mystery of the "biological clock," a remarkable physiological process that enables some animals to find their ways to destinations and others to regulate vital activities. Dr. Frank A. Brown of Northwestern University, one of the researchers in bio-rhythms, the science of life cycles, has discovered that oysters, which open and close their shells with the rising and falling of the tides, can be transported from New Haven, Connecticut, to his laboratory in Evanston, Illinois, and will continue to swing their shells on the timetable of the tides 1000 miles away.

The built-in biological clockwork of the oyster and fiddler crab is helping the U.S. Navy and Air Force—which have financed most of the research—to perfect complex machines that guide ships and planes with the simplicity and precision of animal timers.

Frogs, horseshoe crabs, and beetles have played a prominent role in the scientific development of everything from improved reading machines to plans for landing unmanned vehicles on the moon. And although scientists have not been able to demonstrate how the "homing instinct" works, a great deal of research is being concentrated on birds because of their time and direction senses. In communications research, for example, it has been found that bird calls recorded in one location do not have a uniform meaning for birds of the same species in other geographical locations.

It has been found that some animals can sense such subtle things as electromagnetism, radar waves, infrared rays and inertial forces; and animal research has helped in such important scientific discoveries as radar and sonar.

Air Force scientists are delving into such problems as: why the back wings of flies are perfect vibrating gyroscopes; why the honeybees know how to fly a straight course to flowers from miles away; why electric eels are able to generate enough voltage (by means of 6000 to 10,000 tiny disc-shaped cells or "generators") to shock anyone nearby. The Navy is conducting studies of the albatross on Midway Island, and also sponsoring research on the Tasmanian Shearwater, a bird that annually returns to its home nest the same week yearly after a flight that circles the Pacific. The understanding of these animal sensory mechanisms may have far-reaching results for man.

Man has evolved from his animal ancestors. From the mysterious and primitive depths of his brain, inherited from these ancestors, come sensory perceptions and powers already proven but not yet understood.

Is man really in danger of losing his senses through disuse? Or, how far can he go in using his own uniquely developed brain and his technological inventions to take the place of senses he lacks or to extend those he has beyond their natural limits?

Enough is known today about the capabilities of the brain to provide science with its greatest challenge. The power of suggestion that can cause the primitive aborigine to will himself to die, the power of conditioning that can develop superhuman strength in the Yogi, the power of faith that creates immunity from burns for the Fijian fire-walker—all seem to share the same mental, emotional, or sensory mechanism. As science lifts the curtain of mystery from man's primitive past, it becomes evident that we are only scratching the surface of human potentialities.

It is a long journey from the primordial sea of our animal ancestry to a modern cybernetics laboratory, but the living brain has made it. The future of the brain under the explosive impact of scientific exploration is staggering to contemplate. Yet, science is not omniscient. It may be a long time before computer machines can replace the human soul or the role of free will in the affairs of men.

Until then the limitless future of the brain with its unfolding secrets holds the key for shaping the destiny of mankind.

The Source of All Power

by W. Clement Stone

In this book we have made a sincere and unsparing attempt to record the efforts that are going on in the world to penetrate the secrets of the human mind. We responded with enthusiastic dedication to the challenge to "investigate mind phenomena."

Religion, naturally, was not included within the bounds of our investigation. Lourdes was visited not because it is a religious shrine, but because the phenomena occurring there could not be ignored.

But it is my belief that one cannot talk about the mind of man without being aware, always and ever, of the brilliant light from a divine source cast on that mind—which would otherwise dwell in darkness.

There are many practical scientists of great eminence who, as they penetrated into the secrets of natural laws, became more and more convinced of the existence and power of a Supreme Intelligence. This has been most beautifully expressed by Wernher von Braun, Director of the George C. Marshall Space Flight Center of the National Aeronautics and Space Administration. He wrote:

"The two most powerful forces shaping our civilization today are science and religion.

"Through science man strives to learn more of the mysteries of creation. Through religion he seeks to know the Creator.

"Neither operates independently. It is as difficult for me to understand a scientist who does not acknowledge the presence of a superior rationality behind the existence of the universe as it is to comprehend a theologian who would deny the advances of science.

"Far from being independent or opposing forces, science and religion are sisters. Both seek a better world. While science seeks control over the forces of nature around us, religion controls the forces of nature within us.

". . . Finite man cannot comprehend an omnipresent, omniscient, omnipotent, and infinite God. Any effort to visualize God, to reduce him to our comprehension, to describe him in our language, beggars his greatness.

"I find it best through faith to accept God as an intelligent will, perfect in goodness, revealing Himself in the world of experience more fully down through the ages, as man's capacity for understanding grows.

"For spiritual comfort I find assurance in the concept of the fatherhood of God. For ethical guidance I rely on the corollary concept of the brotherhood of man.

"Scientists now believe that in nature, matter is never destroyed. Not even the tiniest particle can disappear without a trace. Nature does not know extinction—only transformation. Would God have less regard for His masterpiece of creation, the human soul?"

And the great psychiatrist, Dr. C. G. Jung, gives a seven-word summary of what I feel is the spirit of our age in the title of his book, *Modern Man in Search of a Soul*. Also, in this book, he makes an interesting statement:

> "Among all my patients in the second half of life—that is to say, over thirty-five—there has not been one whose problem in the last resort was not that of finding a religious outlook on life. It is safe to say that every one of them fell ill because he had lost that which the living religions of every age have given to their followers, and none of them has been really healed who did not regain his religious outlook."

And we are all aware of the great religious reformation of worldwide significance that is taking place in our time to promote harmony, understanding, peace, and spiritual enlightenment among all peoples. The movement was initiated by Pope John XXIII and is being continued by Pope Paul VI. Hardly a day passes buy that the metropolitan press carries a story indicating a trend toward the unity of understanding among church leaders of all denominations.

Again, let me repeat:

You are a mind with a body.

You are the product of heredity, environment, physical body, conscious and subconscious minds, experiences and particular position and direction in time and space—and something more, including powers known and unknown.

You have the power to affect, use, control, or harmonize with all of the facets of your being. And you can direct your thoughts, control your emotions, and ordain your destiny.

I believe in the power of prayer; I believe in miracles. And, in my study of mind phenomena in research for this book, I found that all paths eventually lead through *the other side of the mind* to the source of all power—God.

Glossary of Terms

acetylcholine—A complicated chemical substance associated with electrical changes in the brain.

age regression—An apparent alteration of personality in which the subject exchanges his present personality for one he had when he was younger; usually induced under hypnosis.

alpha rhythm—The pattern of brain waves associated with forms of ideas and the nature of images.

amygdala—A part of the brain which controls various emotions, such as rage and fear.

analgesia—Loss of sensitivity to pain.

animal magnetism—Mesmer's term for hypnosis, based on the incorrect notion that the phenomena observed were due to the emanation of a magnetic fluid or force.

beta rhythm—The pattern of brain waves common in tension and chronic anxiety states.

biological thought transmission (see *telepathy*)

bionics—A newly coined word from the Greek root *bion*, which means "living," used to define a new science of systems which function similarly to living systems.

biotechnology—A technical term applied generally to the study of life functions.

brain wave—Rhythmic fluctuations of voltage between parts of the brain resulting in a flow of electric current.

cataplexy, plastics—A condition of muscular rigidity sometimes accompanied by unconsciousness.

cerebral cortex—The "grey matter" of the brain, responsible for all higher mental activities.

clairvoyance—Purportedly the cognition of objects or events by means other than through the five senses.

clonus—A forced series of alternating contractions and partial relaxations of the same muscle.

cortical function—Pertaining to the function of the brain.

cybernetics—Comparative study of the control system formed by the nervous system and the brain, and mechanical-electrical communication systems.

dissociation, personality—A psychological state in which mental activity seems to operate independently of the normal conscious personality.

electrochemical energy—The combination of electrical and chemical energy, used here with reference to brain energy.

electroencephalograph (EEG)—An apparatus for detecting and recording brain waves.

electromagnetism—Magnetism developed by a current of electricity.

electronic brain stimulation (ESB)—Stimulation of the brain by the implantation of electrodes.

electrosurgery—A new medical art involving the use of electricity or electrical instruments to kill nerve cells and dissolve blood clots. Used especially in diseases of the brain and nervous system.

engram—A permanent impression left on protoplasm as the result of a stimulus.

extrasensory perception—Defined, in the *Journal of Parapsychology* as "response to an external event not presented to any known sense." It embraces telepathy, clairvoyance and precognition.

faith-healing—A method or practice of treating diseases by prayer and exercise of faith in God.

feedback—The returning of a fraction of the output of an electrical oscillation to the input to which the fraction is added at the proper phase.

genetic memory—Pertaining to hereditary memory.

gyroscope—A complicated stabilizing instrument or steering apparatus.

hallucinogenic drugs—Drugs which produce hallucinations or visions.

hibernation—State of passing the winter in a torpid or lethargic condition, as many animals do.

hippocampus—A region of the brain.

hyperacuity—An unusual degree of sensitiveness of sight, hearing, touch, smell or taste; due to psychological causes.

hyperaesthesia—An unusual degree of sensitivity of the actual sense organs.

hypothalamus—A tiny rectangular piece of the brain located near the thalamus; chiefly responsible for the feeling of pleasure.

hypothermia—A new medical term denoting the "cooling down" or "freezing" of body temperature during surgery; used mainly in heart surgery.

kymograph—An automatic apparatus on which curves of pressure may be traced.

leucotomy—A medical term denoting the insertion of electrodes in the brain, used for treating mentally ill patients.

Medium see also, *Sensitive Psychic*—A person who claims or believes in his or her ability to contact the spirits of the dead; one who claims extrasensory or psychic powers in general.

neurophysiology—A medical term for the study of the brain and nervous system.

neurons—Nerve cells.

non-verbal suggestion (see *telepathy*)

nucleic acid—Any of a group of acids, combinations of a sugar or a derivative of a sugar with phosphoric acid and a base, found in nuclear material.

occultism—Occult theory or practice; belief in hidden or mysterious powers and the possibility of human control over them.

paranormal—The parapsychologist's term for what the scientist would call the supernatural.

parapsychology—The study of such purported phenomena as telepathy, precognition, clairvoyance, psychokinesis, and the occult powers of mediums.

plethysmograph—An instrument for measuring bodily changes during emotional reactions.

poltergeist—A noisy ghost.

Psychic [noun] (see *Medium*)

psychochemistry—New term denoting psychological and chemical relationship in study of the human psyche or personality.

psychokinesis—The purported movement of objects by merely "willing" them to move or otherwise without physical means.

psychosomatic—Pertaining to the functional interrelationship between mind and body, as in psychosomatic medicine which deals with bodily disorders induced by mental or emotional ills.

reincarnation—The belief that the souls of the dead return to earth in new forms or bodies.

schizophrenia—A type of insanity characterized by loss of contact with environment and by disintegration of personality.

Sensitive [noun] (see *Medium*)

septal region—The term for a certain area of the brain, sometimes associated with schizophrenia.

servo-mechanism—A control mechanism.

somnambulism—A sleep or sleep-like state in which walking and other acts are performed.

stimulus deprivation—State of being without external sensory stimuli, often artificially induced for experimental purposes.

stroboscope—An instrument for studying the successive phases of a periodic or varying motion by means of light periodically interrupted.

subliminal perception—A psychological term meaning perception below the threshold of consciousness or beyond the reach of personal awareness. Similar to subconscious perception.

supernormal—Exceeding the natural powers of man.

synapse—A physiological term meaning the point at which the nervous impulse passes from one neuron to another.

telepathy—Purportedly the communication between one mind and another by means other than through the five senses.

thalamus—A part of the brain sometimes known as the "inner" brain, about the size of a finger, which governs sensations of pain.

thanatomania—A term used by anthropologists to denote that suggestion, intense expectation, fear or belief in magic, may among primitive communities produce coma resulting in death.

theta rhythm—The pattern of brain wave that is usually associated with pleasure.

thought transference (see *telepathy*)

trance—A state of partly suspended animation or of inability to function. A daze or stupor.

vacuum tube—A sealed tube with the contained gas exhausted to a pressure low enough to permit the passage of electrical discharges between metallic electrodes projecting into the tube from the outside.

yoga—A collective term for the various systems of mental and physical training (in India) designed to make the mind function at higher levels than normal.

APPENDIX B

Bibliography of Works Consulted

Abbott, D., *Behind the Scenes With the Mediums*, Chicago, 1907

Abramowski, E., *The Phenomena of Cryptoamnesia in Telepathy*, Paris, 1914

Adrian, E., *The Physical Background of Perception*, London, 1947

Allen, M., *Morphological Creativity*, Englewood Cliffs, N.J., 1962

Aradi, Z., *The Book of Miracles*, N.Y., 1956

Ashby, W., *Design for a Brain*, London, 1952

Baird, A., *One Hundred Cases for Survival After Death*, N.Y., 1944

Barcroft, J., *Features in the Architecture of Physiological Function*, London, 1934

Bauer, R., *The New Man in Soviet Psychology*, Cambridge, Mass., 1959

Behanan, K., *Yoga*, N.Y., 1937

Behari, B., *Sufis, Mystics, and Yogis of India*, Bombay, 1962

Bernstein, M., *The Search for Bridey Murphy*, N.Y., 1956

Besterman, T., *Crystal Gazing*, London, 1924

Besterman, T., *Some Modern Mediums*, London, 1930

Blackmore, S., *Spiritism, Facts and Frauds*, London, 1924

Blanton, M., *The Miracle of Bernadette*, N.Y. 1939

Brazier, M., *The Electrical Activity of the Nervous System*, London, 1951

Broad, C., *Religion, Philosophy and Physical Research*, N.Y., 1953

Bromage, B., *Tibetan Yoga*, London, 1959

Cadwallader, M., *Hydesville in History*, Chicago, 1917

Carrington, H., *The Physical Phenomena of Spiritualism*, London, 1934

Carrington, H., *The Invisible World*, N.Y. 1946

Carrington, H., *A Primer of Psychic Research*, N.Y., 1932

Carrington, W., *Telepathy*, London, 1945

Cerminara, G., *Many Mansions*, N.Y., 1950

Conklin, G., *The Supernatural Reader*, N.Y., 1953

Cook, J., *Remedies and Rackets*, N.Y., 1958

Coover, J., *Experiments In Psychical Research at Leland Stanford University*, California, 1917

Cousins, R., *The Will to Think*, N.Y., 1957

Craik, K., *The Nature of Explanation*, London, 1934

Cranston, R., *The Miracle of Lourdes*, N.Y., 1955

Cuddon, E., *Hypnosis: Its Meaning and Practice*, London, 1938

Diamond, E., *The Science of Dreams*, N.Y., 1962

Dingwall, E., *Ghosts and Spirits of the Ancient World*, London, 1930

Doyle, A., *The Case for Spirit Photography*, N.Y., 1923

Ducasse, C., *The Belief in a Life After Death*, Springfield, Ill., 1961

Dunne, J., *An Experiment with Time*, London, 1927

Dunninger, J., *Inside the Medium's Cabinet*, N.Y., 1935

Edwards, F., *Stranger Than Science*, N.Y., 1959

Edwards, F., *Strangest of All*, N.Y., 1956

Elkin, A., *The Australian Aborigines*, Sydney, 1938

Erickson, M., Hershman, S., and Sector, I., *The Practical Application of Mental and Dental Hypnosis*, N.Y., 1961

Esdaile, J., *The Introduction of Mesmerism into the Public Hospitals of India*, London, 1856

Estabrooks, G., *Hypnosis: Current Problems*, N.Y., 1962

Eysenck, H., *Sense and Nonsense in Psychology*, Middlesex, England, 1957

Eysenck, H., *Uses and Abuses of Psychology*, London, 1953

Fodor, N., *The Haunted Mind*, N.Y., 1959

Ford, A., and Bro, M., *Nothing So Strange*, N.Y., 1958

Freytag, F., *The Hypnoanalysis of an Anxiety Hysteria*, N.Y., 1958

Gardner, M., *Fads and Fallacies*, N.Y., 1952

Gardner, M., *In the Name of Science*, N.Y., 1952

Gibbs, F. and Gibbs, E., *Atlas of Electroencephalography*, Cambridge, Mass., 1950

Gresham, W., *Houdini: The Man Who Walked Through Walls*, N.Y., 1959

Gudas, F., *Extrasensory Perception*, N.Y., 1961

Gurney, E., Myers, F. and Podmore, F., *Phantasms of the Living*, London, 1886 (abridged 1918)

Hall, T., *The Spiritualists*, London, 1963

Harney, W., *Brimming Billabongs*, London, 1947

Hart, H., *The Enigma of Survival*, London, 1959

Hebb, D., *The Organization of Behavior*, N.Y., 1949

Helle, J., *Miracles*, N.Y., 1952

Heywood, R., *Beyond the Reach of Sense*, N.Y., 1961

Heywood, R., *The Sixth Sense*, London, 1959

Hill, N., and Stone, W. Clement, *Success Through a Positive Mental Attitude*, Englewood Cliffs, N.J., 1960

Houdini, H., *A Magician Among the Spirits*, N.Y., 1924

Houdini, H., *Miracle Mongers and Their Methods*, N.Y., 1920

Hubbard, R. *Dianetics, the Modern Science of Mental Health*, London, 1951

Hudson, T., *The Law of Psychic Phenomena*, Chicago, 1905

Hull, C., *Hypnosis and Suggestibility*, N.Y., 1933

Huxley, J., *Knowledge, Morality and Destiny*, N.Y., 1957

Jaensch, E., *Eidetic Memory*, London, 1930

Janet, P., *The Major Symptoms of Hysteria*, N.Y., 1907

Jastrow, J., *Error and Eccentricity in Human Belief*, N.Y., 1935

Johnson, R., *The Imprisoned Splendour*, N.Y., 1953

Jung, C., *Collected Works*, London, 1960

Lambert, H., *A General Survey of Psychical Phenomena*, N.Y., 1928

Lancaster, E., and Poling, J., *The Final Face of Eve*, N.Y., 1958

Latil, P. de, *Thinking by Machine*, London, 1953

Lethbridge, T., *Ghost and Ghoul*, N.Y., 1962

Leuret, F., and Bon, H., *Modern Miraculous Cures*, N.Y., 1957

Lockwood, D., *I, the Aboriginal*, Adelaide, 1962

Lorenz, K., *King Solomon's Ring*, London, 1952

MacKay, C., *Extraordinary Popular Delusions and the Madness of Crowds*, London, 1841

McCabe, J., *The Lourdes Miracles*, London, 1925

Milne, L., and Milne, M., *The Senses of Animals and Men*, N.Y., 1962

Mountford, C., *The Tiwi—Their Art, Myth and Ceremony*, London, 1958

Mowrer, O., *The Crisis in Psychiatry and Religion*, Princeton, New Jersey, 1961

Mullholland, J., *The Art of Illusion*, N.Y., 1934

Murchison, C., *The Case For and Against Psychical Belief*, Mass., 1927

Murphy, G., *Challenge of Psychical Research*, N.Y., 1961

Myers, F., *Human Personality and Its Survival of Bodily Death*, New Hyde Park, N.Y., 1961

National Spiritualists Association, *The Spiritualists Manual*, Washington, D.C., 1911

Omez, R., *Psychical Phenomena*, N.Y., 1958

Osty, E., *Supernormal Faculties in Man*, London, 1923

Pask, G., *An Approach to Cybernetics*, London, 1961

Penfield, W., and Rasmussen, T., *The Cerebral Cortex of Man*, N.Y., 1950

Pratt, J., *Parapsychology: An Insider's View of ESP*, N.Y., 1964

Price, H., *Leaves From a Psychist's Case Book*, London, 1933

Price, H., *Confessions of a Ghost-Hunter*, London, 1936

Price, H., *Fifty Years of Psychical Research*, London, 1939

Price, H., *The Most Haunted House in England*, London, 1940

Price, H., *Poltergeist Over England*, London, 1945

Price, H., *The End of Borley Rectory*, London, 1946

Prince, M., *The Dissociation of Personality*, N.Y., 1906

Proskauer, J., *Spook Crooks*, N.Y., 1932

Proskauer, J., *The Dead Do Not Talk*, N.Y., 1946

Puharich, A., *The Sacred Mushroom*, N.Y., 1959

Puharich, A., *Beyond Telepathy*, N.Y., 1962

Rawcliffe, D., *Illusions and Delusions of the Supernatural and the Occult*, N.Y., 1959

Reynolds, J., *Gallery of Ghosts*, N.Y., 1949

Richardson, J., *The Great Psychological Crime*, N.Y., 1928

Richet, C., *Thirty Years of Psychical Research*, London, 1923

Rhine, J., *The Reach of the Mind*, N.Y., 1947

Rhine, J., *New World of the Mind*, N.Y., 1953

Rhine, J., and Pratt, J., *Parapsychology*, Springfield, Ill., 1957

Rhine, L., *Hidden Channels of the Mind*, N.Y., 1961

Roberts, K., *Henry Gross and His Dowsing Rod*, N.Y., 1951

Ropp, R. de, *Drugs and the Mind*, N.Y., 1957

Ross, R., *Living Magic*, Chicago, 1956

Roth, W., *Ethnological Studies Among the North-West-Central Queensland Aborigines*, Brisbane, 1897

Salter, W., *Ghosts and Apparitions*, London, 1938

Sargent, W., *Battle for the Mind*, N.Y., 1957

Scarne, J., and Rawson, C., *Scarne On Dice*, Harrisburg, Pa., 1946

Schmeidler, G., and McConnell, R., *ESP and Personality Patterns*, New Haven, 1958

Shackleton, E., *South*, N.Y., 1962 (original publication 1920)

Sinclair, U., *Mental Radio*, London, 1930

Singer, C., *From Magic to Science*, N.Y., 1958

Sinnott, E., *Cell and Psyche*, N.Y., 1959

Sinnott, E., *The Biology of the Spirit*, N.Y., 1961

Sitwell, S., *Poltergeists*, N.Y., 1959

Skinner, B., *Science and Human Behavior*, N.Y., 1953

Soal, S., and Bateman, F., *Modern Experiments in Telepathy*, New Haven, 1953

Stearn, J., *The Door to the Future*, N.Y., 1963

Stern, K., *The Third Revolution*, N.Y., 1961

Stone, W. Clement, *The Success System That Never Fails*, Englewood Cliffs, N.J., 1962

Sudre, R., *Parapsychology*, N.Y., 1960

Tabori, P., *Harry Price: The Biography of a Ghost-Hunter*, London, 1950

Thigpen, C., and Cleckley, H., *The Three Faces of Eve*, N.Y., 1957

Thouless, R., *An Introduction to the Psychology of Religion*, Cambridge, 1928

Thurston, H., *Ghosts and Poltergeists*, Chicago, 1954

Tyrell, G., *Science and Psychic Phenomena*, New Hyde Park, N.Y., 1961

Underhill, E., *Mysticism*, London, 1911

Vasiliev, L., *Experiments in Mental Suggestion*, Hampshire, Eng., 1963

Vasiliev, L., *Long Distance Suggestion*, (In Russian) Moscow, 1962

Vogt, E., and Hyman, R., *Water Witching, USA*, Chicago, 1959

Von Bonin, G., *Essay on the Cerebral Cortex*, Springfield, Ill., 1950

Walker, K., *The Extra-Sensory Mind*, N.Y., 1961

Wallace, A., *Miracles and Modern Spiritualism*, London, 1896

Walter, W. Grey, *The Living Brain*, London, 1953

Weitzenhoffer, *Hypnotism*, N.Y., 1953

West, D., *Psychical Research Today*, London, 1954

Yogananda, P., *Autobiography of a Yogi*, Los Angels, 1959

Young, J., *Doubt and Certainty in Science*, Oxford, 1951

In addition to the above books, a good number of periodicals were consulted in the preparation of this work; among them: *The Proceedings and Journals of the Society for Psychical Research* (London), *Bulletins and Journals of Parapsychology* (Duke University Press), *The International Journal of Parapsychology* (The Parapsychology Foundation Inc., New York), *Proceedings and Journal of the American Society for Psychical Research* (New York), *Revue Metaphysique* (Paris), *Revue Internationale de Radiesthesie* (Brussels), *Scientific American* (New York), *New Scientist* (London).

APPENDIX C

Acknowledgments

While it is not possible to list all those who have helped in the preparation of this book, either through research, interviews, advice and guidance, or specialized contributions, we wish especially to thank the following:

Dr. W. Grey Walter, head of the Burden Neurological Institute, Bristol, England; Mr. and Mrs. Guy Lambert; Rosalind Heywood; Dr. Letitia Fairfield and Dr. D. J. West of the London Society for Psychical Research; Mr. and Mrs. Gordon Pask of London; Stephen Abrams of Oxford; A. D. Cornell of Cambridge; C. E. M. Hansel of the University of Manchester; George Zorab of the Dutch Psychical Research Society; Dr. J. M. Kooey, astro-physicist at the Royal Netherlands Military Academy, Breda, Holland; Dr. Arthur Kline, dean of the post-graduate medical school, University of Vienna; Louis Couffignal, inspector general for the Ministry of Education and president of the Association for Cybernetical Pedagogy in Paris; Dr. Antoine Remond, of the Salpetriere Hospital in Paris; French science writer Pierre de Latil; Professor and Mrs. Hans Bender and Dr. Inge Strauch of the psychology department, University of Freiburg, Germany.

Dr. J. G. Pratt, Dr. Milan Ryzl, and Pavel Stepanek for permission to observe and photograph ESP experiments in Prague, Czechoslovakia; Surjit Singh, Sikh guide of New Delhi, India; H. N. Banerjee of Sri Ganganagar; Dr. K. Sampurnanda, Governor of Rajasthan; Dr. D. S. Kothari, chairman of the Physics Department, University of New Delhi; the medical directors of the All India Institute of Medical Sciences in New Delhi.

Dr. Hiroshi Motoyama, Director of the Institute of Religious Psychology in Tokyo, and his mother, for warm hospitality as well as help in research; Captain Stanley Brown, skipper of the *Maroro* and an authority on the Fiji firewalkers.

Rene Henri and Alan Stewart, guides in the Australian Outback country; Neville Bell, Australian bush pilot; Harry Sidgwick, Superintendent of the Manangrida government reservation; Mr. and Mrs. Kevin Miller of Manangrida; Mrs. John Morrison of Mudgenberri Station, for her fine buffalo meat sandwiches; Douglas Lockwood, prizewinning journalist in Darwin, whose book *I, the Aboriginal* introduced us to Waipuldanya, a full-blooded aboriginal of the Alawa tribe; various Darwin government officials who gave permission to enter Arnhem Land.

Dr. J. B. Rhine of Duke University; Dr. Ward Halstead of the University of Chicago; Dr. Gardner Murphy of the Menninger Clinic; Dr. Karl Osis, Director of the American Society for Psychical Research, New York; Oliver Caldwell of the U.S. Department of Health, Education and Welfare; Dr. Eugene Konecci of NASA; Sidney Schneider of Chicago; Lydia Bacon, secretary to Mr. Stone; Bill and Martha Smith, of Traverse City, Michigan, for enormous help in meeting a deadline; Mrs. Winifred Feely; Howard A. Moffett, M.D.; and Capt. Harry A. Adams, U.S.N. (Ret.).

Finally, we must acknowledge a debt to Jessie V. Stone and Russ Ogg who nobly endured the ordeals of this collaboration. Without them and all the others, this book would not have been possible.

APPENDIX D

Special Acknowledgment

by N. L. Browning

Once in a blue moon you meet a man like W. Clement Stone, a man who has made a phenomenal success in the hardheaded world of business but who has dedicated his life to a Magnificent Obsession of *giving* to an incredible range of worthy causes. This book grew out of our common interest in the twilight zone of the mysteries of the opportunity of spending a full year of research and writing in one special field of interest, and with carte blanche permission to go wherever necessary to seek the answers. I am deeply grateful to both Mr. and Mrs. W. Clement Stone not only for financially sponsoring this assignment but for such generous giving of themselves in the arduous pains of co-authorship, for their encouragement and understanding and patience, for the tremendous investment of their own time and energies, as well as funds, and for their unwavering moral support through a long and difficult project. Both my husband and I owe them a special debt of gratitude and hope that the project has been worthy of its sponsors.

I owe a special debt, too, to Editor Don Maxwell of *The Chicago Tribune* for making it possible for me to be relieved of

other assignments in order to devote full time to this book—
and to *The Tribune* for permitting me to draw freely upon
previously published articles. We are also indebted to Dr. Joe
Maddy of Interlochen who gave my husband a four months'
leave of absence from his work at the Interlochen Arts Academy to accompany me on our around-the-world research trip.

Printed in the USA
CPSIA information can be obtained
at www.ICGtesting.com
JSHW012020140824
68134JS00033B/2795

9 781722 501068